Incredibly Indispensable Irish Web Directory

2002
Second Edition

Compiled by Steffen Higel, Sheena Lavery, Pauline McCaffrey, Dolores Vischer and Liam Donnelly

•

Clive and Bettina Zietman

in association with Irish Times Books

Dedication

In memory of Irene Stanley
and Margarita Habgood

Publishers' note

This edition published in 2001

Kogan Page Limited
120 Pentonville Road
London N1 9JN

Kogan Page (US) Limited
163 Central Avenue, Suite 4
Dover, NH 03820, USA

Kogan Page website: www.kogan-page.co.uk

The Irish Times website: www.ireland.com

This 2002, second Irish edition is based on and includes material from the
The Incredibly Indispensable Web Directory compiled by
Clive and Bettina Zeitman, and also published by Kogan Page.

British Library Cataloguing in Publication Data

A CIP record for this book is available from the British Library.

ISBN 0 7494 36573

Cover design by anú design www.anu-design.ie
Design concept Brenda McNiff
Typeset by Saxon Graphics Ltd, Derby
Printed and bound in Great Britain by Thanet Press Ltd, Margate

contents

government 104

healthcare 114

help! 127

hobbies and leisure 132

information sources 145

living 153

personal finance 165

places 169

science and nature 182

shopping 188

sport 203

technology 223

travel 227

introduction

Household names on the Internet for Irish users

This directory is different to all others. It is aimed at all Irish users who are frustrated with the Web generally, in particular the failings of search engines. It is ideal for beginners, non-surfers, families, researchers and business users. It is a cherry-picked selection of household names on the Web, chosen from an essentially Irish perspective. Be it Liam Neeson or the Office of Public Works, RTÉ or BMW, this book contains them all. It is a neat and crystal-clear list of official household names, familiar to everyday Irish users. For those who wish to go directly to the sites for Temple Bar, Punchestown Racecourse or Aer Lingus this book will be incredibly indispensable. It is *not* cluttered with the weird or the obscure. It is *not* dominated by American sites nor does it contain anything but official sites supported by well-known companies and institutions. The National Gallery, Dublin Zoo and Tesco are in. The Utah Elvis Appreciation Society and The Klingon Dictionary are out. The websites listed are self-explanatory and thus the book does not contain commentary or descriptions. James Dean, Trinity College, The Northern Ireland Executive and AIB need no introduction.

Searching the Web

People who have just bought a computer may not be familiar with the mystique, language and workings of the Internet. Because the Internet was born and has grown in an unstructured and largely unregulated fashion it can be very difficult to navigate. Most people search the Web by inserting keywords into search engines. The search engines produce lists of websites (often in no particular order) which are triggered by the selected word. Say, for example, you are looking for the Irish Museum of Modern Art website. By inserting the words "irish", "museum", "modern" and "art" into a search engine, you may, with luck, be led in the right direction. Often however, you will be led astray. Why?

- There is a skill in using search engines. This is a skill which mere mortals don't necessarily possess. People who spend their lives working with computers assume that everyone in the world thinks like they do. The truth is that they don't.
- Even the most powerful and sophisticated search engines only cover about 15% of all websites.
- Search engines are not human brains. They therefore do not think like the human brain, in particular they do not think like yours. Although you know what you are looking for, the search engine may well have very different ideas.
- It is so easy to set up a website that the Web has already become full to the point of overflowing with websites of dire quality. The search engines find it hard to sift the wheat from the chaff.
- Different search engines have different rules about refining searches. To use a particular search engine properly you have to learn the rules.
- Even the choice of search engine is overwhelming. There are scores of search engines and some are better at searching particular subjects. At the last count, there were approximately 4,000 in existence. Which search engine to use can be mystifying.

Although the Web is a wonderful source of information and the search engines can do the trick, there is an alternative. If you know the precise company or institution you are looking for, it is far easier and quicker to go straight to it by typing in the web address. All computers linked to the Internet have an address box. Type the address, press enter on your keyboard and you will be taken directly to your chosen destination. YOU DO NOT NEED TO USE A SEARCH ENGINE. This book enables you to circumvent the search engines completely if the website you are looking for is listed here.

Please note that not every famous name has a website. For example, only new films seem to have official websites. Films that pre-date the Internet do not. Similarly, many large institutions have not yet caught up with the Internet age. Some have sites under construction and others may well have changed their website address between the time this book was compiled and the date of publication. When companies are taken over or merge, this also tends to affect the website address. To some extent this book is aiming at a moving target and future editions will incorporate as many additions and changes as possible.

preface to the second edition

In the world of the internet and e-commerce things move and change at a rapid pace. In the year since the first edition of this Web directory was published, thousands of new web sites have been created for Irish organisations and firms, hundreds have ceased to exist and many others have been improved and extended. Our compilers were given the task of developing the most comprehensive directory available in Ireland and for people in other countries with an interest in researching any Irish subject.

For this new edition, we have checked all those sites listed in the first edition to ensure that they are still live, removing those sites now 'dead'. In researching and selecting new sites for inclusion, our brief was to select organisations and companies whose names would immediately indicate the business or service offered, or its role. We concentrated on developing a more comprehensive directory of websites that collectively provide an information reference point on all aspects of Irish life. From the arts and entertainment fields to travel, the many sections in the book include all the authoritative Irish sites that our research uncovered, and other UK and international sites that will provide relevant information. In many sections the listings have been sub-divided into two – Irish and International.

This easy-to-use book has grown in extent: the original first edition contained approximately 6,000 websites, this new edition contains over 8,800 sites. We believe that these sites all have relevance for people living in Ireland (North and South) and for anyone searching for information on any aspect of Irish life or culture. By using this directory's clear contents headings or index, your search for a specific web address will be substantially speeded up.

Thanks must go the team of four compilers, each of whom lives, studies and works in Ireland and who share a passion for the internet and for gathering and selecting new information for this second edition: Steffen Higel, Sheena Lavery, Pauline McCaffrey and Liam Donnelly. The support of co-publishers, **The Irish Times**, and of their New Media division, **ireland.com** and the General Services department in particular, has been invaluable in bringing this book together, and is acknowledged here.

If you know of a website for a household name company or organisation that deserves to be included in the next edition of this book – or if you have any other comments – please e-mail your suggestions to irishweb@koganpage.co.uk.

Dolores Vischer
October 2001

arts and entertainment

artists, galleries & exhibitions
clubs
comedy
dance
events/festivals
fashion
film
funding and regulation
literature
magazines and websites
music
professional bodies
radio
television
theatre
tickets
video

arts and entertainment

artists, galleries & exhibitions

Anne Stahl	www.clubi.ie/stahl
Appollo Gallery	www.appollogallery.ie
Apsleys Crafty Copy	www.craftycopy.co.uk
Ark (Children's Cultural Centre)	www.ark.ie
Art.ie	www.art.ie
Artboxx.co.uk	www.artboxx.co.uk
Arthouse	www.arthouse.ie
Arts Council for Ireland	www.artscouncil.ie
Arts Council for Northern Ireland	www.artscouncil-ni.org
Austin Street Gallery	www.asg-arts.com
Bank of Ireland Arts Centre	www.bankofireland.ie
Bell Gallery	www.bellgallery.com
Belltable Arts Centre	www.commerce.ie/belltable
Brian McCarthy	http://indigo.ie/~bmccart
Brushwood Studios	www.brushwoodstudios.com
Butler Gallery	www.butlergallery.com
Carole Ward	www.bodyartist.ie
Charles Gilmore Galleries	www.charlesgilmoregalleries.co.uk
Chester Beatty Library	www.cbl.ie
Clotworthy Arts Centre	www.antrim.gov.uk
Colin Gibson	www.colingibson.com
Combridge Fine Arts	www.cfa.ie
Courtauld Institute	www.courtauld.ac.uk
Crawford Municipal Art Gallery	www.synergy.ie/crawford
Dalriada Galleries	www.irishart.co.uk
Darlene Garr	www.darlenegarr.com
Douglas Hyde Gallery	www.douglashydegallery.com
Dyehouse Gallery	www.dyehouse-gallery.com
Eakin Gallery	www.eakingallery.co.uk
Eastwood Gallery	www.eastwoodgallery.co.uk
Elaine Somers Gallery	www.elainesomers.com
Elizabeth Cope	www.elizabethcopeart.com
Emer Gallery	www.emergallery.com
Engine Room Gallery	www.artnorth.co.uk
Felim Egan	www.felimegan.ie/one.html
Fergus Costello	www.ferguscostello.com/nindex2.html
Fiona Woods	www.fionawoods.com
foto-ART8	www.fotoart8.org
Gallery 148	www.gallery148.com
Gallery of Photography	www.irish-photography.com
Galway Arts Centre	www.galwayartscentre.ie
Galway Bay Gallery	www.galwaybaygallery.com
Graham Knuttel	www.knuttel.com
Greenart Corporate Gallery	www.greenart.co.uk

Greenlane Gallery	www.greenlanegallery.com
Horner Gallery	www.dublincorp.ie/services
Hugh Lane Gallery	www.dublincorp.ie/services
Irish Art Group, The	www.irishart.demon.co.uk
Irish Art Studio	www.irishartstudio.com
Irish Landscape Paintings	http://liamjones.irish-art.net
Irish Museum of Modern Art	www.modernart.ie
Kenny's Art Gallery	www.kennys.ie/gallery
Kerlin Gallery	www.kerlin.ie
Martin Toland Gallery	www.martintoland.com
Michael Killen, Sculptor	www.michaelkillen.ie
Michael O'Clery	www.oclery.com
National Gallery	www.nationalgallery.ie
National Gallery UK	www.nationalgallery.org.uk
National Portrait Gallery UK	www.npg.org.uk
Ormeau Baths Gallery	www.ormeaubathsgallery.co.uk
Photo Art	www.photoart.ie
Pictures of Ireland	www.picturesofireland.com
Project Arts Centre	www.project.ie
q gallery	www.qgallery.co.uk
RHA Gallagher Gallery	http://homepage.tinet.ie
Riverview Art Gallery	www.irishpaintings.net
Roisin O'Shea	www.roisinoshea.ie
Royal Academy UK	www.royalacademy.org.uk
Sam Fleming	www.samfleming.com
Sculptors Society of Ireland	www.sculptors-society.ie
Sheldonart	www.sheldonart.com
Stephen Bennett	www.stephenbennett.net
Stunned ArtZine	www.stunned.org
Tate Gallery	www.tate.org.uk
Taylor Gallery	www.taylorgallery.co.uk
Tyrone Guthrie Centre	www.tyroneguthrie.ie
Ulster Museum	www.ulstermuseum.org.uk
Waldock Gallery	www.irishpaintings.com
White Cube	www.whitecube.com

clubs

Ireland

Docs Nightclub	www.docs.ie
Earth (Drogheda)	www.earthdrogheda.com
Equinox Nite Club (Sligo)	www.equinoxniteclub.ie
Grill (Letterkenny)	www.thegrillniteclub.ie
GPO Nightclub (Galway)	www.gpoclub.ie
Parliament (Belfast)	www.theparliament.co.uk
Playhouse Nightclub (Dublin)	www.playhousedublin.com
Pod	www.pod.ie
Temple Theatre (Dublin)	www.templetheatre.ie
Velure (Dublin)	www.velure.com
Zoo (Dublin)	www.zoonightclub.com

Northern Ireland

Boom Boom Rooms (Bangor)	www.boomboomroom.club24.co.uk
Dempsey's International (Belfast)	www.dempseysterrace.co.uk
Elk (Toome)	www.the.elk.co.uk
Kelly's Complex (Portrush)	www.kellys-portrush.com
M Club (Belfast)	www.mclub.co.uk
Met (Armagh)	www.themet.co.uk
Milk (Belfast)	www.clubmilk.com
Nero's (Portrush)	www.nerosniteclub.com
Parliament (Belfast)	www.theparliament.co.uk
Shine@Queens (Belfast)	www.shine.net
Shelter (Dublin)	
Thompsons (Belfast)	www.thomponsbelfast.com

club and pub guides

Big Blue Spot	www.bigbluespot.com/belfast/bars.asp
Bbm Magazine	www.bbmag.co.uk
Clubbing.com	www.clubbing.com
Cybersonik Magazine	www.cybersonik.com
Dance Link	www.dance-link.com
Dance Magazine.com	www.dance-magazine.com
DJ List	www.thedjlist.com
Dublin Drinking	www.dublindrinking.com
Innkeeper, The	www.theinnkeeper.co.uk
Irish DJs Online	www.irishdj.cjb.net
Ministry of Sound	www.ministryofsound.com
Nightclub Network	www.nightclub.com
Nightclubs by county	www.accessentertainment.co.uk/nightclubs
Privilege	www.privilege-ibiza.com
Northern Ireland DJ	www.northernirelanddj.com
Ulster Pub Guide	www.go2pub.com
UK Clubs	www.ukclubs.co.uk
V-club	www.v-club.co.uk
Where to tonight	www.wheretotonight.com

comedy

2irish	www.2irish.com
Acme Comedy Management & Exploitation	http://irishcomedy.com
City Limits Comedy Club	www.dmcwebs.com/citylimits
Comedy Cellar	www.comedycellar.cc
Comedy Store	www.thecomedystore.co.uk
Comic Relief	www.comicrelief.org.uk
D'Unbelievables	www.irishcorner.com
Ed Byrne	www.edbyrne.com
Eddie Izzard	www.izzard.com

French & Saunders	www.frenchandsaunders.com
Graham Norton	www.grahamnorton.co.uk
Ha'penny Laugh	www.iol.ie/~damianr/hapenny
Kevin Gildea	www.dmcwebs.com/kevingildea
Make'em Laugh	www.rte.ie/tv/makeemlaugh
Monty Python Online	www.pythonline.com
Navanman	www.navanman.ie
Reeves & Mortimer	www.boehme.demon.co.uk/phil/rm/rm.html

dance

Ballet Companies.com	http://balletcompanies.com
Ballet Ireland	www.dancecompanies.net/countries/ireland.html
Bellydance Ireland	www.bellydance-irl.com
CoisCéim Dance Theatre	www.iol.ie/~coisceim
Daghdha Dance Company	www.ul.ie/~ddc
Dance Collective Northern Ireland	www.niinternet.com/dance
English National Ballet	www.ballet.org.uk
Irish Dancing.com	www.irishdancing.com
Irish National Youth Ballet Company	http://homepage.eircom.net/~inybco/home
Kirov Ballet	www.webcom.com/shownet/kirov
Michael Flatley's Lord of the Dance	www.lordofthedance.com
National Performing Arts School	www.npas.ie
Riverdance	www.riverdance.com
Royal Academy of Dancing	www.rad.org.uk

events/festivals

Anamu	www.topgold.com/anamu
BAFTA Awards	www.bafta.org
Belfast Carnival	www.belfastcarnival.org
Belfast Festival at Queen's	www.belfastfestival.com
Booker Prize	www.bookerprize.com
Brit Awards	www.brits.co.uk
Cannes Film Festival	www.festival-cannes.fr
Cathedral Quarter Arts Festival	www.cqaf.com
Celtronic Dance Festival	www.celtronic.com
Cinemagic	www.cinemagic.org.uk
Cork Film Festival	www.corkfilmfest.org
Docklands – Ireland's Documentary Film Festival	www.doclands.ie
Dublin Dog Show	www.dogsireland.com/dublindss.htm
Dublin Film Festival	www.ireland.iol.ie/dff
Dublin Fringe Festival	www.fringefest.com

Dublin Literary Pub Crawl	www.dublinpubcrawl.com
Dublin Theatre Festival	www.eircomtheatrefestival.com
Dublin Writers Festival	http://homepage.eircom.net/~dwf
Edinburgh Festival	www.edinburghfestivals.co.uk
Edinburgh Fringe Festival	www.edfringe.com
Feile An Phobail	www.feilebelfast.com
Feile Iorras	www.feileiorras.org
Fiddlers Green Folk Festival	www.fiddlersgreenfestival.com
Film Fleadh	www.filmfleadh.com
Fleadh Cheoil na hÉireann	www.fleadhcheoil.com
Fleadh Festival	www.fleadhfestival.com
Foyle Film Festival	www.foylefilmfestival.com
Galway Arts Festival	www.galwayartsfestival.com
Glastonbury Festival	www.glastonbury-festival.co.uk
Glyndebourne	www.glyndebourne.com
Guinness Jazz Festival	www.corkjazzfestival.com
Heart of the Glens Festival	www.nacn.org/cushendall
International IMPAC Dublin Literary Award	www.impacdublinaward.ie
International Music Festival	www.icorch.com/festival00.html
Irish Times Literary Prize	http://ireland.com/dublin/entertainment/books/featurea0409.htm
Kilkenny Arts Festival	www.kilkennyarts.ie
London Fashion Week	www.londonfashionweek.co.uk
London Festival of Literature	www.theword.org.uk
London Film Festival	www.lff.org.uk
London International Festival of Theatre	www.lift-info.co.uk
Mobo Awards	www.mobo.net
Montreux Jazz Festival	www.montreuxjazz.com
Moscow State Circus	www.moscowstatecircus.co.uk
Motor Show	www.motorshow.co.uk
Murphy's Cat Laughs Comedy Festival	www.thecatlaughs.com
Music Festivals Worldwide	www.festivals.com
Oscars (Academy of Motion Picture Arts & Sciences)	www.oscars.org
Puck Fair Festival	www.puckfair.ie
Pulitzer Prize	www.pulitzer.org
Reading Festival	www.readingfestival.co.uk
Roe Valley Folk Festival	www.folk-festival.com
Rose of Tralee	www.roseoftralee.ie
St. Patrick's Festival	www.paddyfest.ie
Venice Film Festival	www.doge.it/mostra/56
Wexford Festival Opera	www.wexfordopera.com
Whitbread Book Awards	www.whitbreadbookawards.co.uk

Witness	www.witnness.com
Womad	www.womad.org
Yeats Summer School	www.itsligo.ie/yeats/ss99/ssppbroc.htm

fashion

Eddie Shanahan – The Agency	www.theagency.ie
Fashion Planet	www.fashion-planet.com
Image	www.image.ie
Irish Fashion	www.irish-fashion.com
Marc O'Neill	www.marconeill.com

film

actors & actresses

Adam Sandler	www.adamsandler.com
Aidan Quinn	www.fusic.com/enasp/aidanquinn.asp
Alicia Silverstone	www.alicia-silverstone.net
Alyssa Milano	www.alyssa.com
Anna Friel	www.netshopuk.co.uk/annafriel
Anthony Hopkins	www.nasser.net/hopkins
Antonio Banderas	www.antoniobanderasfans.com
Arnold Schwarzenegger	www.schwarzenegger.com
Audrey Hepburn	www.audreyhepburn.com
Ava Gardner	www.avagardner.org
Ben Affleck	www.affleck.com
Bob Hope	www.bobhope.com
Brad Pitt	www.celebsites.com/html/bradpitt
Bruce Lee	www.brucelee.org.uk
Bruce Willis	www.brucewillis.net
Burl Ives	www.burlives.com
Cameron Diaz	www.cameron-diaz.com
Carrie Fisher	www.carriefisher.com
Cary Grant	www.carygrant.co.uk
Cheryl Ladd	www.cherylladd.com
Christian Bale	www.christianbale.org
Claire Danes	www.claire-danes.com
Clint Eastwood	www.clinteastwood.net
Courteney Cox	www.courteneycox.net
Daniel Day-Lewis	www.danielday.org
David Boreanaz	www.celebrityblvd.com/davidboreanaz
David Schwimmer	www.davidschwimmer.net
Denzel Washington	www.celebsites.com/html/denzelwashington
Dervla Kirwan	www.geocities.com/hollywood
Don Johnson	www.donjohnson.com

Doris Day	www.dorisday.com
Errol Flynn	www.errolflynn.net
Ewan McGregor	www.ewanspotting.com
Gail Porter	www.gail-porter-world.co.uk
George Clooney	www.welcome.to/clooney
Gillian Anderson	http://gaws.ao.net
Gwyneth Paltrow	www.gwyneth.cjb.net
Harold Lloyd	www.haroldlloyd.com
Harrison Ford (Fan Club)	www.harrisonford.indy-world.com
Helena Bonham-Carter	www.helena-bonham-carter.com
Ian McKellen	www.mckellen.com
Ingrid Pitt	www.pittofhorror.com
Jack Ryder	www.jackryder.cjb.net
James Dean	www.jamesdean.com
Jennifer Aniston	www.celebsites.com/jenniferaniston
Jeremy Irons	www.casenet.com/people/jeremyirons.htm
Jim Carrey	www.jimcarreyonline.com
Jimmy Stewart	www.jimmy.org
John Lynch	http://home.earthlink.net
John Travolta	http://dev.celebsites.com/johntravolta/index_f.htm
John Wayne	www.johnwaynebirthplace.org
Joseph Smith	www.joesmith.com
Kate Winslet	www.kate-winslet.org
Keanu Reeves	www.keanunet.com
Kelly Brook	www.kellybrookonline.com
Kevin Spacey	www.spacey.com
Kristen Johnston	www.kristenjohnston.net
Leonard Nimoy	www.nimoy.com
Leonardo di Caprio	www.leonardodicaprio.com
Liam Neeson	www.geocities.com/hollywood
Mark Wahlberg	www.markwahlberg.com
Martin Lawrence	www.martin-lawrence.com
Matt Damon	www.mattdamon.com
Maureen O'Hara	www.users.uswest.net/~aknot/lelajay.htm
Maureen O'Sullivan	www.geocities.com/hollywood
Meg Ryan	www.megryan.net
Mel Gibson	www.geocities.com/hollywood
Melanie Griffith (Fan Club)	www.antoniobanderasfans.com/melanie_griffith
Melissa Joan Hart	www.melissa-joan-hart.com
Michael Douglas	www.michaeldouglas.com
Nicolas Cage	www.cage-cave.avalon.hr
Nicole Kidman (Fan Club)	www.nicolekidman.org
Pamela Anderson Lee	www.pamelaandersonlee.com

Peter O'Toole	www.hame.toronto.on.ca/otoole
Pierce Brosnan	http://piercebrosnan.jamesbond-online.com
Richard Harris	www.geocities.com/hollywood
Robson Green	www.robsongreen.com
Roy Rogers	www.royrogers.com
Sandra Bullock	www.sandra.com
Sean Connery	www.thespiannet.com/actors/c/connery_sean/index.shtml
Stephen Collins	www.stephencollins.com
Thomas Dolby	www.thomas-dolby.com
Timothy Dalton	www.timothydalton.com
Tom Cruise (Fan Club)	www.tomcruise.fans.net
Tony Curtis	www.tonycurtis.com
Tony Hancock (Fan Club)	www.staff.ncl.ac.uk/nigel.collier/index2.html
Tori Spelling	www.tori-spelling.com
Val Kilmer	http://vkn.com
Wes Craven	www.wescraven.com
Will Smith	www.willsmith.net
William Shatner	www.williamshatner.com
Winona Ryder	www.winonaryder.org

cinemas

IFC	www.fii.ie
Imax	www.imax.com
Lisburn Omniplex	www.filminfo.net
Movie House Cinemas	www.moviehouse.co.uk
Ormonde Stillorgan	www.ormondecinemas.com
Queen's Film Theatre, Belfast	www.qub.ac.uk/qft
Roxy	www.roxycinema.co.uk
Sheridan Imax, Belfast	www.belfastimax.com
Ster Century	www.stercentury.net
Strand, The	www.strand4screens.co.uk
Thirteen Denzille	www.13denzille.com
UCI	www.uci-cinemas.co.uk
Virgin	www.virgin.net/cinema
Warner Village Cinemas	www.warnervillage.co.uk

films

A.I. Artificial Intelligence	http://aimovie.warnerbros.com
America's Sweethearts	www.spe.sony.com/movies/americassweethearts/home/index.html
American Beauty	www.americanbeauty-thefilm.com
American Pie 2	www.americanpiemovie.com
Angela's Ashes	www.angelasashes.com
As Good As It Gets	www.spe.sony.com/movies/asgoodasitgets

Austin Powers	www.austinpowers.com
Back to the Future	www.bttf.com
Batman & Robin	www.batman-robin.com
Being John Malkovich	www.beingjohnmalkovich.com
Big Lebowski	www.lebowski.com
Billy Elliot	www.billyelliot.com
Blair Witch Project	www.blairwitch.co.uk
Boogie Nights	www.boogie-nights.com
Bread and Roses	www.breadandrosesthemovie.com
Bridget Jones Diary	www.miramax.com/bridgetjonesdiary
Bully	www.bullythemovie.com
Captain Corelli's Mandolin	www.captain-corellis-mandolin.com
Carry On	www.carryonline.com
Cats and Dogs	www.catsanddogsmovie.warnerbros.com
Celebrity	www.miramax.com/celebrity
Chicken Run	www.chickenrun.co.uk
Crazy/beautiful	http://studio.go.com/movies/crazybeautiful
Crouching Tiger, Hidden Dragon	www.spe.sony.com/cthv/crouchingtiger
Dancer in the Dark	www.tvropa.com/tvropa1.2/dancer/main.asp
Dinosaur	http://disney.go.com/disneypictures/dinosaur/dinomain.html
Divorcing Jack	www.divorcingjack.com
Driven	www.what-drives-you.com
East is East	www.eastiseast.co.uk
End of the Affair	www.spe.sony.com/movies/endoftheaffair
Erin Brockovich	www.erinbrockovich.com
Essex Boys	www.essexboysthemovie.com
Evolution	www.countingdown.com/evolution
Eyes Wide Shut	www.eyeswideshut.com
Fast & the Furious	www.thefastandthefurious.com
Final Fantasy	www.finalfantasy.com
Galaxy Quest	www.galaxyquest.com
Girl, Interrupted	www.girlinterrupted.com
Gladiator	www.gladiator-thefilm.com
Grease	www.greasemovie.com
Hannibal	www.mgm.com/hannibal
High Fidelity	http://studio.go.com/movies/highfidelity
Highlander	www.highlander-official.com

How to Cheat in the Leaving Certificate	www.tadhg.net/htc/making.html
I Went Down	www.iftn.ie/iwentdown
Independence Day	www.id4.com
Inspector Gadget	http://disney.go.com/disneyvideos/familyfilm/shelves/gadget
Into the West	www.littlebird.ie
Jackie Brown	www.jackiebrown.co.uk
James Bond	www.jamesbond.com
Jaws	www.jawsmovie.com
Jurassic Park 3	www.jurassicpark.com
Knight's Tale, A	www.aknightstale.com
Legally Blonde	www.mgm.com/legallyblonde/main.html
Lock, Stock & Two Smoking Barrels	www.lockstock2barrels.com
Lord of the Rings	www.lordoftherings.net
Magnolia	www.magnoliamovie.com
Matrix, The	http://whatisthematrix.warnerbros.com
Me, Myself & Irene	www.memyselfandirene.com
Michael Collins	www.michaelcollins.warnerbros.com
Mission Impossible	www.missionimpossible.com
Moulin Rouge	www.moulinrougemovie.com
Nightmare on Elm Street	www.elmstreet.co.uk
Notting Hill	www.notting-hill.com
Nutty Professor II	www.klumps.com
Pearl Harbour	http://studio.go.com/movies/pearlharbour/html/index.html
Perfect Storm	www.perfectstorm.net
Planet of the Apes	www.planetoftheapes.com
Pokémon	www.pokemonthemovie.com
Prince of Egypt	www.prince-of-egypt.com
Psycho	www.universalstudios.com/home
Rocky Horror Picture Show	www.rockyhorror.com
Rugrats Movie	www.rugratsmovie.com
Rush Hour 2	www.rushhour2.com
Saving Private Ryan	www.rzn.com/pvt.ryan
Scary Movie	www.scarymovie.com
Shaft (2000)	www.shaft-themovie.com
Shakespeare in Love	www.miramax.com/shakespeareinlove
Shrek	www.shrek.com
Snatch	www.snatch-themovie.com
Snow Falling on Cedars	www.snowfallingoncedars.com
South Park the Movie	www.southparkmovie.com
Spinal Tap	www.spinaltap.com

Star Trek	www.startrek.com
Star Wars	www.starwars.com
Stuart Little	www.stuartlittle.com
Summer Catch	http://summercatch.warnerbros.com
Sweet and Lowdown	www.spe.sony.com/classics/sweetandlowdown
Swordfish	www.operationswordfish.com
Tarzan (Disney's)	www.tarzan.co.uk
The Beach	www.virgin.net/thebeach
The Butcher Boy	www.thebutcherboy.com
The Closer You Get	www.foxsearchlight.com
The General	www.spe.sony.com/classics/general
The Mummy	www.themummy.com
The Patriot	www.spe.sony.com/movies/thepatriot
The Phantom Menace	www.starwars.com/episode-i
The Talented Mr Ripley	www.talentedmrripley.com
The World is Not Enough	www.jamesbond.com/bond19
Thomas Crown Affair	www.mgm.com/thethomascrownaffair
Titan A.E.	www.titanae.com
Titanic	www.titanicmovie.com
Tomorrow Never Dies	www.tomorrowneverdies.com
Toy Story 2	http://disney.go.com/worldsofdisney/toystory2
Trainspotting	www.miramax.com/trainspotting
U-571	www.u-571.com
What's Cooking	www.whatscookingthefilm.com
Wizard of Oz	www.thewizardofoz.com
X-Men	www.x-men-the-movie.com

organisations

Academy of Motion Picture Arts & Sciences	www.orcars.org
American Film Institute	www.afionline.org
Association of Independent Video and Filmmakers	www.aivf.org
Association of Motion Picture Sound	www.amps.net
BAFTA	www.bafta.org
Bord Scannán na hÉireann	www.filmboard.ie
British Board of Film Classification	www.bbfc.co.uk
British Film Commission	www.britfilmcom.co.uk
British Film Institute	www.bfi.org.uk
British Screen Finance	www.britishscreen.co.uk
British Universities Film & Video Council	www.bufvc.ac.uk
British Video Association	www.bva.org.uk

Ceol n Irish Traditional Music Centre	www.ceol.ie
County Wicklow Film Commission	www.wicklow.ie/film
Directors' Guild of Great Britain	www.dggb.co.uk
Film Institute of Ireland	www.fii.ie
Film Makers Ireland	www.filmmakersireland.ie
Galway Film Centre	www.galwayfilmcentre.ie
Independent Production Unit RTE	www.rte.ie/ipu
Irish Actors Equity	www.iftn.ie
Irish Cinema	www.irishcinema.com
Irish Film & Television Academy	www.ifta.ie
Irish Film Board	www.filmboard.ie
Irish Film Centre	www.fii.ie/ifc
New Producers Alliance	www.npa.org.uk
Northern Ireland Film Commission	www.nifc.co.uk
Oscars	www.oscar.com
Screen Commission Ireland	www.screencommireland.com
Screen Training Ireland	www.screentrainingireland.ie
Women in Film and Television	www.wif.org

production companies & studios

20th Century Fox UK	www.fox.co.uk
Ardmore Studios Ireland	www.ardmore.ie
Armed Eye Film Production & Education	www.armedeyefilm.com
Bollywood	www.bollywood.org.uk
Buena Vista International	www.bvimovies.com
Castle Rock	www.castle-rock.com
Claddagh Films	www.claddagh.ie
Columbia Tristar	www.spe.sony.com/movies
Dimension Films	www.dimensionfilms.com
Disney Studios	www.disney.com/disneypictures
Dreamchaser Productions	www.iftn.ie/dreamchaser
Ealing Studios	www.ealingstudios.co.uk
Elstree Film Studios	www.elstreefilmstudios.co.uk
FilmFour	www.filmfour.com
Fine Line Features	www.flf.com
HDS Studios	www.hds-studios.com
Hollywood	www.hollywood.com
Hummingbird	www.iftn.ie/production/h/hummingbird.html
Laganside Studios	www.laganside-studios.com
Leavesden Studios	www.leavesdenstudios.com
Lucas Film	www.lucasfilm.com
MCA Universal	www.mca.com
Merlin Films Group Limited	www.merlin.ie
MGM Studios	www.mgm.com
Miramax	www.miramax.com
Network Ireland Television	www.network-irl-tv.com

New Line	www.newline.com
Northern Visions Media Centre	www.northernvisions.org
October Films	www.octoberfilms.com
Orion	www.orionpictures.com
Paramount Studios	www.paramount.com/motionpicture
Pathé	www.pathé.co.uk
Picture Palace Productions	www.picturepalace.com
Polygram Video	www.polygramvideo.co.uk
Poolbeg Productions	www.poolbeg.ie
Radius Television Productions	www.iftn.ie/production/r/radius.html
RTÉ Facilities and Engineering	www.rte.ie/about/facilities
Sony Pictures Entertainment	www.spe.sony.com
Steven Spielberg Dreamworks	www.spielberg-dreamworks.com
Teddington	www.teddington.co.uk
Telegael Teo	www.iftn.ie/facilities/t/telegael.html
The Yard	www.theyard.ie
Three Mills Island	www.threemills.com
Tyrone Productions	www.tyroneproductions.com
United International Pictures	www.uip.com
Universal Studios	www.universalstudios.com
Walt Disney Studios	www.disney.go.com
Warner Brothers Studios	www.movies.warnerbros.com

funding and regulation

Aosdána	www.artscouncil.ie/aosdana
Arts Council for England	www.artscouncil.org.uk
Arts Council for Ireland	www.artscouncil.ie
Arts Council of Northern Ireland	www.artscouncil-ni.org
Arts, Heritage Gaeltacht & the Islands (Dept of)	www.irlgov.ie/ealga
British Copyright Council	www.britishcopyright.org.uk
Broadcasting Standards Commission	www.bsc.org.uk
Community Development Foundation	www.cdf.org.uk
Copyright Licensing Agency	www.cla.co.uk
Department for Culture, Media & Sport	www.culture.gov.uk
Independent Radio and Television Commission	www.irtc.ie
Independent Television Commission	www.itc.co.uk
National Lottery Charities Board	www.nlcb.org.uk
New Opportunities Fund	www.nof.org.uk
Office of the Director of Telecommunications Regulation	www.odtr.ie

literature

authors & societies

Anne Frank	www.annefrank.com
Danielle Steele	www.daniellesteele.com
Danny Morrison	www.dannymorrison.com
Fay Weldon	www.tile.net/weldon
Flann O'Brien	www.hellshaw.com/flann
George Bernard Shaw	www.georgebernardshaw.com
Ian Fleming	www.ianfleming.org
Ireland Literature Exchange	www.indigo.ie/~ilew
Irish Poets Worldwide	www.irishpoetsworldwide.com
Irish Translators' Association	homepage.eircom.net/~translation
James Joyce	www.jamesjoyce.ie
John Connolly	www.johnconnolly.co.uk
John Grisham	www.jgrisham.com
John Steinbeck	www.steinbeck.org
Ken Follett	www.ken-follett.com
Lewis Carroll	www.lewiscarroll.org/carroll
London Review of Books	www.lrb.co.uk
Maeve Binchy	www.randomhouse.com/features/binchy
Margaret Drabble	www.tile.net/drabble
Martina Devlin	www.martinadevlin.com
Mary A Larkin	www.marylarkin.co.uk
PG Wodehouse (Fan Club)	www.serv.net/~camel/wodehouse
Poetry Book Society	www.poetrybooks.co.uk
Poetry Ireland	www.poetryireland.ie
Poetry Review	www.poetrysoc.com
Roddy Doyle	www.penguinputnam.com/roddydoyle/start.htm
Rudyard Kipling	www.kipling.org.uk
Samuel Beckett	www.reading.ac.uk/serdepts/vl/lib/bif/bif.html
Seamus Heaney	www.ibiblio.org/dykki/poetry
Shakespeare Birthplace Trust	www.shakespeare.org.uk
Stephen King	www.stephenking.com
World-Wide Wilde Web	www.showgate.com/tots/gross/wildeweb.html
Yeats Society Sligo	www.yeats-sligo.com

irish language associations

Comhaltas Ceoltóirí Éireann	www.comhaltas.com
Féile Pan-Cheilteach	www.panceltic.com
Gaelscoileanna	www.iol.ie/gaelscoileanna
oideas Gael	www.oideas-gael.com

publishers

A & A Farmer	www.farmerbooks.com
Appletree Press	www.appletree.ie
Blackstaff Press	www.blackstaffpress.com
Clo Iar-Chonnachta	www.cic.ie
Cois Life	www.coislife.ie
Collins Press	www.collinspress.com
Colourpoint Books	www.colourpoint.co.uk
Gill & Macmillan	www.gillmacmillan.ie
Kogan Page	www.kogan-page.co.uk
Mentor Books	www.mentorbooks.ie
Mercier Press	www.indigo.ic/mercier
O'Brien Press	www.obrienpress.ie
Oaktree Press	www.oaktreepress.com
Poolbeg Press	www.poolbeg.com
Salmon Publishing	www.salmonpoetry.com
Wolfhound Press	www.wolfhound.ie

magazines and websites

Amateur Stage	www.uktw.co.uk/amstage
Amnet	www.amnet.ie
Art Guide	www.artguide.org.uk
Art Libraries of UK & Ireland	http://arlis.nal.vam.ac.uk
Art Review	www.art-review.co.uk
Arts Business	www.arts-business.co.uk
Arts Worldwide	www.artsworldwide.org.uk
BBC Music	www.bbcworldwide.com/musicmagazine
BlankMag.com	www.blankmag.com
Blather	www.blather.net
Bookview Ireland	www.bookviewireland.ie
Casting Weekly	www.ndirect.co.uk/~castingw
Ceili.ie	www.ceili.ie
Celebrities.com	www.celebrities.com
Circa Art Magazine	www.recirca.com
CLÉ	www.irishbooks.org
CLUAS	www.cluas.com
Comedy Central	www.comedycentral.com
Comhaltas Ceoltoiri Eireann	www.comhaltas.org
Culture Ireland	www.cultureireland.com
Daily Tonic	www.dailytonic.com
Dotmusic	www.dotmusic.com
Economist	www.economist.co.uk
Empire	www.empireonline.co.uk
Entertainment Ireland	www.entertainmentireland.ie
Event Guide	www.eventguide.ie
Extreme Ireland	www.extremeireland.com
Film Find	www.filmfind.tv
Film Institute of Ireland	www.fii.ie

Film net	www.filmnet.ie
FilmInfo	www.filminfo.net
Galleries Magazine	www.artefact.co.uk
Hibernia Magazine	www.twoh.com
Hot Press	www.hot-press.com
In Belfast Magazine	www.inbelfastmagazine.com
In Dublin	www.indublin.ie
International Directory of Art Libraries	http://iberia.vassar.edu/ifla-idal
International Movie Database	www.imdb.com
Irish Classical Music Guide	www.geocities.com
Irish Drum and Bass magazine	www.irishdrumandbass.com
Irish Film & Television Net	www.iftn.ie
Irish Music Net	www.imn.ie
Irish Tatler (IT)	www.smurfit.ie/comms
Irish Traditional Music Archive	www.itma.ie
Irish Visions	www.irishvisions.com
Irish Writer's Centre	www.writerscentre.ie
Irish Writer's Guide	http://homepage.eircom.net
Live Art Magazine	http://art.ntu.ac.uk/livemag
Magill	www.hoson.com
Magpie	www.magpie.ie
Media Week	www.mediaweek.co.uk
MP3	www.mp3.com
Mr Showbiz	http://mrshowbiz.go.com
Muse	www.muse.ie
Music Network	www.musicnetwork.ie
MusicWeb Ireland	www.musweb.com
New Musical Express	www.nme.com
Northern Ireland Entertainment Centre	www.onthetowntonite.com
Official London Theatre	www.officiallondontheatre.co.uk
Out On The Town	www.outonthetown.ie
Phoenix Magazine	www.phoenix-magazine.com
Poetry Ireland Review	www.poetryireland.ie
Q	www.qonline.co.uk
Radio Times	www.radiotimes.co.uk
Radiowaves	www.radiowaves.fm
Rolling Stone	www.rollingstone.com
RTÉ Guide	www.rteguide.ie
Satellite World	www.satelliteworld.demon.co.uk
Scroll Internet Magazine	www.scroll.ie
SHOWBIZ Ireland	www.showbizireland.com
Skip Music	www.skipmusic.co.uk
Smash Hits	www.c3.vmg.co.uk
Source Magazine	www.source.ie
Stinging Fly	www.stingingfly.org
Teletext	www.teletext.co.uk

Text-me	www.text-me.ie
The Stage	www.thestage.co.uk
Theatre	www.uktw.co.uk/theatremag
Time	www.time.com
Time Out	www.timeout.com
TV Times	www.tvtimes.co.uk
Ultimate Band List	www.ubl.com
Uncut Magazine	www.uncut.net
Warner ESP (Music Catalogue)	www.warneresp.co.uk
What's on Where	www.wow.ie
World Pop	www.worldpop.com

music

music artists

4 of Us	www.the4ofus.com
911	www.c3.vmg.co.uk/911
Abba	www.abbasite.com
Aerosmith	www.aerosmith.com
Alanis Morisette	www.alanismorisette.com
All Saints	www.theallsaints.com
Altan	www.altan.ie
Another Level	www.anotherlevel.co.uk
Aqua	www.aqua.dk
Ash	www.ash-official.com
Aslan	www.aslan.ie
Atomic Kitten	www.atomickitten.co.uk
B*Witched	www.b-witched.com
Backstreet Boys	www.backstreetboys.com
Barry Manilow	www.manilow.com
BB King	www.bbking.com
Beach Boys	www.beachboys.com
Beatles	http://emanon.net/~ringo/beatles.htm
Beck	www.beck.com
Bee Gees	www.beegees.net
Belle & Sebastian	www.jeepster.co.uk/belleandsebastian
Billie Piper	www.billiepiper.com
Billy Idol	www.billyidol.com
Björk	www.bjork.co.uk/bjork
Björn Again	www.bjornagain.com
Black Sabbath	www.black-sabbath.com
Blondie	www.blondie.net
Blur	www.blur.co.uk
Bob Dylan	www.bobdylan.com
Bob Marley	www.bobmarley.com
Boy George	www.boy.george.net
Boyzone	www.boyzone.co.uk
Brian Kennedy	www.briankennedy.co.uk

Britney Spears	www.britneyspears.co.uk
Bruce Springsteen	www.brucespringsteen.net
Cardigans	www.cardigans.net
Catatonia	www.catatonia.com
Celine Dion	www.celineonline.com
Charlie Parker	www.charlieparker.com
Cher	www.cher.com
Chris de Burgh	www.cdeb.com
Christina Aguilera	www.christina-aguilera.com
Christy Moore	www.christymoore.net
Clannad	www.clannad.com
Cleopatra	www.cleopatramusic.com
Cliff Richard	www.cliffrichard.org
Coldplay	www.coldplay.com
Corrs	www.corrs.com
Craig David	www.craigdavid.co.uk
Cranberries	www.the-cranberries.net
Crash Test Dummies	www.crashtestdummies.com
Cure	www.thecure.com
Daniel O'Donnell	www.infowing.ie/donegal/daniel/daniel.htm
David Bowie	www.davidbowie.com
David Gray	www.davidgray.com
David Holmes	www.davidholmes.com
Davy Spillane	www.davyspillane.com
Deep Purple	www.deep-purple.com
Del Amitri	www.delamitri.com
Des'ree	www.desree.co.uk
Destiny's Child	www.destinyschild.com
Diana Ross	www.dianaross.com
Divine Comedy	www.thedivinecomedy.com
Donny & Marie Osmond	www.donnyandmarie.com
Doors	www.thedoors.com
Duke Ellington (Fan Club)	www.duke.fuse.net
Elton John	www.eltonjohn.com
Elvis Costello	www.elvis-costello.com
Elvis Presley	www.elvis-presley.com
Eminem	www.eminemworld.com
Emma Bunton	www.emma-bunton.net
Enya	www.repriserec.com/enya
Eric Clapton	www.repriserec.com/ericclapton
Everything but the Girl	www.ebtg.com
Five	www.5ive.co.uk
Frames	http://listen.at/theplateau
Frank Sinatra	www.sinatrafamily.com
Fugees	www.fugees.net
Gabrielle	www.gabrielle.co.uk
Garbage	www.garbage.com
Genesis	www.genesis-web.com

George Michael	www.aegean.net
Geri Halliwell	www.gerihalliwell.co.uk
Gerry Marsden & the Pacemakers	www.gerrymarsden.com
Gloria Estefan	www.gloriafan.com
Grateful Dead	www.dead.net
Hanson	www.hansonline.com
Heaven 17	www.heaven17.com
Hollies	www.hollies.co.uk
Honeyz	www.honeyz.co.uk
Hootie & the Blowfish	www.hootie.com
Iron Maiden	www.ironmaiden.co.uk
Isaac Hayes	www.isaachayes.com
Jamiroquai	www.jamiroquai.co.uk
Janet Jackson	www.friendsofjanet.com
Jean Michel Jarre	www.jeanmicheljarre.com
Jennifer Lopez	www.jenniferlopez.com
Jewel	www.jeweljk.com
Jimi Hendrix	www.jimi-hendrix.com
JJ72	www.jj72.org
Joan Armatrading	www.joanarmatrading.com
Joan Baez	www.baez.woz.org
Johnny Cash	www.johnnycash.com
Joni Mitchell	www.jonimitchell.com
Julian Cope	www.juliancope.com
Kelis	www.kelis.com
Kenny Rogers	www.kennyrogers.net
Kula Shaker	www.kulashaker.co.uk
Kylie Minogue	www.kylie.com
Led Zeppelin	www.atlantic-records.com/led_zeppelin
Lenny Kravitz	www.virginrecords.com/kravitz
Leonard Bernstein	www.leonardbernstein.com
Leonard Cohen	www.leonardcohen.com
Level 42	www.level42.com
Levellers	www.levellers.co.uk
Lightning Seeds	www.lightningseeds.com
Lou Reed	www.loureed.org
Macy Gray	www.macygray.com
Madonna	www.wbr.com/madonna
Manic Street Preachers	www.manics.co.uk
Mansun	www.mansun.co.uk
Mariah Carey	www.mariahcarey.com
Mariah Carey (Fan Club)	www.mariahcarey-fanclub.com
Marilyn Manson	www.marilynmanson.net
Mary J Blige	www.mjblige.com
Massive Attack	www.massiveattack.co.uk
Melanie C	www.northern-star.co.uk
Metallica	www.metclub.com
Michael Jackson	www.mjnet.com

Michael Nyman	www.december.org/nyman
Moby	www.moby.org
Moloko	www.moloko.co.uk
Natalie Imbruglia	www.natalie-imbruglia.co.uk
Neneh Cherry	www.nenehweb.com
Nsync	www.nsync.com
Oasis	www.oasisinet.com
Ocean Colour Scene	www.oceancolourscene.com
Patsy Cline	www.patsy.nu
Paul Brady	www.paulbrady.com
Peter Gabriel	www.geffen.com/gabriel
Phil Coulter	www.philcoulter.com
Phil Lynott	www.roisindubh.com
PJ Harvey	www.pjh.org
Placebo	www.placebo.co.uk
Placido Domingo	www.placido-domingo.com
Pogues	www.pogues.com
Portishead	www.portishead.co.uk
Prince	www.love4oneanother.com
Prodigy	www.theprodigy.co.uk
Public Enemy	www.public-enemy.com
Puff Daddy	www.puffdaddy.com
Pulp	www.rise.co.uk/pulp
Queen	www.queen-fip.com
Radiohead	www.radiohead.co.uk
Ramones	www.officialramones.com
Ray Charles	www.raycharles.com
REM	www.wbr.com/rem
Ricky Martin	www.rickymartin.com
Robbie Williams	www.robbiewilliams.co.uk
Rod Stewart	www.wbr.com/rodstewart
Rolling Stones	www.the-rolling-stones.com
Ronan Keating	www.ronankeating.net
Roy Orbison	www.orbison.com
S Club 7	www.sclub7.co.uk
Samantha Mumba	www.samanthamumba.com
Seal	www.wbr.com/seal
Shania Twain	www.shania-twain.com
Sheryl Crow	www.sherylcrow.com
Simon & Garfunkel	www.sonymusic.com/artists/simonandgarfunkel
Sinéad O'Connor (Fan Club)	www.sinead-oconnor.com
Sixpence None the Richer	www.sixpence-ntr.com
Smashing Pumpkins	www.smashing-pumpkins.net
Smokey Robinson & the Miracles (Fan Club)	www.edgenet.net/smokey_miracles
Spice Girls	http://c3.vmg.co.uk/spicegirls
Status Quo	www.statusquo.co.uk
Stephen Gately	www.stephengately.co.uk
Stephen Sondheim	www.sondheim.com

Steps	www.stepsofficial.com
Stereophonics	www.stereophonics.co.uk
Suede	www.suede.co.uk
Supergrass	www.supergrass.com
Thin Lizzy	www.hmccavera.freeserve.co.uk
Tina Turner	www.tina-turner.com
Tom Jones	www.tomjones.com
Tom Petty	www.tompetty.com
Toni Braxton	www.tonibraxton.net
Tori Amos	www.tori.com
Travis	www.travisonline.com
U2	www.u2.com
Ultimate Band List	www.ubl.com
Ultravox	www.ultravox.org.uk
Van Morrison	www.harbour.sfu.ca/~hayward/van/van.html
Vengaboys	www.vengaboys.com
Verve	www.the-raft.com/theverve
Westlife	www.westlife.co.uk
Wet Wet Wet	www.wetwetwet.co.uk
Whitney Houston	www.whitney-houston.co.uk
Whitney Houston (Fan Club)	www.whitney-fan.com
Will Smith	www.willsmith.net
Wyclef Jean	www.wyclef.com

promoters

Aiken Promotions	www.aikenpromotions.ie
MCD	www.mcd.ie
Note Productions	www.note.ie
Pat Egan Sounds	www.gmpublicity.com
Verve Marketing	www.verve.ie
Wonderland Promotions	www.wonderlandpromotions.co.uk

opera

Anna Livia International Opera Festival	www.operaannalivia.com
Castleward Opera	www.castlewardopera.faithweb.com
Cork Opera House	http://homepage.eircom.net
English National Opera	www.eno.org
Grand Opera House Belfast	www.goh.co.uk
Irish Opera Online	www.geocities.com
Irish Tenors	www.theirishtenors.com
Opera Ireland	www.opera-ireland.ie
Opera Theatre Company	www.imn.ie/otc
Wexford Festival Opera	www.wexfordopera.com

orchestras

Association of British Orchestras	www.abo.org.uk

BBC Symphony	www.bbc.co.uk/orchestras/so
Berlin Philharmonic	www.berlin-philharmonic.com
Boston Symphony	www.bso.org
Chicago Symphony	www.chicagosymphony.org
Contemporary Music Centre	www.cmc.ie
Hibernian Orchestra	www.geocities.com
Irish Chamber Orchestra	www.icorch.com
London Philharmonic	www.lpo.co.uk
London Symphony	www.lso.co.uk
Los Angeles	www.la.phil.org
National Association of Youth Orchestras	www.nayo.org.uk
National Symphony Orchestra of Ireland	www.rte.ie/music/nso
National Youth Orchestra of Ireland	http://homepage.tinet.ie/~nyoi
New York Philharmonic	www.nyphilharmon.org
Philharmonia	www.philharmonia.co.uk
Royal Philharmonic	www.rpo.co.uk
RTÉ Concert Orchestra	www.rte.ie/music/rteco
Ulster Orchestra	www.ulster-orchestra.org.uk
Ulster Youth Jazz Orchestra	www.sackbutt.demon.co.uk
Vanbrugh String Quartet	www.rte.ie/music/vanbrugh
Vienna Philharmonic	www.vienna.at/philharmoniker/vph
Vienna Symphony	www.weiner-symphoniker.at

organisations

British Music Information Centre	www.bmic.co.uk
British Phonographic Industry	www.bpi.co.uk
Comhaltas Ceoltóirí Éireann	www.comhaltas.com
Irish Music Rights Organisation	www.imro.ie
Irish Recorded Music Association	www.iol.ie/~ppiltd/irma.html
Irish Traditional Music Archive	www.itma.ie
Irish World Music Centre	www.ul.ie/~iwmc
Mechanical Copyright Protection Society	www.mcps.ie
Music Industries Association	www.mia.org.uk
Music Network	www.musicnetwork.ie
Performing Rights Society	www.prs.co.uk
Phonographic Performance Ireland	www.iol.ie/~ppiltd
Royal Academy of Music	www.riam.ie

record companies

21st Century Music	www.21stcentury.co.uk
A&M	www.amrecords.com
Ainm-Music.com	www.iol.ie/trend/ainm
Aran Records	www.aranmusic.co
Arista	www.aristarec.com
Atlantic	www.atlantic-records.com
Beggars Banquet	www.beggars.com

Blast Furnace Recording Studio	www.blast-furnace.com
BMG	www.bmg.com
CB Productions	www.cbproductions.co.uk
Celtic Collections	www.celtic-collections.com
Celtic Heartbeat	www.celticheartbeat.com
Celtic Note	www.celticnote.ie
Chandos	www.chandos-records.com
Cherry Moon	www.cherrymoon.com
Claddagh Records	http://indigo.ie/~claddagh
Columbia	www.columbiarecords.com
Creation	www.creation.co.uk
Decca	www.decca.com
Dolphin Discs	www.dolphindiscs.com
ECM	www.ecmrecords.com
Emerald Music	www.emeraldmusiconline.com
EMI Chrysalis	www.emichrysalis.co.uk
Epic	www.epicrecords.com
Geffen	www.geffen.com
Golden Discs	www.goldendiscs.ie
HMV	www.hmv.co.uk
Hyperion	www.hyperion-records.co.uk
Island	www.island.co.uk
Legacy Recordings	www.legacyrecordings.com
MCA	www.mcarecords.com
Mercury	www.mercuryrecords.com
Ministry of Sound	www.ministryofsound.co.uk
Naxos & Marco Polo	www.hnh.com
Nimbus	www.nimbus.ltd.uk
Parlophone	www.parlophone.co.uk
Polydor	www.polydor.co.uk
Polygram	www.polygram.com
QED Productions	www.qed-productions.com
Sony	www.sonymusic.co.uk
Sony Classical	www.sonyclassical.com
Tara	www.taramusic.com
Telstar	www.telstar.co.uk
Tower	www.towereurope.com
Universal	www.umusic.com
Virgin	www.virginrecords.com
Warner Brothers	www.wbr.com

stadia & venues

Birmingham NEC	www.nec.co.uk
Earls Court Olympia	www.eco.co.uk
Grand Opera House Belfast	www.goh.co.uk
HQ	www.imhf.com
King's Hall, Belfast	www.kingshall.co.uk
London Arena	www.londonarena.co.uk
National Concert Hall	www.nch.ie
Odyssey Arena	www.odysseyarena.co.uk

RDS	www.rds.ie
Roisin Dubh	http://roisindubh.net
Slane	www.csn.ul.ie
Temple Bar Music Centre	www.tbmc.ie
University Concert Hall Limerick	www.uch.ie
Vicar Street	www.vicarstreet.com
Waterfront Hall, Belfast	www.waterfront.co.uk
Wembley	www.wembley.co.uk
Whelans	www.whelanslive.com

professional bodies

Association of Art Historians	www.gold.ac.uk/aah
Association of Illustrators	www.aoi.co.uk
Association of Irish Musical Societies	www.aims.ie/main.htm
Association of Mouth & Foot Painting Artists Worldwide	www.amfpa.com
British Arts Festivals Association	www.artsfestivals.co.uk
British Society of Master Glass Painters	www.bsmgp.org.uk
Cartoonists' Guild	www.pipemedia.net/cartoons
Communications Workers Union Ireland (CWU)	www.cwu.ie
Directors' Guild of Great Britain	www.dggb.co.uk
English Regional Arts Boards	www.arts.org.uk
Equity British Actors' Union	www.equity.org.uk
Fine Art Trade Guild	www.fineart.co.uk
Guild of Film Production Accountants & Financial Administrators	www.gfpa.org.uk
Guild of Television Cameramen	www.gtc.org.uk
Heritage Council	www.heritagecouncil.ie
Impact Trade Union	www.impact.ie
Incorporated Society of Musicians	www.ism.org
Institute of Contemporary Arts	www.ica.org.uk
International Federation of Journalists	www.ifj.org
Irish Congress of Trade Unions	www.ictu.ie
Irish Writers Centre	www.writerscentre.ie
London Arts Board	www.arts.org.uk/directory/regions/london
London Association of Art & Design Education	www.laade.org
Magic Circle	www.themagiccircle.co.uk
Mandate Trade Union	www.iol.ie/arena/mandate
National Acrylic Painters Association	www.artarena.force9.co.uk/napa
National Archives of Ireland	www.nationalarchives.ie
National Art Library UK	www.nal.vam.ac.uk
National Portraiture Association	www.natportrait.com
National Union of Journalists	http://indigo.ie/~nujdub

New Broadcasters Association	www.irtc.ie/bassoc.htm
Producers' Alliance for Cinema & Television	www.pact.co.uk
Production Managers' Association	www.pma.org.uk
SIPTU	www.siptu.ie
Society of Authors	www.writers.org.uk/society
Society of Television Lighting Directors	www.stld.org.uk
Writers' Guild of Great Britain	www.writers.org.uk/guild

radio

103FM Cork	www.103fm.ie
2FM	www.rte.ie/2fm
95FM	www.95fm.ie
96FM Cork	www.96fm.ie
98FM The Sound of the City	www.98fm.ie
Anna Livia	www.irtc.ie/annalivi.htm
Atlantic	www.atlantic252.com
BBC Local Radio	www.bbc.co.uk/england
BBC Northern Ireland	www.bbc.co.uk/northernireland
BBC Radio 1	www.bbc.co.uk/radio1
BBC Radio 2	www.bbc.co.uk/radio2
BBC Radio 3	www.bbc.co.uk/radio3
BBC Radio 4	www.bbc.co.uk/radio4
BBC Radio 5	www.bbc.co.uk/radio5
BBC World Service	www.bbc.co.uk/worldservice
Capital FM (London)	www.capitalfm.com
Capital Gold (London)	www.capitalgold.co.uk
CKR FM	www.ckrfm.com
Clare FM	www.clarefm.ie
Classic FM	www.classicfm.co.uk
Classic Gold	www.classicgold828.co.uk
Classic Hits 98FM	www.98fm.ie
Cool FM (Belfast)	www.coolfm.co.uk
Donegal Highland Radio	www.highland.radio.com
Downtown Radio	www.downtown.co.uk
East Coast Radio	www.eastcoastradio.net
Emerald Radio Student Radio	www.emeraldradio.com
Energy FM	www.energy94.com
FM 104	www.fm104.ie
Galway Bay FM	www.wombat.ie/gbfm
Highland Radio	www.highlandradio.com
Jazz FM (London)	www.jazzfm.com
Kiss FM (London)	www.kissfm.co.uk
LBC (London)	www.lbc.co.uk
LM FM	www.lmfm.com
Lyric FM	www.lyricfm.ie
Manx Radio	www.manxradio.com
NEAR FM 101.6	www.nearfm.ie

News Direct (London)	www.newsdirect.co.uk
Phantom FM	www.phantomfm.com
Pirate FM	www.piratefm102.co.uk
Q102.9FM	www.q102-fm.com
Q97.2 FM	www.q97-fm.com
Radio Caroline	www.radiocaroline.co.uk
Radio Foyle	www.bbc.co.uk/northernireland
Radio Kerry	www.radiokerry.ie
Raidió na Gaelteachta	www.rnag.ie
Raidió na Life	www.iol.ie/~rnl102
RTE	www.rte.ie/radio
Shamrock Radio	www.shamrockradio.com
Southeast Radio	www.southeastradio.ie
Talk Radio	www.talk-radio.co.uk
Tipp FM Radio	www.tippfm.com
Today FM	www.todayfm.com
Virgin Radio	www.virginradio.com
Voice of America	www.voa.gov
WLR FM	www.wlrfm.com

television

organisations

Irish Film & Television Network	www.iftn.ie
Royal Television Society	www.rts.org.uk

production companies

Aardman Animations	www.aardman.com
About Face Media	www.aboutface.co.uk
Addictive Television	www.addictive.com
Claddagh Films	www.claddagh.ie
Footprint TV	www.footprint-tv.com
Ginger Media Group	www.ginger.com
Hat Trick Productions	www.hat-trick.co.uk
Little Bird	www.littlebird.ie
Mentorn	www.mentorn.co.uk
MGTV Ltd	www.mgtv.co.uk

programmes

2TV	www.rte.ie/tv/2tv
Alan Partridge	www.alan-partridge.co.uk
Ally McBeal	www.foxworld.com/ally
Babylon 5	http://babylon5.warnerbros.com
Ballykissangel	www.bbc.co.uk/ballykissangel
Baywatch	www.baywatchtv.com
BBC Comedy Zone	www.comedyzone.beeb.com
BBC Schools	www.bbc.co.uk/education/schools
Beverly Hills 90210	www.helicon7.com/90210

Bewitched	www.bewitched.net
Beyond the Hall Door	www.rte.ie/tv/beyondthehalldoor
Big Breakfast	www.bigbreakfast.channel4.com
Big Brother	www.bigbrother.terra.com
Blind Date	www.blinddate.co.uk
Brookside	www.brookie.com
Buffy the Vampire Slayer	www.buffyslayer.com
Bull Island	www.rte.ie/tv/bullisland
Castaway 2000	www.bbc.co.uk/castaway2000
Casualty	www.bbc.co.uk/casualty
Changing Rooms	www.bbc.co.uk/changingrooms
Charlie's Angels	www.charliesangels.com
Cold Feet	www.coldfeetonline.co.uk
Coronation Street	www.coronationstreet.co.uk
Dawson's Creek	www.dawsons-creek.com
Den2	www.rte.ie/tv/den2
Don't Feed the Gondolas	www.rte.ie/tv/dftg
Dot.what?	www.rte.ie/tv/dotwhat
Due South	www.duesouth.com
Eastenders	www.bbc.co.uk/eastenders
Echo Island	www.rte.ie/tv/echo
Emmerdale	www.emmerdale.co.uk
ER	www.ertv.com
Fair City	www.rte.ie/tv/faircity
Father Ted	www.geocities.com
Fawlty Towers	www.fawlty-towers.com
Frasier	www.frasier.mcmail.com
Friends	www.friends.warnerbros.com
Gardeners' World	www.gardenersworld.beeb.com
Gladiators	www.lwt.co.uk/gladiators
GMTV	www.gmtv.co.uk
Have I Got News For You	www.haveigotnewsforyou.com
Holby City	www.bbc.co.uk/holbycity
Holiday	www.takeoff.beeb.com
Hollyoaks	www.merseytv.com/hollyoaks.com
Home & Away	www.homeandaway.seven.com.au
Irish Dreamtime	www.rte.ie/tv/irishdreamtime
Jerry Springer Show	www.universalstudios.com/tv/jerryspringer
Kavanagh QC	www.kavanaghqc.co.uk
Knight Rider	www.knight-rider.com
Late Late Show	www.rte.ie/tv
Men Behaving Badly	www.menbehavingbadly.com
Monty Python	www.montypython.net

Morbegs	www.rte.ie/tv/morbegs
Mr Bean	www.mrbean.co.uk
Neighbours	www.baxendale.u-net.com/ramsayst
No Frontiers	www.rte.ie/tv/nofrontiers
NYPD Blue	www.nypdblue.com
Oprah Winfrey	www.oprahshow.com
Patrick Kielty Almost Live	www.bbc.co.uk/northernireland
Peak Practice	www.peakpractice.co.uk
Planet of the Apes	www.foxhome.com/planetoftheapes
Prime Time	www.rte.ie/news/primetime.html
Questions & Answers	www.rte.ie/news/qanda.html
Red Dwarf	www.reddwarf.co.uk
Seinfeld	www.seinfeld.com
South Park	www.southpark.co.uk
Star Trek	www.startrek.com
Streetwise	www.rte.ie/tv/streetwise
Talk TV	www.talktv.co.uk
TFI Friday	www.tfifriday.com
The Bill	www.thebill.com
The Fast Show	www.comedyzone.beeb.com/fastshow
The Prisoner	www.the-prisoner-6.freeserve.co.uk
The Saint	www.saint.org
The Sweeney	www.thesweeney.com
They Think It's All Over	www.talkback.co.uk/theythink
This Morning with Richard & Judy	www.g-wizz.net/thismorning
Tomorrow's World	www.bbc.co.uk/tw
Top Gear	www.topgear.beeb.com
Top of the Pops	www.totp.beeb.com
Who Wants to be a Millionaire?	www.rte.ie/tv/millionaire/millionaire.htm
Who Wants to be a Millionaire?	www.phone-a-friend.com
Wish You Were Here?	www.wishyouwerehere.com
World in Action	www.world-in-action.co.uk
X-Files	www.fox.com/thexfiles

television channels

BBC	www.bbc.co.uk
BBC News	www.news.bbc.co.uk
Beeb.com	www.beeb.com
Bravo	www.bravo.co.uk
Carlton	www.carltontv.co.uk
Carlton Select	www.carltonselect.com
Central	www.centraltv.co.uk
Channel 4	www.channel4.co.uk

Channel 5	www.channel5.co.uk
Christian Channel	www.godnetwork.com
CNN	www.cnn.com
Discovery	www.discovery.com
Disney Channel	www.disneychannel.co.uk
E4	www.e4.com
Emmys (Academy of Television Arts & Sciences)	www.emmys.org
Euro TV	www.eurotv.com
Film Four	www.filmfour.com
Golf Channel	www.thegolfchannel.com
Grampian	www.grampiantv.co.uk
Granada	www.granadatv.co.uk
Granada Plus	www.gplus.co.uk
Granada Sky	www.gsb.co.uk
HTV	www.htv.co.uk
ITV	www.itv.co.uk
ITV Digital	www.dubinfo.co.uk/itvdigital
Living	www.livingtv.co.uk
LWT	www.lwt.co.uk
MTV	www.mtv.co.uk
National Geographic	www.nationalgeographic.com
NBC	www.nbc.com
Nickelodeon	www.nickelodeon.co.uk
Paramount	www.paramount.com/television/index.html
RTÉ	www.rte.ie
S4C (Wales)	www.s4c.co.uk
Sci-Fi Channel	www.scifi.com
Sky	www.sky.com
Tara Television	www.taratv.net
TG4	www.tnag.ie
UTV (Ulster)	www.utvlive.com
Web TV	www.webtv.com

theatre

companies

Aisling Ghear	www.beal-feirste.com
Barnstorm Theatre Company	www.barnstorm.ie
Centre Stage	www.argonet.co.uk/users/cstage
Impact Theatre Company	www.impacttheatrecompany.com
Prime Cut Productions Ltd	www.primecutproductions.co.uk
Siamsa Tire	www.siamsatire.com
Team Theatre	www.teamtheatre.ie

organisations

National Association for Youth Drama	www.youthdrama.ie
Theatre Shop	www.theatreshop.ie

productions

Art	www.dewynters.com/art
Beautiful Game	www.beautifulgamemusical.com
Buddy Holly Story	www.mpcgroup.co.uk/buddy
Carousel	www.shubert.com/carousel.html
Cats	www.reallyuseful.com/cats
Chicago	www.chicagothemusical.com
Doctor Dolittle	www.doctordolittle.co.uk
Evita	www.thenewevita.com
Fosse the Musical	www.fosse.uk.com
Graduate	www.thegraduate.uk.com
Grease	www.grease-tour.com
Houdini The Musical	www.houdinithemusical.com
Jekyll & Hyde	www.jekyll-hyde.com
Les Misérables	www.lesmis.com
Lord of the Dance	www.lordofthedance.com
Macnas	www.failte.com/macnas
Mamma Mia!	www.mamma-mia.com
Miss Saigon	www.miss-saigon.com
Phantom of the Opera	www.thephantomoftheopera.com
Rent	www.rentdublin.com
Riverdance	www.riverdance.com
Rocky Horror Picture Show	www.rockyhorror.com
Saturday Night Fever	www.nightfever.co.uk
Spend, Spend, Spend	www.spendspendspend.net
Spirit of the Dance	www.spiritofthedance.com
Tap Dogs	www.tapdogs.com
The King and I	www.kingandi.co.uk

theatres

Abbey Theatre	www.abbeytheatre.ie
An Grianan	www.angrianan.com
Andrew's Lane Theatre	www.homepage.eircom.net/~irishtheatre
Ark	www.ark.ie
Belltable	www.commerce.ie/belltable
City Arts Centre	http://homepage.eircom.net/~cityarts
Conway Mill	www.conwaymill.org
Crypt Arts Centre	www.dublinevents.com/theatre/cryptarts
Everyman Palace Theatre	www.everymanpalace.com

Gaiety Theatre	www.gaietytheatre.net
Gate Theatre	www.gate-theatre.ie
Grand Opera House Belfast	www.goh.co.uk
Lyric Theatre	www.lyrictheatre.co.uk
Market Place Theatre & Arts Centre	www.marketplacearmagh.com
Olympia Theatre	www.olympia.ie
Pavilion Theatre	www.paviliontheatre.ie
Peacock Theatre	www.abbeytheatre.ie
Project Arts Centre	www.project.ie
Royal Shakespeare Company Theatre	www.rsc.org.uk
Samuel Beckett Centre	www.tcd.ie/drama
SFX Entertainment	www.sfx.com
Temple Theatre	www.templetheatre.ie
Theatre Royal Waterford	www.theatreroyalwaterford.com
Town Hall Theatre Galway	www.townhalltheatregalway.com
Watergate Theatre, Kilkenny	www.watergatekilkenny.com

tickets

BBC Ticket Unit	www.bbc.co.uk/tickets
First Call	www.first-call.co.uk
Global Tickets	www.globaltickets.com
Group Line	www.groupline.com
Hot Tickets Direct	www.hotticketsdirect.com
Keith Prowse	www.keithprowse.co.uk
Lastminute.com	www.lastminute.com
London Theatre Bookings	www.londontheatrebookings.com
Requestable Services	www.requestableservices.com
Society of Ticket Agents & Retailers	www.s-t-a-r.org.uk
Ticket King	www.ticketking.ie
Ticket Select	www.stoll-moss.com
Ticketmaster America	www.ticketmaster.com
Ticketmaster Ireland	www.ticketmaster.ie
Tickets Online	www.tickets-online.co.uk
Ticketweb	www.ticketweb.co.uk
Wembley	www.wembleyticket.com
West End Theatre Bookings	www.uktickets.co.uk
What's On Stage	www.whatsonstage.com

video

Advance Vision	www.advancevision.ie
Blockbuster	www.blockbuster.co.uk
Chartbusters	www.chartbusters.ie
Movie Magic	www.moviemagic.ie
Movie Master	www.moviemaster.ie
Xtravision	www.xtravision.ie

accountants
advertising agencies
agriculture
architects
automotive
business magazines & websites
chambers of commerce
chemicals
communication portals
computer training
couriers
electrical & technological
energy
engineering
finance
food & beverages
insurance
irish gifts
manufacturing
marketing
metals & mining
model agencies
office supplies & equipment
paper & packaging
pharmaceutical
printing & publishing
private investigators
professional bodies
property
recruitment
retail
services
shipbuilding/repair
solicitors
stock exchanges & financial listings
telecommunications
transportation & logistics
trade unions
travel & transport
us corporations
utilities

business

accountants

Access Accounts Ltd	www.access-accounts.ie
Accuris	www.accuris.ie
Ardagh Horan	www.ahca.ie
Arthur Andersen	www.arthurandersen.com
ASM Horwath	www.asmhorwath.com
Association of Chartered Certified Accountants	www.acca.ie
Baxter Associates	www.baxterworld.com
BDO Stoy Hayward	www.bdo.co.uk
Boylan & Dodd	www.boylandodd.com
Brendan J McGinn & Co.	www.bjmglobal.com
Caldwell McClintock	www.caldmcc.com
Cavanagh JJ & Co	www.jjcavanagh.com
Central Business Services	www.central-business-systems.co.uk
Chartered Institute of Public Finance & Accountancy	www.cefni.co.uk
CJS Payroll Management Consultancy Ltd	www.cjspayroll.co.uk
Conlan, Crotty, Murray & Co	www.conlancrottymurray.com
Cooney Carey	www.cooneycarey.ie
Coopers & Lybrand Deloitte	www.coopers.co.uk
Cremin McCarthy O'Connor	www.cmoc.ie
Daly Park & Co	www.dalypark.com
Deloitte & Touche	www.deloitte.co.uk
eRatings.com	www.eratings.com
Ernst & Young	www.e-y.ie
Farrell & Company	www.come.to/farrell
Finnegan & Co	www.fgibson.co.uk
FitchCampbell	www.fitchcampbell.co.uk
Fitzpatrick Morris Barrett	www.fmb.ie
Flanagan Jennings & Co	www.wlflanagan.com
Flannagan Edmonds & Bannon	www.niac.org.uk
FPM	www.fpmca.com
Gahan & Co.	www.gahan.ie
Glenn & Company	www.glennaccounts.com
Glover M & Co.	www.mglover&co.com
Grant Thornton	www.grantthornton.co.uk
Hamilton Morris & Co	www.hamiltonmorris.co.uk
Hanna Thompson	www.hannathompson.com
Harbinson Mulholland	www.harbinson-mulholland.com
Harvey & Co	www.harvey-accountants.co.uk
Institute of Chartered Accountants Ireland	www.icai.ie
JA McNicholl & Co Ltd	www.mcnicholl.net

Jackson Andrews	www.jackson-andrews.co.uk
JL Grant & Co	www.jlgrant.com
John Graves & Co	www.johngravesaccountants.com
John MacMahon	www.johnmacmahon.com
Johnston Kennedy	www.johnston-kennedy.com
Joseph M. Casey	www.josephmcasey.ie
Kinnear Chartered Accountants	www.kinnear.ie
KPMG	www.kpmg.ie
Listing Of Accountants in Ireland by County	www.euroka.com/accountants
Marsh Mackey	www.marshmackey.com
Mazars	www.mazars.ie
MB McGrady & Co	www.mbmcgrady.co.uk
McClure Watters	www.mcclure-watters.co.uk
McKee & Co, JR	www.jrmckee.co.uk
Michael Cuddy Accountants	www.mpcuddyaccountants.com
Molloy, Edward F.	www.efmolloy.com
Mooney Moore	www.mooneymoore.co.uk
Moore Stephens	www.msca.co.uk
Muir & Addy	www.muiraddy.co.uk
Nolan & Associates	www.solomon.ie/nolan
Noone Casey	www.noonecasey.ie
O'Brien Cahill & Co	http://indigo.ie/~obc
O'Hare & Associates	www.oha.ie
O'Mahony Donnelly	www.omahonydonnelly.ie
O'Reilly McCarthy	www.ormc.ie
O'Shaughnessy's, Chartered Accountants	www.osca.ie
Opus Accountancy Services	www.theopusgroup.co.uk
OSK Accountants	www.osk.ie
PricewaterhouseCoopers	www.pwcglobal.com
Russel Brennan Keane	www.rbk.ie
Savage R & Co	www.rsavage.co.uk
SD Brown	www.sdbrown-co.com
Sheehan Quinn & Co	www.sheehanquinn.ie
Shriver Price & Co	www.shriverprice.com
T McGaffin	www.tommcgaffin.com
Thomson Caldwell McClintock	www.caldmacc.com
Tumalty & Dawson & Co	www.tumalty-dawson.co.uk
Victor Skillen	www.diamondskillen.co.uk
WJ Miscampbell	www.miscampbell.co.uk

advertising agencies

2020 Advertising	www.2020advertising.co.uk
Adculture.net	www.adculture.net
AdeptWeb	www.adeptweb.ie
Adnet	www.adnet.ie
Advertising Standards Authority of Ireland	www.asai.ie

Adworld	www.adworld.ie
Anderson Spratt Group	www.asgh.com
Ardmore Advertising	www.ardmore.co.uk
Association of Advertisers in Ireland	www.aai.ie
AV Brown	www.avb.co.uk
Bates Ireland	www.batesireland.ie
BBC Advertising	www.bbcad.ie
Brian Wallace Advertising	www.brianwallace.ie
Concept Advertising	www.conceptads.ie
Doherty Advertising	www.doherty.ie
Doubleclick	www.doubleclick.net
GCAS Advertising	www.gcasgroup.com
Genesis Advertising	www.genesis-advertising.co.uk
Helme Partnership	www.helme.ie
ICAN Interactive Advertising	www.ican.ie
Institute of Advertising Practitioners in Ireland	www.iapi.ie
Levy McCallum	www.levymccallum.co.uk
McCann-Erickson	www.mccann-belfast.com
McConnells Advertising Services	www.mcconnells.ie
MediaLive	www.medialive.ie
Millennium Advertising & Marketing Ltd	www.millennium-advertising.co.uk
MRB Creative	www.mrbcreative.com
Navigator Blue	www.navigatorblue.com
Owens DDB	www.owensddb.com
Paragon Design	www.paragondesign.ie
Proactive Media	www.proactive.ie
Realty Design	www.realitydesign.ie
Screen Media	www.screencentral.co.uk
TDP Advertising	www.tdpadvertising.co.uk
Walker Communications	www.walkercommunications.co.uk
Wyncroft International	www.wyncroft.com
Young Advertising	www.youngadvertising.com

agriculture

AgriAware	www.agriaware.ie
Agridata	www.agridata.ie
AgriNet	www.agrinet.ie
AgriTech	www.agritech.ie
Arramara Teo	www.arramara.ie
Bibby Ireland	www.bibbyireland.co.uk
Coillte	www.coillte.ie
Conor Engineering	www.conor-eng.ie
Dairy Master Farming Systems	www.dairymaster.ie
Department of Agriculture and Food	www.irlgov.ie/daff
Farm.ie	www.farm.ie

Farm2Trade	www.farm2trade.ie
Farmdirect	www.farmdirect.ie
Farmer's Weekly	www.fwi.co.uk
Farmhand	www.farmhand.ie
Farmsoft	www.farmsoft.ie
Farmweek Journal	www.mortonnewspapers.com
Goulding Chemicals	www.gouldings.ie
Holstein UK & Ireland	www.holstein-uki.org
HVS Animal Health	www.hsvanimalhealth.com
IAM Agricultural Machinery	www.iam.ie
Irish Cattle Traders' and Stockowners' Association	www.icsaireland.com
Irish Dairy Board	www.idb.com
Irish Farmer's Journal	www.farmersjournal.ie
Irish Fertilizer Industries	www.ifi.ie
Irish Holstein Fresian Association	www.ihfa.ie
Kerry Algae	www.kerryalgae.ie
Lakelands Dairies	www.lakeland.ie
Masstock	www.masstock.com
McHale Engineering	www.mchale.net
Model Nursery Liners	www.modelnurseryliners.com
Pest Prevention Services	www.amireland.com/pps
Progressive Genetics	www.progressivegenetics.ie
South East Growers	www.se-growers.ie
South Western Services	www.sws.ie
Tanco Engineering	www.tanco.ie
Tasc Software	www.tasc.ie
Teagasc	www.teagasc.ie
Tractor Spares International	http://indigo.ie/~rayltd
Wexford Organization for Rural Development	http://indigo.ie/~word

architects

Alan Patterson Design	www.alanpattersondesign.com
Building Information Centre	www.bild.ie
Burnside Jane D Architects	www.janeburnsidearchitects.co.uk
David Ferguson & Associates	www.niarchitects.co.uk
Hamilton Architects	www.hamiltonarchitects.com
Herron Michael J Architect	www.herronarchitect.co.uk
Irish Planning Institute	irishplanninginstitute.ie
Loughrey.Agnew.Architects	www.loughrey-agnew.com
Mackel & Doherty Architects	www.macdoh.com
Ward Design	www.ward-design.com

automotive

car hire

Argus Rent-A-Car	www.argus-rentacar.com
Atlas Car Rentals	www.atlascarhire.com

Autorental	www.autorentals.ie
Capital Car Hire	www.capital-car-hire.com
Country Car Rental	www.countrycar.com
Dan Dooley	www.dan-dooley.ie
Galway Motor Club	www.iol.ie/~jordane
Hamill Rent-A-Car	www.hamills.com
Hertz	www.hertz.ie
Malone Car Rental	www.malonecarrental.com
Michael Tynan Motors	www.tynanmotors.ie
Motor Vehicle Repairers Association	www.mvra.com
Murray's Europcar	www.europcar.ie
Payless Bunratty Car Rentals	www.iol.ie/paylessbcr
Pierse Motors	www.piersemotors.ie

clubs & associations

Autofinder	www.autofinder.ie
Automobile Association	www.aaireland.ie
Motorsport Ireland	www.motorsportireland.com
SIMI	www.simi.ie

manufacturers

Alfa Romeo Ireland	www.alfaromeo.ie
Audi	www.audi.co.uk
BMW Ireland	www.bmw.ie
Daewoo	www.daewoo-cars.co.uk
Ford	www.ford.com
General Motors	www.gm.com
Honda	www.honda.co.uk
Lexus Ireland	www.lexus.ie
Mazda	www.mazda.ie
MG	www.mgcars.co.uk
Nissan Ireland	www.nissan.ie
Opel Ireland	www.opel.ie
Peugeot	www.peugeot.ie
Renault Ireland	www.renault.ie
Renault UK	www.renault.co.uk
Rover	www.rover.co.uk
Saab Ireland	www.saab.ie
Seat	www.seat.co.uk
Toyota Ireland	www.toyota.ie
Volvo	www.volvocars.co.uk

motorsports

Mondello Park	www.mondellopark.ie
Rally Experience	www.rallyexperience.com

parts & accessories

AA Shop	www.aaireland.ie
Chequered Flag Shop	www.calfacts.com
Cleary Nissan & Sons	www.clearynissan.com
Kwik-Fit	www.kwik-fit.com
McCoy Motors	www.mccoymotors.ie

Montash	www.montash.ie
Mr Bull Bar	www.mrbullbar.ie
Murray Motorsport	www.murraymotorsport.ie
Pat Hickey Truck & Trailer Spares	www.pathickey.com
Tallaght Autoparts	www.tallaghtautoparts.ie

sales & service

Allens Honda	www.allenshonda.com
Appleyard Car Sales	www.peugeot-cars.com
Auto Q	www.autoq.co.uk
Auto Zone	www.autozone.uk.com
Autotronics	www.autotronics.ie
Bavarian	www.bavarianbmw.co.uk
Bells	www.bellscrosgar.com
Bikeworld	www.bikeworld.ie
Bob Mullan Motors	www.bobmullanmotors.com
CAB Motor Company	www.cab-motors.ie
Cara Motorhomes	www.caramotorhomes.ie
Carboy	www.carboy.co.uk
Charles Hurst	www.charleshurstgroup.co.uk
Clontarf Motors	www.clontarfmotors.com
Cotter Motorcycles	www.cottermc.com
Crawfords Motor Group	www.crawfords.ie
Crossan Motorcycles	www.crossan.co.uk
David Prentice BMW	www.davidprenticebmw.co.uk
Donnelly Bros.	www.donnellybros.co.uk
Dornan Motor Group	www.dornanmotorgroup.co.uk
EP Mooney	www.epmooney.com
Fingal Car Auctions	www.irish-auctions.com
Ford Dealers of Ireland	www.fdi.ie
Fort Motors	www.fortmotors.ie
Hog Hill Custom Motorcycles	www.hoghillcustomcycles.com
Hogs R Us	www.hogsrus.net
Irish Classic Car Collection	www.irishclassiccars.com
Isaac Agnew Volkswagen	www.isaacagnew.volkswagen.co.uk
Joe Lynch and Sons	www.jlynchsons.ie
John Kelly	www.johnkelly.ie
Koping Motors	www.kopingmotors.com
Kwik-Fit	www.kwik-fit.com
Landrover Sales & Repairs	www.landroverservicesni.co.uk
Lindsay Cars	www.lindsayford.co.uk
Motor Market	www.motormarket.ie
Motor Zone	www.motorzone.ie
Motornet	www.motorweb.ie
Murphy & Gunn	www.murphygunn.com
New Kawasaki Centre	www.newkc.com
Pierse Motors	www.piersemotors.ie
Ross Motorcycles	www.rossmotorcycles.com
Starting Grid	www.startinggrid.ie

The New Gem	www.thenewgem.com
Triumph Northern Ireland	www.linzgt6.demon.co.uk
WCA Car Auctions	www.wca.ie
Windsor Motor City	www.windsormotorcity.ie

business magazines & websites

Accountancy Ireland	www.icai.ie
Accountancy Age	www.accountancyage.co.uk
Administration	www.ipa.ie
Adworld	www.adworld.ie
Beo	www.beo.ie
Bizplus	www.bizplus.ie
Bowsie	www.bowsie.com
Business & Finance	www.businessandfinance.ie
Business Plus	www.bizplus.ie
Business Week	www.businessweek.com
Cluas	www.cluas.com
Cumasc	www.cumasc.ie
Economist	www.economist.co.uk
Education Ireland	www.educationmagazine.ie
Electric News	www.electricnews.net
Entertainment Ireland	www.entertainmentireland.ie
Euromoney	www.euromoney.com
European Business Forum	www.europeanbusinessforum.com
Farm.ie	www.farm.ie
Farmer's Weekly	www.fwi.co.uk
Farmweek Journal	www.mortonnewspapers.com
Finance Dublin	www.findub.com
Fleet Management	www.fleet.ie
Forbes	www.forbes.com
Harvard Business Review	www.hbsp.harvard.edu/hbr
History Ireland	www.historyireland.com
Image	www.image.ie
Industrial Relations News	www.irn.ie
InEpt	www.inept.com
Investment Week	www.invweek.co.uk
Ireland Today	www.irelandplus.com
Ireland's Eye	www.irelandseye.com
Ireland.com	www.ireland.com
Irish Emigrant	www.emigrant.ie
Irish Farmer's Journal	www.farmersjournal.ie
Irish Fashion Net	www.irish-fashion.com
Irish Forests	www.irishforests.com
iVenus	www.ivenus.com
Job Scene	www.jobscene.ie
LiveIreland.com	www.liveireland.com
Mac-eZine	www.mac-ezine.ie
Marketing Magazine	www.marketing.ie
Messenger	www.messenger.ie

Online.ie	www.online.ie
Six Mag	www.sixmag.com
Slashdot	www.slashdot.org
Tech Central	www.infolive.ie
The Onion	www.theonion.com
The Phoenix	www.phoenix-magazine.com
The World of Hibernia	www.twoh.com
Ulster Business	www.ulsterbusiness.com
Web Ireland	www.webireland.com
What's on Where	www.wow.ie

chambers of commerce

Athlone Chamber of Commerce and Industry	www.athlonechamber.ie
Balbriggan Chamber of Commerce	www.connect.ie/users/balbriggan
Belfast Chamber of Trade and Commerce	www.belfastchamber.co.uk
Boyle Chamber of Commerce	http://ireland.iol.ie/~boylecoc
Bray & District Chamber	www.braychamber.com
Carlow Chamber of Commerce	www.carlowchamber.com
Castlebar Chamber of Commerce	www.castlebar.ie/ccc
Chambers of Commerce of Ireland	www.chambersireland.ie
Clonmel Chamber of Commerce	www.clonmel.ie
Cobh and Harbour Chamber of Commerce	www.cobhharbourchamber.ie
Cork Chamber of Commerce	www.corkchamber.ie
Drogheda Chamber of Commerce	www.droghedachamber.com
Dublin Chamber of Commerce	www.dubchamber.ie
Dublin City Centre Business Association	www.dccba.iol.ie
Dun Laoghaire Rathdown Chamber of Commerce	www.dlrchamber.ie
Dundalk Chamber of Commerce	www.dundalk.ie
East Mayo Chamber of Commerce	www.eastmayo.com
Ennis Chamber of Commerce	www.iol.ie/~enniscc
Euro Chambres	www.eurochambres.be
Galway Chamber of Commerce	www.galwaychamber.com
Greater Blanchardstown Chamber of Commerce	www.gbcoc.org
Killarney Chamber of Commerce	www.killarney-chamber.com
Letterkenny Chamber of Commerce	http://www.letterkennychamber.com
Mullingar Chamber of Commerce	www.mullingar-chamber.ie
Navan Chamber of Commerce	www.navanchamber.com
New Ross Chamber of Commerce	www.newrosschamber.ie
Newbridge Chamber of Commerce	www.newbridgechamber.ie
Northern Ireland Chamber of Commerce & Industry	www.nicci.co.uk

Roscommon Chamber of Commerce	www.irelandwide.com/chamcom/rcc
Sligo Chamber of Commerce	www.sligochamber.ie
South Dublin Chamber of Commerce	www.southdublinchamber.com
Swords Chamber of Commerce	www.swordschamber.ie
Waterford Chamber of Commerce	www.waterfordchamber.com
Westport Chamber of Commerce	www.westportireland.com
Wexford Chamber of Commerce	www.wexchamber.ie
Youghal Chamber of Commerce and Tourism	http://homepage.tinet.ie/~youghal

chemicals

Alkem	www.alkem.ie
Arch Chemicals	www.archchemicals.com
Audit Diagnostics	www.auditdiagnostics.ie
Aughinish Alumina	www.aughinish.com
Bayer	www.bayer.co.uk
Camida	www.camida.com
Corcoran Chemicals	www.corcoranchemicals.com
Hays Chemical Distribution	www.hayschem.co.uk
Healy Chemicals	www.healychemicals.ie
Hygeia	www.hygeia.ie
Kompass	www.kompass.ie
MinChem	www.minchem.ie
Norman Lauder Ltd	www.nll.ie
Northern Ireland Search	www.nisearch.com
Ocon Chemicals	www.oconchemicals.com
Online.ie	www.online.ie
Reheis	www.reheis.com
Solvechem	www.solvechem.com
Taisal Trading	www.taisaltrading.com
UltraChem Systems	www.ultrachemsystems.ie
Yahoo.com	www.yahoo.com
ZPM Europe	www.commerce.ie/cz/zpm

communication portals

Beeb.com	www.beeb.com
Doras	www.doras.ie
EBay.co.uk	www.ebay.co.uk
Ebid	www.ebid.ie
Eircom.ie	www.eircom.ie
Eircom.net	www.eircom.net
Ireland On-Line	www.iol.ie
ireland.com	www.ireland.com

computer training

A 1-2-1 Computer Training	www.a121computertraining.ie
Adelaide Training	www.adelaidetraining.com
Advance Computer Training	www.safebyte.co.uk

Alternative Training	www.alternativetraining.net
Amicus Technology	www.amicustec.ie
Arthouse Training	www.arthouse.ie/training
Ask-Training	www.ask-training.com
Assist Training	www.assisttraining.ie
Astro Computer Training	www.astrotraining.com
BIC Systems	www.bicsystems.com
BCS Training	www.bcs.ie
Business Computer Training	www.bct.ie
Cadco	www.cadco.ie
Cara	www.bullcara.com
Centre for Advanced Technology Training	www.catt.ie
Clonmel Computer Training Centre	www.cctc.ie
Compu-Train	www.computrain.ie
Computer Gym	www.computergym.ie
Computer Learning Centre	www.clci.ie
Computing Advisory Services	www.goodcomputing.co.uk
CyberHouse Computer Training	www.cyberhouse.ie
DMA Computers	www.dmacomputers.ie
Dorset College	www.dorset-college.ie
Eden Training	www.eden.ie
Elite Training	www.elitetraining.com
Essential Computer Training	www.essentialtraining.ie
European Computer Driving Licence	www.ecdl.ie
Everyman Computers	www.everyman.ie
Global Knowledge	www.globalknowledge.ie
Horizon	www.hos.horizon.ie
IT Training Enterprise	www.ittenterprise.com
IBM Training	www.ibm.com/services/learning/ie
Interactive Training Solutions	www.interactive-avenue.ie
Irish Academy of Computer Training	www.iact.ie
Kaysers Computing	www.kayserscomputing.com
Knowledge Pool	www.knowledgepool.com
Micro Computer Solutions	www.mcsgroup.co.uk
NetHouse	www.nethousecafes.com
NS Enterprise Training Ltd	www.nsenterprise.co.uk
Opus Training Services	www.theopusgroup.co.uk
Paradigm	www.paradigm.ie
Pitman Training	www.pitman-training.com
Professa	www.professa.com
Putari	www.putari.com
Quartet	www.mfcomputerservices.ie
Searc	www.searc.ie
Sureskills	www.sureskills.com
SX3	www.sx3.com
Valley Training	www.valleytraining.com
Wood You Like	www.iol.ie/woodyoulike
Write Lines	www.writelines.com

couriers

B-Fast Parcels	www.bfast.co.uk
Data Dispatch	www.datadispatchcouriers.co.uk
DHL	www.dhl.co.uk
Direct Couriers	www.directcouriersni.co.uk
Falcon Couriers	www.falconcouriers.co.uk
Fastrack	www.irishrail.ie/html/freight/fastrack.html
Federal Express	www.fedex.com
K & L Deliveries	www.kandl.ie
Mailit-Europe	www.mailit.ie
Parcel Force	www.parcelforce.co.uk
Parcellink	www.translink.co.uk/parcels.asp
SDS	www.sds.ie
Securicor Omega	www.securicor.co.uk
TNT	www.tnt.co.uk
Transnet Couriers	www.couriersireland.co.uk
UPS	www.ups.com
World Courier	www.worldcourier.com

electrical & technological

manufacturers

Aiwa	www.aiwa.co.uk
Ashbrook Electrical	www.ashbrookelectrical.com
Bosch	www.bosch.co.uk
Braun	www.braun.com
Bridisco	http://indigo.ie/~bridisco
Brother	www.brother.com
Cookson Group	www.cooksongroup.co.uk
DeLonghi	www.delonghi.com
Electrolux	www.electrolux.co.uk
EMDA	www.emda.ie
Ericsson	www.ericsson.com
Excel Electric Group	www.excelelectric.ie
Frentech Engineering	www.frentech.ie
General Electric	www.ge.com
Glen Dimplex	www.glendimplex.com
Hotpoint	www.hotpoint.co.uk
Kenwood	www.kenwood.ie
Lumin8	www.lumin8.com
Mitsubishi	www.mitsubishi.com
Moulinex	www.moulinex.fr
NEC	www.nec.com
Nokia	www.nokia.com
Panasonic	www.panasonic.com
Peats	www.peats.ie
Philips	www.philips.com

Pioneer Electronics	www.pioneerelectronics.com
Power City	www.powercity.ie
PowerPoint	www.powerpoint.ie
Psion	www.psion.com
Renley	www.iol.ie/~renley
Samsung Electronics	www.samsungelectronics.com
Siemens	www.siemens.ie
Suparule	www.suparule.com
Whirlpool	www.whirlpool.ie

services

Ashdale Engineering Ltd	www.ashdale.co.uk
Brownbrook Distributors Ltd	www.brownbrook.co.uk
Cable & Accessories	www.cableaccess.com
Electric Links	www.electriclinks.com
Electrical Manufacturers and Distributors Association	www.emda.ie
Elwood Electrical	www.elwoodelectrical.com
Engineering Support & Services Ltd	www.frentech.ie
Global Electrical	www.globalelectricalireland.com
H Ritchie & Sons	www.hritchie.co.uk
JK Services	www.jkservices.ie
Mercury Engineering	www.mercury.ie
National Electronics Test Centre	www.netc.ie
Park Electrical Services	www.parkelect.co.uk
Pat Smith Engineering	www.pse.ie
PCAS	www.pcas.ie
Register of Electrical Contractors of Ireland	www.reci.ie
S R K Equipment Co	www.srkequipment.com

shops/wholesalers

Botanic Electrical Wholesalers	www.bewl.ie
Clancys Electrical	www.clancyselectrical.com
Comet Store	www.cometstore.ie
Dempsey's	www.dempseys.co.uk
Discount Electrical	www.discountelectrical.ie
Dixons	www.dixons.co.uk
O'Connors	www.oconnors.ie
Prizebuy.com	www.prizebuy.com
Sherwoods	www.sherwoods.ie

energy

Bord Gáis Eireann	www.bge.ie
Bula Resources	www.bularesources.com
Calor Gas	www.calorgas.ie
Celtic Power	www.celticpower.ie
Eirtricity	www.eirtricity.ie
EPower	www.epower.ie
ESB	www.esb.ie

Exxon	www.exxon.com
Flogas	www.flogas.ie
Gulf	www.gulfoil.com
Irish Energy Centre	www.irish-energy.ie
Irish Energy Management	www.iem.ie
Kilronan Windfarm	www.kilronanwindfarm.com
Maxol	www.maxol.ie
Mobil	www.mobil.co.uk
Northern Ireland Electricity	www.nie.co.uk
Phoenix Natural Gas	www.phoenix-natural-gas.com
Shell Transport & Trading Company	www.shell.com
Texaco	www.texaco.com
Tullow Oil	www.tullowoil.ie
Viridian Group PLC	www.viridiangroup.co.uk

engineering

Adtec Engineering	www.adtec.ie
Caldwell Partnership Consulting Engineering	www.the-caldwell-partnership.co.uk
Callaghan Engineering	www.calleng.ie
Carl Bro Group	www.carlbro.com
Davy Hickey Properties	www.citywest.com
Dennis Wilson Partnership	www.dwp.ie
Environmental Engineering Ltd	www.eel.ie
Fehily Timoney	www.fehilytimoney.com
Institution of Chemical Engineers	www.icheme.org
Institution of Electrical Engineers	www.iee.org
Institution of Engineers of Ireland	www.iei.ie
IRTU Design Directorate	www.designdir.com
JP Behan Associates	www.jpbehanassociates.com
MC O'Sulliavan	www.mcos.ie
Mott MacDonald	www.mottmac.com
Nicholas O'Dwyer	www.nicholasodwyer.com
Oscar Faber	www.oscarfaber.com
Parthus Technologies PLC	www.parthus.com
Pegler & Louden	www.pli.ie
Royal Institute of the Architects of Ireland	www.riai.ie
Shannon Engine Support	www.ses.ie
Westward Precision Engineering	www.westwardeng.com

finance

Abbey National	www.abbeynational.co.uk
AccBank	www.accbank.ie
AIB Group	www.aib.ie
Anglo Irish Bank	www.angloirishbank.ie
Bank of Ireland	www.boi.ie
Bank of Scotland	www.bankofscotland.co.uk
Barclays	www.barclays.co.uk

Bishopstown Credit Union	www.bishopstowncu.ie
Central Bank of Ireland	www.centralbank.ie
Citibank	www.citibank.ie
Eagle Star	www.eaglestarlife.ie
EBS Building Society	www.ebs.ie
Euro Finance Group	www.eurofinancegroup.ie
Financial Planning Development Board	www.fpdb.ie
First Active	www.firstactive.com
First Trust Bank	www.ftbni.com
Gandon Capital Markets	www.gandon-capital.ie
Halifax	www.halifax.co.uk
Hibernian Group	www.hibernian.ie
HSBC	www.hsbc.com
ICC Bank	www.icc.ie
ICS Building Society	www.mortgagestore.ie
IDA	www.ida.ie
IIB Bank	www.iib-bank.ie
Institute of Bankers in Ireland	www.instbank.ie
Irish Permanent	www.irishpermanent.ie
Irish Stock Exchange	www.ise.ie
MBNA	www.mbna.com
Morgan Chase	www.chase.com
National Irish Bank	www.nib.ie
Northern Bank	www.nbonline.co.uk
Northern Rock	www.northernrock-ireland.ie
Norwich Union International	www.nuinternational.com
TSB Bank	www.tsbbank.ie
Ulster Bank	www.ulsterbank.com

finance consulting

A&L Goodbody	www.algoodbody.ie
Amarach Consulting	www.amarach.com
Bea.com	www.bea.com
Coface.com	www.coface.com
Dolmen Butler Briscoe	www.dbb.ie
Gartner Group Ireland	www.gartner.com
GE Capital GCF Europe	www.gecapital.ie
Granite.ie	www.granite.ie
hiTouch	www.hitouch.com
Holcom	www.holcom.ie
I-Fusion.net	www.i-fusion.net
ICAN	www.ican.ie
Icarus e-Com	www.icarus-e.com
IFMS ltd	www.ifms.ie
Innovations	www.innovationwebworks.com
Interact	www.interact.ie
Interactivefx	www.interactivefx.ie
International Development Ireland	www.idi.ie
Interxion Ireland	www.interxion.com

Ion Equity	www.ionequity.com
Iontas Creative Solutions	www.iontascreative.ie
ISI Interact	www.interactsi.com
IT Alliance	www.italliancegroup.com
J-I-P Solutions	www.jipsolutions.com
JB O'Sullivan	www.jbos.ie
Kamtech IT Consultants	www.kamtech.ie
Keating & Associates	www.keating.ie
KPMG	www.kpmg.ie
Kratos	www.kratos.ie
Lalor International Holdings	www.lih.ie
Lynx Technology	www.lynxtech.net
Magnitek	www.magnitek.com
Marks & Spencer Financial Services	www.marksandspencer.com/ financialservices
Mediaone	www.mediaone.ie
MERC Partners	www.merc.ie
Mercer	www.wmmercer.com
MF Computer Services	www.mfcomputerservices.ie
Milestone Systems	www.milestone.ie
Mitchell James	www.mitchelljames.com
Nevadatele.com	www.nevadatele.com
NSM Internet Consultants	www.nsm.ie
O'Shaughnessy's Chartered Accountants	www.osca.ie
Octagon Technologies	www.octagon.ie
OSK Accountants & Business Consultants	www.osk.ie
PA Consulting	www.pa-consulting.com
Paul Handley Consultancy	www.phcl.ie
Piercom	www.piercom.ie
Plaut Consulting	www.plaut.ie
PM Centrix	www.pmcentrix.com
Price Waterhouse Coopers	www.pricewaterhousecoopers. com
Prospectus Strategy Consultants	www.prospectus.ie
Pyramid Consulting	www.pyramidconsult.ie
Rabobank	www.rabobank.com
Refresh	www.refresh.ie
Spiders Consulting	www.spiders.ie
Stockex.ie	www.stockex.ie
The Identity Business	www.theidentitybusiness.ie
Trinity VC	www.trinity-vc.ie
Tusa	www.tusa.ie
Virtual Financial Management	www.vfm-asp.com
Westdeutsche Landesbank	www.westlb.com
Woolwich	www.woolwich.co.uk

food & beverages

Antrim Hills Spring Water Co Ltd	www.antrimhills.com
Avonmore	www.glanbia.ie
Bass Ireland Ltd	www.bassbrewers.com
Bewley's	www.bewleys.com
Cadbury's	www.cadbury.ie
Celtic Coast Seafoods	www.celticcoast.com
Dale Farm	www.dalefarm.co.uk
Dawn Farm Foods	www.dawnfarms.ie
Dunns of Dublin	www.dunns.ie
Express Dairy	www.expressdairy.co.uk
Fair Oak Foods	www.fairoakfoods.ie
Guinness	www.guinness.com
HB Ice-Cream	www.hbicecream.ie
Irish Dairy Boards	www.idb.ie
Irish Pride Bakery	www.irishpride.ie
Irish Produce	www.irish4ever.ie
Lily O'Briens	www.lilyobriens.ie
Musgrave	www.musgrave.ie
Superquinn	www.superquinn4food.ie
Tayto	www.tayto.com
Tesco	www.tesco.ie
United Dairy Farmers	www.utdni.co.uk

insurance

123 Insurance	www.123.ie
AA	www.theaa.com
Abbey Insurance Brokers	www.abbey-online.co.uk
Abbey National	www.abbeynational.co.uk
Admiral	www.admiral.uk.com
AIG	www.aig.com
Allianz	www.allianz.ie
Aon	www.aon.com
Autoline	www.autoline.co.uk
Automobile Association	www.aaireland.ie
AXA Direct	www.axadirect.ie
B & P Malone	www.bpmalone.com
Barker Fresson Insurance	www.barkerfresson.ie
Bupa Ireland	www.bupaireland.ie
Canada Life	www.canadalife.ie
Chubb Group	www.chubb.com
Churchill	www.churchill.com
Cotters Insurance Services	www.cotters.co.uk
Culleton	www.culleton.com
DAS	www.das.co.uk
Diamond	www.diamond.uk.com
Diamond Insurance Services	www.diamond-ins.co.uk
Eagle Star	www.eaglestar.ie
Elephant	www.elephant.co.uk

Endsleigh Insurance	www.endsleigh.co.uk
FBD Insurance	www.fbd.ie
First Call Direct	www.firstcalldirect.ie
First Ireland	www.firstireland.ie
FMS	www.fms.ie
Friends First	www.friendsfirst.ie
Hibernian	www.hibernian.ie
Insurance Services Ireland	www.insuranceservices.ie
Insure.ie	www.insure.ie
Irish Brokers Network	www.ibn.ie
Irish Insurance Federation	www.iif.ie
Irish Life	www.irishlife.ie
Life Insurance Association	www.lia.ie
Lifetime	www.lifetime.ie
Loftus Insurance Brokers	www.loftus.ie
McCarthy Insurance Group	www.mccarthyinsurances.ie
McClarty's Insurance	www.mcclartys.co.uk
McCormack Insurance	www.mccormackinsurance.com
Motor Broker	www.motorbroker.com
New Ireland Insurance	www.newireland.ie
O'Mahony Boylan Golden	www.ombg.ie
O'Reilly Cullen Insurances	www.oreilly-cullen.ie
PMPA/AXA	www.pmpa.ie
Prudential	www.pru.co.uk
QBE Europe	www.qbeeurope.com
Quinn Direct	www.quinn-direct.com
Rooney's Insurance	www.rooneys.ie
Royal & Sun Alliance	www.royalsun.co.uk
Royal & Sun Alliance	www.royalsunalliance.ie
SAGA	www.saga.co.uk
Scottish Legal	www.scotlegal.com
Scottish Provident	www.scotprov.ie
St. Paul	www.stpaul.com
Voluntary Health Insurance	www.vhi.ie
Wright Insurance Group	www.wrightgroup.ie

irish gifts

Anything Irish	www.anything-irish.com
Celtic Crafts	www.celtic-crafts.com
Celtic Art	www.celticarts.com
CeltShop.net	www.celtshop.net
Claddagh Jewellers	www.claddaghjewellers.com
Gill & MacMillan	www.gillmacmillan.ie
Guinness Webstore	www.guinness.com/webstore
Horseware Products	www.horseware.com
House of Ireland	www.houseofireland.com
Irish Produce	www.irish4ever.com
Oideas Gael Language Tuition	www.oideas-gael.com
Olive Hurley, Dance Videos	www.olivehurley.com

Paddy Magic	www.paddymagic.com
Roundstone Musical Instruments	www.bodhran.com
Shamrockshop.com	www.shamrockshop.com
Traditional Irish Foods	www.foodireland.com

manufacturing

A & D Controls	http://aanddcontrols.com
Access Plastics	www.accessplastics.com
Accutool	www.accutool.com
Amphion	www.amphion.com
Arno Limited	www.arno.ie
Atlantic Laser Works	www.atlanticlaserworks.com
B/E Aerospace	www.beaerospace.com
BetaTherm Sensors	www.betatherm.com
Burnside Autocyl	www.burnside.ie
Buttimer	www.buttimer.ie
Byrne Mech Engineering	www.byrnemech.ie
CBR	www.cbrinternational.com
ColdChain	www.coldchain.com
Driverite	www.driveriteltd.com
Duggan Steel Group	www.dugganstee lgroup.com
EdPac	www.edpac.com
Elite Electronic Systems Ltd	www.elitees.com
Eurolec Instrumentation	www.eurolec-instruments.com
Excel Electric Group	www.excelelectric.ie
Farran Technology	www.farran.com
Frank McMahon	www.frankmcmahon.ie
H Clissmann & Son	www.hcsirl.com
Harland & Wolff	www.harland-wolff.com
Harrington Precast Concrete	www.hpc.ie
Hi-Spec Engineering	www.hispec.net
Hydraweld	www.hydraweld.com
Infineer	www.infineer.com
Leaf Technologies	www.leafltd.com
Neltronic (NI) Ltd	www.neltronic.ie
Newbridge Metal	www.newbridgemetal.ie
Noone Engineering	www.nooneeng.com
Nuvotem	www.nuvotem.com
Parsec	www.parsec.ie
Powerscreen	www.powerscreen.co.uk
Precast Products	http://precast.ie
Reckitt Benckiser	www.reckitt.com
RS Group	www.rsgroup.ie
Seagate Technology	www.seagate.com
Ship Company	www.ship.org
Simtec Electronics	www.simtec.co.uk
Springco	www.springco.co.uk
Top Tech Solutions	www.toptech.co.uk
Torc Engineering	www.torcengineering.com

marketing

AC Nielsen	www.acnielsen.com
Advanced Internet Marketing	www.aim-irl.com
Advanced Internet Solutions	www.advancedinternet.ie
Aspire Marketing Consultants	www.aspire.ie
BFK Strategic Design	www.bfk.ie
Blazon	www.blazon.ie
Clarke Warner	www.cwdesign.ie
Comms On-line	www.comms-online
Concept Ads	www.conceptads.ie
Contact Sales Marketing	www.contact.ie
Copywriter	www.copywriter.com
DMA	www.dma.ie
DMR Consulting	www.dmr.ie
e23	www.e23.ie
Emarketeer	www.emarketeer.com
French Grant Associates	www.frenchgrant.com
Genesis	www.genesis.ie
I-Map	www.i-map.ie
Inspiration	www.inspiration.ie
Institute of Advertising Practitioners in Ireland	www.iapi.ie
Irish Marketing Surveys	www.imsl.ie
Kearney Stevens	www.kearneystevens.ie
Kinman Public Relations	www.kinman.ie
Marketing Institute Ireland	www.mii.ie
McGann plm	www.mcgannplm.ie
Moytura	www.moytura.com
Net Irl.com	www.netirl.com
New Idiom	www.newidiom.com
New World Commerce	www.newworldcommerce.com
O'Malley & Hogan	www.omhog.ie
O'Sullivan PR	www.osullivanpr.ie
Proactive Group	www.proactive.ie
Public Relations Institute of Ireland	www.prii.ie
Quaestus	www.quaestus.ie
Ray Walshe Marketing	www.rwamarketing.com
Reality Design & Marketing	www.realitydesign.ie
Research & Evaluation Services	www.res.nireland.com
Response Group	www.responsegroup.eu.com
Rothco	www.rothco.ie
SPSS	www.spss.com
Unique Perspectives	www.uniqueperspectives.ie/default.htm
V3Marketing	www.v3marketing.com
Verve Marketing	www.verve.ie
Watermarque	www.watermarque.ie
Web Review	www.webreview.com
Webmarketing	www.webmarketing.ie
Young Advertising	www.youngadvertising.com

metals & mining

Anglo American	www.angloamerican.co.uk
Armal Welding Machines & Accessories	www.armal.com
Balmar	www.balmar.ie
Bodycote International	www.bodycote.com
Bular Resources	www.bularesources.ie
Complex Tooling & Moulding Ireland	www.ctmc.com
Corus Group	www.corusgroup.com
Eutectic & Castolin	www.eutectic.com
Glencar Mining	www.glencarmining.ie
Johnson Matthey	www.matthey.com
NK Coatings Ltd	www.nkcoatings.com
Oerlikon Welding	www.oerlikonweld.com
SGL	www.sperrin-galvanisers.co.uk
Tara Stainless & Engineering	www.tarastain.ie
Walsh Engineering	www.walshengineering.com

model agencies

Asset Models	www.assetsmodels.com
Catwalk Elite	www.catwalkelite.com
Celtic Talent International	www.celtictalent.com
Models I	www.models1.co.uk
Premier Model Management	www.premier-models.com
Scallywags	www.scallywags.co.uk
Storm	www.stormmodels.com
Street TV	www.street.tv

office supplies & equipment

3M Ireland	www.3m.com
Allstat	www.allstat.ie
APW Wright Line	www.wrightline.com
Asdon Business Centre	www.asdon.co.uk
Atlantic Ink Supplies	www.atlanticink.com
Axis Office Supplies	www.axisofficesupplies.com
Balmoral Contract Interiors	www.moffett.co.uk
Bandon Office Supplies Ltd	www.bandonoffice.com
Bison Office Supplies	www.bisonofficesupplies.co.uk
Bizquip	www.bizquip.ie
Boss Novus Office Products	www.bossnovus.ie
Canon	www.canon.co.uk
Castle T Furniture	www.castlet.ie
City Office Supplies	www.cityofficesupplies.ie
Codex	www.iol.ie/~codex
Cookstown Office Supplies	www.cookstownofficesupplies.co.uk
Copy Systems	www.copysystems.ie
Crowley Busness Services	http://cbs.foundmark.com

Dennis Smyth Business Furniture	www.officefurnitureni.com
Desks International	www.desksinternational.com
Donworth & Co	www.donworth.ie
Eagle Office	www.eagleoffice.net
EDCO	www.edco.co.uk
Fagan Office Supplies	www.faganofficesupplies.ie
Farrell Office	www.farrelloffice.com
Filofax	www.filofax.com
Fitzwilliam Business Centre	www.fitzbiz.com
Flanigan & Son	www.flaniganfurniture.com
Flynn Letters Ltd	www.flynns.ie
G & A Manifold	www.gamanifold.ie
Gemini	www.gemini.ie
Glasnevin Business Centre	www.glasnevinbusinesscentre.com
Graham Business Supplies	www.grahambusinesssupplies.com
Green Office	www.greenoffice.ie
Guilbert N.I.	www.guilbert.co.uk
Harry Roberts	www.officeshop.ie
Hobbs Office Supplies	www.hobbs.ie
Ikon	www.kallkwik.co.uk
Kennedy Office Supplies	www.kos.ie
Knights Group	www.knights.ie
KVS Distribution	www.scandac.tripod.com
M2 Office Supplies	www.m2officesupplies.ie
MMM Office Interiors	www.mmmshopfitters.co.uk
Office Centre	www.officecentre.ie
Office Direct	www.officedirect.ie
Office Evolutions	www.officeevolutions.ie
Office World Interiors	www.2000complex.co.uk/officeworld
OfficeIE.com	www.officeie.com
Paperman	www.paperman.ie
Paperweight	www.paperweight.ie
Paul Haycock	www.phos.ie
PremGroup	www.premgroup.com
Print & Display	www.printanddisplay.ie
Ruane Office Supplies	www.ruane-office-supplies.ie
SCI Interiors	www.sci.ie
Sellotape Ireland	www.iol.ie/sellotape
Sheelin Office	www.sheelinoffice.ie
Slevin Group	www.slevin-group.com
Stanley Office	www.stanleyoffice.ie
TICo	www.tico-group.ie
Typetec	www.typetec.ie
Universal Office Supplies	www.uos.co.uk
Viking	www.vikingop.com

paper & packaging

Ac Tape	www.actape.ie
Alert Packaging	www.alertpackaging.com
Ambassador Packaging	www.safe-pak.net
Bag Trader	www.bagtrader.ie
Carrigaline Print	www.carrigalineprint.ie
Eurotech	www.eurotech.ie
GetBags	www.getbags.net
Glenpak	www.glenpak.com
Gosheron Packaging	www.gosheron-packaging.com
Ire-tex	www.ilp.ie
JMC	www.jmcpaper.ie
Kenilworth Products	www.kenilworth.ie
Norske Skog	www.norske-skog.com
O'Hagan Corrugated	www.ohagancorrugated.com
Packaging Industries Ltd	www.packagingindustries.ie
Paper Pieces	http://paperpieces.net
Premier Paper	www.premierpaper.ie
Propac	www.nefab.com
Raflatac	www.raflatac.com
Security Pak Systems	www.securitypak.ie
Smurfit	www.smurfit.ie
Snazzybags	www.snazzybags.com
Spanboard Products Ltd	www.sonae-industria-tafisa.com
Tetrapak	www.tetrapak.com
TQ Paper	www.tqpaper.com
UPM Kymmene	www.upm-kymmene.com
Venture	www.venture.ie
Western Plastics	www.westernplastics.ie
Xerox	www.xerox.com
Zebra Packaging	www.zebrapackaging.ie

pharmaceutical

3M	www.3m.com
Abbott	www.abbott.ie
Allergan	www.allergan.com
Alltracel	www.alltracel.com
Amersham International	www.amersham.co.uk
Asta Medica	www.astamedica.com
Astra Zeneca	www.astrazeneca.com
BASF	www.basf.com
Bayer	www.bayer.com
Bristol Myers Squibb	www.bms.com
Celltech	www.medeva.co.uk
CompuPharma	www.compupharma.net
Dura	www.durapharm.com
Elan	www.elancorp.com
Eli Lilly	www.lilly.com

Fischer	www.dr-fischer.com
Galan Holdings plc	www.galanplc.com
Get Lenses	www.getlenses.ie
Glaxo Smith Kline	www.gsk.com
Glaxo Wellcome	www.glaxowellcome.com
H Lundbeck A/S	www.lundbeck.com
Hoechst	www.hoechst.com
Hollister	www.hollister.com
Johnson & Johnson	www.jnj.com
Mallinckrodt	www.mallinckrodt.com
Merck	www.merck.com
Monsanto	www.monsanto.com
Norbrook Laboratories Ltd	www.norbrook.co.uk
Novartis	www.novartis.com
Novo Nordisk	www.novo.dk
Nycomed Amersham	www.amersham.co.uk
Organon	www.organon.com
Perfecseal	www.perfecseal.com
Pfizer	www.pfizer.ie
Pharmacia & Upjohn	www.pharmacia.com
Pinewood Healthcare	www.pinewood.ie
Roche	www.roche.com
Rowa	www.rowa.ie
Searle	www.monsanto.com
Shire Pharmaceuticals Group	www.shiregroup.com
Solvay	www.solvay.com
Takeda	www.takedapharm.com
Unichem	www.unichem.co.uk
UniPhar	www.allphar.ie
United Drug	www.united-drug.ie
Warner-Lambert	www.warner-lambert.com
Yamanouchi	www.yamanouchi.com

printing & publishing

irish printers

Action Press	www.actionpress.co.uk
Advantage Printers	www.advantageprinters.ie
Allied Print	www.alliedprint.ie
Anglo Printers	www.angloprinters.ie
Antrim Printers	www.antrimprinters.co.uk
Argus Press	www.arguspressltd.com
Bowater (NI) Ltd	www.bowater.com
Brayprint	www.brayprint.com
CB Forms	www.cbforms.ie
Chanel Wedding Stationery	www.chanelweddings.com
Chroma	www.chroma.ie
Color Print	www.colorprint.ie
Colorman	www.colorman.ie
Colour Books	www.colourbooks.ie

Craftprint	www.craftprint.ie
Cube Printing	www.cubeprinting.ie
Derreen Printing	www.derreenprinting.com
Docuprint	www.docuprint.ie
Dorman & Sons Ltd	www.dormans-print.co.uk
E-Print	www.eprint.ie
Easyprint	www.easyprint.co.uk
Edenderry Print	www.edenderry.sagenet.co.uk
Euroscreen Group	www.es-group.ie
Gemini	www.gemini.ie
Graham & Heslip Ltd	www.grahamandheslip.com
Hughes Print	www.hughes-print.ie
Jaycee Printers	www.jcprint.ie
Limestreet Print Works	www.limestreet.ie
Microprint	www.microprint.ie
Murphy Print & Design	www.murphyprint.com
Nicholson & Bass Ltd	www.nicholsonbass.com
Ormond Printing Company	www.ormond.ie
Print and Display	www.printanddisplay.ie
Print Works Group	www.printworksgroup.com
Printco	www.printco.com
Printlines	www.printlines.ie
Rennicks	www.rennicks.com
Snap Printing	www.snapprinting.ie
The Printed Image	www.tpi.ie
W&G Baird	www.wgbaird.com

irish publishers

Appletree Press	www.appletree.ie
CB Publications	www.cbweb.net
Citis	www.citis.ie
Cló Mhaigh Eo	www.leabhar.com
Collins Press	www.collinspress.com
Colourpoint	www.colourpoint.co.uk
Columbia Press	www.columbia.ie
Compuscript	www.compuscript.com
Cork University Press	www.ucc.ie/corkunip
CPG Group	www.cpg.ie
DBA Publishing	www.dbapublishing.ie
Donard Publishing	www.donardpublishing.com
Educational Company of Ireland	www.edco.ie
Fish Publishing	www.fishpublishing.com
Folens	www.folens.ie
Gill & Macmillan	www.gillmacmillan.ie
Irish Academic Press	www.iap.ie
Lilliput Press	www.lilliputpress.ie
Mentor Books	www.mentorbooks.ie
Mercier Press	www.indigo.ie/mercier
O'Brien Press	www.obrien.ie
Oak Tree Press	www.oaktreepress.com

Poolbeg	www.poolbeg.com
Round Hall	www.roundhall.ie
Salmon Poetry	www.salmonpoetry.com
Veritas	www.veritas.ie

non-irish publishers

Addison Wesley Longman	www.awl.com
Dorling Kindersley	www.dk.com
Harper Collins	www.harpercollins.co.uk
Kogan Page	www.kogan-page.co.uk
Liturgical Press	www.litpress.org
Macmillan	www.macmillan.co.uk
McGraw-Hill	www.mcgraw-hill.co.uk
Osborne Books	www.osbornebooks.co.uk
Oxford University Press	www.oup.co.uk
Paulist Press	www.paulistpress.com
Pearson	www.pearson.co.uk
Prim-Ed	www.prim-ed.com
Puffin	www.puffin.co.uk
Rough Guides	www.roughguides.com

private investigators

1st Priority Investigations	www.priorityinvestigations.com
Abacus Investigations	www.abacusinv.co.uk
Blue Shield Security	www.blueshieldsecurity.com
Carratu	www.carratu.com
Confidential Investigators Athlone Ltd	www.cia.ie
Elliot & Associates	www.prvt-eye.com
Foley & Associates	www.mpfoley.com
Impact	www.impactssa.co.uk
International Federation of Associations of Private Investigators	www.i-k-d.com
JC Associates	www.surveillance.org.uk
Minerva Protective Services	www.consultminerva.com

professional bodies

Association for Civil/Social/Political Education Teachers	www.cspeteachers.ie
Association of Advertisers in Ireland	www.aai.ie
Bar Council	www.lawlibrary.ie/barcouncil
Bord Altranais	www.nursingboard.ie
Bord Bia – Food Board	www.bordbia.ie
British Medical Association	www.bma.org.uk
Chartered Institute of Arbitrators	www.arbitration.ie
Chartered Institute of Housing	www.cih.org
Confederation of British Industry	www.cbi.org.uk

Dublin City Centre Business Association	www.dccba@iol.ie
eCommerce Association of Ireland	www.ecai.ie
Engineering Employers Association	www.eef.org.uk
Federation of Small Business	www.fsb.org.uk
Federation of the Retail Licensed Trade (NI)	www.ulsterpubs.com
Forfás	www.forfas.ie
Freight Transport Association Ltd	www.fta.co.uk
Institute of Accounting Technicians in Ireland	www.icai.ie/iati
Institute of Chartered Accountants (England and Wales)	www.icaew.co.uk
Institute of Chartered Accountants in Ireland	www.icai.ie
Institute of Personnel & Development	www.cipd.co.uk
Institution of Engineers	www.iei.ie
Insurance Institute of Ireland	www.insurance-institute.ie
Irish Accounting and Finance Association	www.wit.ie/bussacc/iafa/home.html
Irish Auctioneers and Valuers Institute	www.iavi.ie
Irish Business and Employers Confederation	www.ibec.ie
Irish Business Bureau	www.ibb.be
Irish Coalition of Service Industries	www.icsi.ie
Irish Congress of Trade Unions	www.ictu.ie
Irish Dairy Board	www.idb.ie
Irish Exporters Association	www.irishexporters.ie
Irish Hardware Association	www.irishhardware.ie
Irish Hotels Federation	www.ihf.ie
Irish Institute of Purchasing and Materials Management	www.iipmm.ie
Irish Institute of Training & Development	www.iitd.com
Irish Internet Association	www.iia.ie
Irish Life Insurance Association	www.lia.ie
Irish Management Institute	www.imi.ie
Irish Marine Institute	www.marine.ie
Irish Master Printers Association	www.rnan.ie
Irish Medical Organisation	www.imo.ie
Irish Nurses Organisation	www.ino.ie
Irish Security Industry Association	www.isia.ie
Irish Small and Medium Enterprises Association	www.isme.ie
Irish Trade Web	www.itw.ie
Leinster Society of Chartered Accountants	www.lsca.ie
Marketing Institue of Ireland	www.mii.ie

Mental Health Association of Ireland	http://mhai.healthyirish.com
Midas Ireland	www.midasireland.ie
National House Building Council	www.nhbc.co.uk
National Institute for Transport & Logistics	www.nitl.ie
Northern Ireland Dairy Association	www.nida.co.uk
Northern Ireland Food and Drink Association	www.nifda.co.uk
Northern Ireland Seafood	www.niseafood.co.uk
Public Relations Institute of Ireland	www.prii.ie
SIPTU	www.siptu.ie
The Northern Ireland Textiles & Apparel Association Ltd	www.nita.co.uk

property

A & L Goodbody	www.algoodbody.ie
Abbott & Matthews	www.abbottmatthews.com
Advantage Home Buyers	www.advantage-home-buyers.com
Alastair Stevenson	www.thepropertyspot.co.uk
Anderson Estate Agents	www.andersonestateagents.com
Arthur Cox	www.arthurcox.ie
Belfast Real Estate	www.advertni.co.uk/bre
Best Property Services	www.bestpropertyservices.com
Billy O'Sullivan	www.billyosullivan.ie
Brady Auctioneers	www.jgbrady.com
Branch32.com	www.branch32.com
Brendan O'Meara Properties	www.bomearaproperties.com
Byrne Auctioneers	www.byrneauctioneers.com
Campbell Stafford	www.campbellstafford.com
Casey & Kingston	http://homepage.eircom.net/~caseyandkingston
Casey-Property.com	www.casey-property.com
Charles Scott and Company	www.charles-scott.co.uk
Charlie Robinson	www.robinson.ie
Colliers International	www.colliers.com
Colm McEvoy	www.colmmcevoy.ie
Coyle Hamilton	www.coylehamilton.com
Daniel Hannon & Sons	www.irishcrafts.com/hannon
Dick Barry & Son	www.barryestateagents.com
Diyhousesales.com	www.diyhousesales.com
Douglas Newman Good	www.dng.ie
Dunloe Ewart	www.dunloe.com
Emerald Auctioneers	www.emeraldauctioneers.com
ERA Ireland	www.eraireland.ie
Eric Cairns	www.ericcairns.co.uk

F & V Sheehan	www.fvsheahan.ie
Ferguson & Associates	www.ferga.com
Flynn & Associates	www.flynnassociates.ie
Grimes	www.grimes.ie
Gunne	www.gunne.ie
Hamilton Osborne King	www.hok.ie
Harry Brann	www.harrybrann.com
Hawthorn Properties	www.hawthornproperties.com
Heskin	www.heskinauctioneers.com
Home Finders	www.property.com/homefinders
Home Locators	www.homelocators.ie
HomeFront	www.homefront.ie
Hunter Campbell	www.huntercampbell.co.uk
Ireland's Property Market	www.property.ie
Irish & European	www.irish-and-european.ie
Irish Stone Houses	www.irishstonehouses.ie
Irish Times Property	www.ireland.com/property
J B Kelly (Dublin)	www.kelly.ie
Jones Lang Lasalle	www.joneslanglasalle.com
Jordan	www.jordan-auctioneers.ie
JP & M Doyle	www.jpmdoyle.ie
Kelly & Co	www.kellyco.ie
Kenneally McAuliffe	www.kenneallymcauliffe.ie
Lambert, Smith, Hampton	www.lsh-ni.co.uk
LetByNet Ireland	www.letbynet.com
Leyden	www.leyden.ie
Lisney	www.lisney.com
Mason Estates	www.masonestates.ie
McClelland & Salter	www.mcclellandsalter.co.uk
McCullagh & Ritchie	www.mccullaghritchie.com
McHale	www.mchaleauctioneers.com
McInerney Holdings	www.mcinerney.ie
McKay Property Services	www.mckps.co.uk
McKeever-Rowan	www.mckeever-rowan.ie
McNally Handy	www.mcnallyhandy.ie
MyHome.ie	www.myhome.ie
National Association of Estate Agents (UK)	www.naea.co.uk
Neal J Doherty	http://njdohertyproperty.com
Nolan & Brophy	www.nolan-brophy.com
Northern Ireland Property	www.niproperty.net
O'Mahony Farrelly	www.omahonyfarrelly.ie
Paddy Vaughan	www.paddyvaughan.com
Philip Johnston And Company	www.philipjohnston.co.uk
Property Ireland	www.propertyireland.ie
Property Partners	www.propertypartners.ie
PropertyNews.com	www.propertynews.com
Reddy Charlton McKnight	www.rcmck.com
Remax Ireland	www.remax-ireland.com

Richmond Business Campus	www.iol.ie/~richmond
Royal Institution of Chartered Surveyors	www.rics.org
SEM	www.sem.ie
Sheehy Residential	www.sheehyres.ie
Sherry Fitzgerald	www.sherryfitz.ie
T & J Gavigan	www.tjgavigan.com
Templeton Robinson	www.templetonrobinson.co.uk
Terry Halpenny	www.terryhalpenny.com
The Property Shop	www.propertyshop.ie
Thomas F Kehoe	www.tfkehoe.com
Thomas J O'Driscoll	www.tjodriscoll.com
Vincent Finnegan	www.finnegan.ie
William Harvey	www.william-harvey.ie
Wyse Estate Agents	www.wyse.ie
Young's Auctioneers	www.youngsauctioneers.com

recruitment

agencies

3 Q Catering	www.3qcatering.ie
Abbey Recruitment	www.abbeyrecruitment.ie
Abbey Training and Recruitment	www.unite.net/customers/abbey
Access Recruitment	www.accessrecruitment.com
Ace Personnel	www.acepersonnel.ie
Achievers Group	www.achieversgroup.ie
Acorn Computer Recruitment	www.acornrecruit.ie
Acumen	www.acumenrecruit.ie
Adecco	www.adecco.co.uk
Adecco	www.adecco.ie
Allen	www.allenrec.com
Ambassador Recruitment	www.ambassador-recruit.com
AMR Human Resources	www.amr.ie
Amrop International	www.amrop.ie
Ann Kilgallon Recruitment	www.akrecruits.ie
Ants	www.ants.ie
Approach People	www.approachpeople.com
Asset Recruitment	www.assetrecruitment.ie
Atlas Personnel Group	www.atlaspg.ie
Bell Recruitment	www.bellrecruitment.co.uk
Berkley Recruitment	www.berkleyrecruitment.com
Best Personnel	www.bestpersonnel.ie
Better Placement Decision	www.bpd.ie
Blue Print	www.blueprintappointments.com
Brendan Long Associates	www.bla.ie
Butler Carolan	www.butlercarolan.ie
Buzz Professional	www.buzz.ie
Calibre	www.calibre-recruitment.com

Career management International	http://indigo.ie/~cmitechr
CCI Recruitment	www.cci.ie
CCM Recruitment	www.ccmrecruitment.com
Centre Point Group	www.centrepointgroup.com
Clark Recruitment	www.clarkrecruitment.ie
CMS Group	www.cms.ie
Collins McNichols	www.commerce.ie/cmcn
Compustaff	www.compustaff.ie
Computer People	www.computerpeople.com
Computer Staff Recruitment	www.csr.ie
Contact Recruitment	www.contact-recruitment.ie
Contract People	www.contractpeople.com
CPL	www.cpl.ie
CRC International	www.crc-international.com
Creative Financial Staffing	www.cfstaffing.com
Dawson Recruitment Group	www.dawsonrecruit.com
Design Staff	www.designstaff.ie
Diamond IT Recruitment	www.diamondit.com
Diamond Recruitment	www.diamond-rec.co.uk
DP Group, The	www.thepdgroup.com
Dublin Childcare Recruitment Agency	www.childcare-recruitment.com
Eden Recruitment	www.edenrecruitment.ie
Elan IT	www.elanit.ie
Ellis Employment	www.agency.ie
Eolas Recruitment	www.eolas.ie
Euro Select	www.euroselect-recruitment.com
Executive Edge	www.executiveedge.ie
Executive Market	www.ex-mark.com
Executive Network	www.exnetwork.com
Financial Recruitment Specialists	www.recruitmentvillage.com
Financial Services Recruitment	www.fsr.ie
First Choice Selection Services Ltd	www.first-choice-rec.com
First Place Personnel	www.firstplacepersonnel.com
Firstaff Personnel Consultants	www.firstaffjobs.com
FK International	www.fkinternational.com
Flexiskills	www.flexiskills.demon.co.uk
Future Focus	www.futurefocus.ie
Future Path	www.futurepath.ie
Gerard O'Malley & Associates	www.omalley-intersearch.com
Global Personnel Services	www.globalpersonnelservices.com
Grafton Recruitment	www.grafton-group.com
Harry Walsh Associates	www.hwapeople.com
Hay Group	www.haygroup.com
Helm Recruitment	www.helm.ie
Henderson Recruitment	www.henderesonrecruitment.com
High Skills Pool	www.highskillspool.ie

Homebased	www.homebased.ie
Howard Recruitment	www.howardrecruitment.com
HRM	www.hrm.ie
ICDS Group	www.icds.ie
Inbucon	www.inbucon.ie
Kennedy Recruitment	www.kennedyrecruitment.co.uk
Key Personnel	www.key.ie
Keystaff Recruitment	www.keystaff.co.uk
Link Personnel Services	www.linkpersonnel.ie
Lynn Recruitment	www.lynn-recruitment.co.uk
Mark Mitchell	www.markmitchell.ie
Mary B Cremin	www.marybcremin.ie
Maxwell Recruitment	www.maxwellrecruitment.ie
Merlin Ireland	www.merlin-ireland.com
Merrion Resources	www.merrionresources.com
Morgan McKinley	www.morgan-mckinley.co.uk
Mydas Recruitment	www.mydasrecruitment.co.uk
New Media CV	www.newmediacv.com
NRC	www.nrc.ie
Onyx Recruitment	www.onyxrecruitment.ie
Options International	www.optionsrecruitment.com
Osborne Recruitment	www.osborne.ie
Peach Enterprises	www.peach.ie
People On The Move	www.peopleonthemove.ie
Pertemps	www.pertemps.ie
Pery Square Agency	www.perysquareagency.ie
Pharmaceutical Recruitment Consultants	www.pharmrecruitment.com
Planet Recruitment	www.planet-recruitment.com
Preferred Staff	www.preferredstaff.com
Premier Recruitment Group	www.premier-recruitment.com
Pro-Step	www.prosteprecruitment.com
Professional Connections	www.profco.com
Quality Recruitment	www.qualityrecruitment.ie
Recruitment for Technology	www.rftgroup.ie
Recruitment Plus	www.recruitmentplus.ie
Recruitment Resources	www.recruitmentresources.ie
Recruitmentdirect	www.recruitmentdirectni.co.uk
Reed	www.reed.ie
Retail Placement	www.retailplacement.ie
Richmond	www.richmond.ie
Sales Placement	www.sales-placement.ie
Santos	www.santos.ie
Select Appointments	www.selectgroup.com
Select People	www.selectpeopleni.com
SHL Group	www.shlgroup.com
SkillsGroup International	www.skillsgroup.ie
SureSkills	www.sureskills.com
Target Recruitment	www.target-recruit.com

Tcrg.com	www.tcrg.com
The Marlborough Group	www.marlborough.ie
The People Group	www.marketingpeople.com
ThePanel.com	www.thepanel.com
TPM Worldwide	www.tmpw.ie
Transformation Services	www.tslit.com
Vineyard	www.vineyardrecruitment.com
WBS Recruitment	www.wbs.ie
Wolfe Group	www.wolfegroup.com
Work in Ireland	www.workinireland.ca
Zenith Recruitment	www.zenith.ie

job listings

3rd Level.com	www.3rd-level.com
CareerPath.com	www.careerpath.com
College Recruiter	www.collegerecruiter.com
Constructionjobs.ie	www.construction-jobs.ie
Corporate Skills	www.corporateskills.com
eMed Jobs	www.emedjob.coom
Fás Jobs Ireland	www.jobsireland.com
HeadHunter	www.headhunter.net
Irish Jobs	www.irishjobs.ie
IrishCareers.com	www.irishcareers.com
IT Appointments	www.itappointments.com
Jobfinder	www.jobfinder.ie
Jobmarketni.com	www.jobmarketni.com
Jobs.ie	www.jobs.ie
Jobsnation.net	www.jobsnation.net
List, The	www.searchthelist.co.uk
Locumotion	www.locumotion.com
Medical Posts	www.medical-posts.com
Monster	www.monster.ie
Nijobs.com	www.nijobs.com
Nixers	www.nixers.com
Planet Graduate	www.planetgraduate.com
Prospects	www.prospects.csu.ac.uk
Recruit Northern Ireland	www.recruitni.com
Recruit OnLine	www.recruit-online.com
RecruitIreland.com	www.recruitireland.com

Softskills	www.softskills.ie
Stepstone	www.stepstone.ie
The Irish Times - Recruitment	www.ireland.com/jobs
Yahoo! Classifieds	http://uk.classifieds.yahoo.com/uk/emp

retail

Aldi	www.aldi-stores.co.uk
Arcadia	www.arcadia.co.uk
Argos	www.argos.co.uk
Arnotts	www.arnotts.ie
Body Shop International	www.the-body-shop.com
Boots	www.boots-plc.com
Buy4Now	www.buy4now.ie
Centra	www.centra.ie
Champion Sports	www.champion.ie
Clerys	www.clerys.ie
Debenhams	www.debenhams.co.uk
Dixons	www.dixons.ie
Dunnes Stores	www.dunnes.ie
Great Universal Stores	www.gusplc.co.uk
Habitat	www.habitat.co.uk
Home Shopping Channel	www.shop-tv.co.uk
House of Fraser	www.hofbi.co.uk
Iceland	www.iceland.co.uk
J Sainsbury	www.j-sainsbury.co.uk
JJB Sports	www.jjb.co.uk
John Lewis Partnership	www.john-lewis-partnership.co.uk
Kingfisher	www.kingfisher.co.uk
Marks & Spencer	www.marks-and-spencer.com
MFI Furniture	www.mfigroup.co.uk
Next	www.next.co.uk
Peats	www.peats.ie
Power City	www.powercity.ie
QVCUK	www.qvcuk.com
Safeway	www.safeway.co.uk
Selfridges	www.selfridges.co.uk
Somerfield	www.somerfield.co.uk
Spar	www.spar.ie
Super Valu	www.supervalu.ie
Superquinn	www.superquinn.ie
Tesco	www.tesco.ie
Wm. Morrison Supermarkets	www.morrisons.plc.uk
Wolsey	www.wolsey.com

services

A1 Catering	www.a1cateringservices.com
Addgards	www.addgards.com
Ambassador Chauffeur Drive	www.ambassador.ie
American Super Stretch Limousines	www.limousinesireland.com
Association of Exhibition Organisers	www.aeo.org
Avis Europe	www.avis-europe.com
Big Services	www.big.ie
Bitewise Foods	www.bitewise.ie

Call-A-Wash	www.callawash.com
Chauffeur Drive by Quinton Hill	www.quintonhill.com
Chauffeur Drive Ireland	www.iol.ie/~jimnolan
Chauffeur Service Ireland	www.chauffeurservice ireland.ie
Chauffeured Classics	www.cclassics.com
ClubIreland	www.clubireland.ie
Company Occasions	www.companyoccasions.ie
Crystal Clean	www.crystalclean.ie
David Fields Cleaning Service	www.cleaningservice.ie
Dedicated Chauffeur Drive	www.irishchauffeurs.com
Delaney Marketing Group	www.dmc.ie
Drain Surgeons	www.drainsurgeons.net
Dyno-Rod	www.dyno-rod.com
Emerald Contract Cleaners	www.emeraldcleaning.ie
Enterprise Ireland	www.enterprise-ireland.com
Eventive Group	www.eventive.ie
Excellent Choice	www.excellentchoice.ie
Expo-Events	www.expo-events.com
Facilities Management	www.facilitiesmanagement.ie
Femcare Ireland	www.femcareireland.com
Forfas	www.forfas.ie
Golden Pages	www.goldenpages.ie
Green Sunrise Group	www.gsholdings.ie
Grosvenor Services	www.grosvenorservices.com
Hire All Party Hire	www.partyhire.ie
Hooper Catering	www.hooperscatering.com
House Finder	www.housefinder.ie
IMS Group	www.imsgroup.com
Independent Directory	www.independent-directory.ie
Indiqu	www.indiqu.com
Innovate	www.innovate.ie
Interference	www.interference.ie
International Conference Organisers	www.ico.ie
Irish Film & Television Network	www.iftn.ie
Key Events	www.keyevents.ie
Kompass	www.kompass.ie
Mailit-Europe	www.mailit.ie
Martin Services	www.martin-services.ie
Master Clean	www.masclean.com
McKechnie Cleaning Service	www.mckechnie-cleaning.ie
MedMedia	www.medmedia.ie
Michael Carroll	www.itsupportsystems.com
Nolans Mobile Pressure Cleaning	www.nolansmpc.com
Ovation Group	www.incentive-conf.ie
Photo-Me International	www.photo-me.co.uk
Powerstation	www.power-station.ie
Swan Chauffeur Drive	www.swanchauffeur.ie
Theme Events	www.events.ie
With Taste Banqueting Service	www.withtastebanqueting.ie

Writelines	www.writelines.com

shipbuilding/repair

Cork Dockyard	www.corkdockyard.com
Harland & Wolff	www.harland-wolff.com

solicitors

A & L Goodbody Solicitors	www.algoodbody.ie
ABC Legal Services	www.abclegalservices.com
Arthur Cox	www.arthurcox.ie
Binchys	www.binchys.com
Boland & Co	www.boland-solicitors.com
C & H Jefferson	www.jefferson.u-net.com
C&H Jefferson	www.chjefferson.co.uk
Cafferky Solicitors	www.cafferkysolicitors.com
Campbell Fitzpatrick	www.campbell-fitzpatrick.co.uk
Campbell Stafford Solicitors	www.campbellstafford.com
Carson & McDowell	www.carson-mcdowell.com
Carvill	www.carvill.ie
Casey & Casey	www.casey-casey.com
Children's Law Centre	www.childrenslawcentre.org
Clarke Jeffers & Co	www.clarkejeffers-law.com
Cleaver Fulton & Rankin	www.cfrlawonline.com
Connolly O'Neill	www.accident-compensation.net
Copeland	www.copelandmccaffrey.co.uk
Cunningham Ellis & Buckle	www.cunningham&lynsey.co.uk
Davison & Co	www.davison-co.com
Dillon-Eustace	www.dilloneustace.ie
Donnelly Neary & Donnelly Solicitors	www.dndlaw.com
Doyle O'Driscoill & Associates	www.doyleodriscoll.com
Duncan Grehan & Partners	www.duncan-grehan.com
Edwards & Company Solicitors	www.edwardsandcompany.co.uk
Elliott Duffy Garrett	www.edgsolicitors.co.uk
Eugene F. Collins Solicitors	www.efc.ie
First Legal	www.dpc.ie
FR Kelly	www.frkelly.ie
Francis Hanna & Co	www.fhanna.co.uk
Frank Lanigan Malcomson & Law	www.lowwwe.com/flml
Gallagher Shatter Solicitors	www.gallaghershatter.ie
Gary-Matthews Solicitors	www.gary-matthews.com
Harry J. Ward & Co.	http://indigo.ie/~hjward
Hewitt & Gilpin	www.hewittandgilpin.co.uk
Highland Law	www.highlandlaw.com
Holland Condon	www.hollandcondon.com
Holmes & Moffitt	www.holmof.co.uk
J.W. O'Donovan	http://indigo.ie/~jwod
John Glynn & Co.	www.tallaght.com/lawyer
John Hussey & Co. Solicitors	www.iol.ie/johnhussey

JohnsElliot	www.johnselliot.com
Kearney Sefton Solicitors	www.kearneysefton.co.uk
Kennedy McGonagle Ballagh	www.kmb.ie
Kenny Stephenson Chapman	www.ksc.ie
Kirwan & Co	www.kirwan.net
L'Estrange and Brett	www.mccann-fitzgerald.ie/lestrange_brett
Law Centre NI	www.lawcentreni.org
Law Society of Ireland	www.lawsociety.ie
Law Society of Northern Ireland	www.lawsoc-ni.org
Ledwidge	www.ledwidge.com
Legal Island	www.legal-island.com
LennonHeather	www.lennonheather.ie
LK Shields	www.lkshields.ie
Macauley & Ritchie	www.nidex.com/m&r
Madden & Finucane	www.madden-finucane.com
Malcomson Law	www.mlaw.ie
Mason Hayes & Curran	www.mhc.ie
Matheson Ormsby & Prentice	www.mop.ie
McAteer & Co Solicitors	www.geocities.com/mcateersolicitors
McCann FitzGerald Solicitors	www.mccann-fitzgerald.ie
McCartan Turkington & Breen	www.mtb-aw.co.uk
McCarthy & Co	www.mccarthy.ie
McKeever Rowan Solicitors	www.mckeever-rowan.ie
McKinty & Wright	www.mckinty-wright.co.uk
McShane and Company	www.mcshaneandco.com
ML White	www.mlwhitesolicitors.com
Napier & Sons	www.napiers.com
Nelson-Singleton	www.nelson-singleton.co.uk
Northern Ireland Ombudsman	www.ni-ombudsman.org.uk
O'Mahony Farrelly	www.omahonyfarrelly.ie
O'Reilly Consultants	www.orc.ie
O'Reilly-Stewart Solicitors	www.oreilly-stewart.co.uk
Oliver Ryan-Purcell	www.euroirishagrilaw.com
Oliver Shanley & Co	www.shanley-law.com
Patterson Donelly	www.pdshaw.co.uk
Peter Dornan & Co	www.peterdornan.co.uk
Peter McDonnell & Associates	www.petermcdonnell.ie
PJ McGrory & Co	www.pjmcgrory.co.uk
PJ O'Driscoll & Sons Solicitors	www.pjodriscoll.ie
Psychological Services (NI) Ltd	www.psychoservices.com
Quinn & Co	www.quinnsolicitors.ie
Reddy, Charlton & McKnight	www.rcmck.com
Ronan Daly Jermyn	www.rdj.ie
Sheldon & Stewart Solicitors	www.sheldon-stewart.co.uk
SJ Diamond & Sons	www.diamondheron.com
Stokes & Co	www.stokesco.ie
Thompson Mitchell	www.thompsonmitchell.co.uk
Tughan & Co	www.tughan.co.uk

Vincent P Fitzpatrick & Co	www.campbell-fitzpatrick.co.uk
Walker McDonald	www.walkermcdonald.com
Watson & Neill	www.watsonandneill.com
Wilson Nesbitt	www.wilson-nesbitt.co.uk
Wood, Kieron	http://indigo.ie/~kwood

stock exchanges & financial listings

America	www.amex.com
Amsterdam	www.aex.nl
Australia	www.asx.com.au
Baltic Exchange	www.balticexchange.co.uk
Berlin	www.berlinerboerse.de
Bermuda	www.bsx.com
Brussels	www.stockexchange.be
Bucharest	www.bvb.ro
Canadian Venture Exchange	www.cdnx.com
Cayman Islands	www.csx.com.ky
Chicago	www.chicagostockex.com
Dow Jones	www.dowjones.com
Dublin	www.ise.ie
EASDAQ	www.easdaq.be
Finfacts	www.finfacts.ie
Frankfurt	www.exchange.de
Helsinki	www.hse.fi
Hong Kong	www.hkex.com.hk
Irish Times Money Mate	http://moneymate.ireland.com
Johannesburg	www.jse.co.za
LIFFE	www.liffe.com
Lisbon	www.bvl.pt
London	www.londonstockexchange.com
London Metal Exchange	www.lme.co.uk
Madrid	www.bolsamadrid.es
Montreal	www.me.org
NASDAQ	www.nasdaq.com
New York	www.nyse.com
Paris	www.bourse-de-paris.fr
Stockholm	www.stockholmsborsen.se
Switzerland	www.swx.ch
Taiwan	www.tse.com.tw
Tokyo	www.tse.or.jp
Toronto	www.tse.com
Warsaw	www.gpw.com.pl

telecommunications

Alphyra/ITG	www.itg.ie
British Telecom	www.bt.com
Broadcom Eireann	www.broadcom.ie
Cable & Wireless	www.cwplc.com
Chorus	www.chorus.ie

COLT Telecom	www.colt-telecom.com
Dome Telecom	www.dometelecom.com
E-Merge	www.e-merge.ie
Ebone	www.gtsireland.com
Eircom	www.eircom.ie
Esat	www.esat.ie
Etel	www.etel-group.com
Imagine	www.imagine.ie
NTL	www.ntl.com
Ocean	www.ocean.ie
Swiftcall	www.swiftcall.ie
Technico	www.technico.ie
Telenor	www.telenor.com
WorldCom Ireland	www.wcom.ie

trade unions

ASLEF	www.aslef.org.uk
Association of Professional Staffs in Colleges of Education	www.ifnet.ie
Association of Secondary Teachers in Ireland	www.asti.ie
ATGWU	www.tgwu.org.uk
Communications Union of Ireland	www.cwu.ie
Construction Industry Federation	www.cif.ie
Fire Brigades Union (FBU)	www.fbu.org.uk
GMB	www.gmb.org.uk
GPMU (UK general union)	www.gpmu.org.uk
ILDA	www.ilda.net
International Labour Office	www.ilo.org
International Confederation of Free Trade Unions (ICFTU)	www.icftu.org
Irish Business and Employers Confederation	www.ibec.ie
Irish Congress of Trade Unions	www.ictu.ie
Irish Federation of University Teachers	www.ifut.ie
Irish Municipal Public and Civil Trade Union	www.impact.ie
Irish National Organisation of the Unemployed	www.inou.ie
Irish National Teachers Organisation (INTO)	www.into.ie
Irish Nurses Organisation	www.ino.ie
Irish Small & Medium Enterprises Association	www.isme.ie
Labour Relations Agency	www.lra.org.uk
Labour Relations Commission	www.lrc.ie
MANDATE	www.mandate.ie
MSF	www.msf.org.uk
National Union of Journalists (NUJ)	http://indigo.ie/~nujdub

Pdforra	www.pdforra.ie
Public Service Executive Union	www.pseu.ie
SIPTU	www.siptu.ie
Small Firms Association	www.sfa.ie
Teachers Union of Ireland (TUI)	www.tui.ie
Trades Union Congress (UK)	www.tuc.org.uk
Union of Shop, Distributive & Allied Workers	www.usdaw.org.uk
Unison	www.unison.org.uk

transportation & logistics

Breen International Transport	www.breentrans.com
Chartered Institute of Transport in Ireland	www.ccs.ie/citi/citi.htm
Irish Road Haulage Association	www.irha.ie
Leamore Transport	www.leamore.ie
McArdle Transport	www.mccardletransport.ie
O'Dwyer Transport	www.o-dwyertransport.com
Securispeed	www.securispeed.com
Travel Management Solutions	www.tmsolutions.ie
Virginia Transport	www.virginia-transport.ie

travel & transport

Aer Arann	www.aerarann.ie
Aer Lingus	www.aerlingus.com
Air France	www.airfrance.ie
AirCoach	www.aircoach.ie
American Airlines	www.aa.com
Argus Rent-a-car	www.argus-rentacar.com
Baltimore/Washington International Airport	www.bwiairport.com
BMI British Midlands	www.flybmi.com
Boston's Logan International Airport	www.massport.com/logan
British Airways	www.british-airways.com
Bus Éireann	www.buseireann.ie
C.I.É	www.cie.ie
Chicago O'Hare International Airport	www.chicagoairports.com/ohare
Citybus	www.translink.co.uk/citybus
CityLink	www.citylink.ie
Continental Airlines	www.continental.com
Cork Airport	www.cork-airport.com
Delta Airlines	www.delta.com
Dublin Airport	www.dublin-airport.com
Dublin Bus	www.dublinbus.ie
Düsseldorf International Airport	www.duesseldorf-international.de
Frankfurt Airport	www.frankfurt-airport.de
Iarnród Éireann/Irish Rail	www.irishrail.ie

Irish Ferries	www.irishferries.com
JFK International Airport (New York)	www.panynj.gov/aviation/ jfkframe.htm
Kilkenny Airfield	www.kinair.com
Knock International Airport	www.west-irl-holidays.ie
London Gatwick Airport	www.baa.co.uk/main/ airports/gatwick
London Heathrow Airport	www.baa.co.uk/main/ airports/heathrow
Motorweb.ie	www.motorweb.ie
NI Railways	www.translink.co.uk
Railtours	www.railtours.ie
Rapid Taxis	www.rapidtaxis.com
Ryanair	www.ryanair.ie
San Francisco International Airport	www.flysfo.com
Sligo Airport	www.sligoairport.com
Translink	www.translink.co.uk
Ulsterbus	www.translink.co.uk
USIT	www.usitnow.ie
Virgin Express	www.virgin-express.com

us corporations

American Express	www.americanexpress.com
Boeing	www.boeing.com
Canon	www.canon.com
Chevron	www.chevron.com
Coca-Cola	www.thecoca-colacompany. com
Dell	www.dell.com
Delta Airlines	www.delta-air.com
Du Pont	www.dupont.com
Eastman Kodak	www.kodak.com
Exxon	www.exxon.com
Federal Express	www.fedex.com
Gateway	www.gateway.com
General Electric	www.ge.com
General Motors	www.gm.com
Goodyear	www.goodyear.com
IBM	www.ibm.com
Intel	www.intel.com
Johnson & Johnson	www.jnj.com
JP Morgan	www.jpmorgan.com
Kodak	www.kodak.com
McDonalds	www.mcdonalds.com
Merck	www.merck.com
Microsoft	www.microsoft.com
Novell	www.novell.com
Proctor & Gamble	www.pg.com
Sears Roebuck	www.sears.com
Sun	www.sun.com

Union Carbide	www.unioncarbide.com
United Airlines	www.ual.com
United Technologies	www.utc.com
Wal-Mart	www.wal-mart.com
Walt Disney	www.disney.go.com
Xerox	www.xerox.com

utilities

Bord Gáis	www.bordgais.com
Bord Na Móna	www.bnm.ie
Calor Gas	www.calorgas.ie
Eirtricity	www.eirtricity.ie
EPower	www.epower.ie
ESB	www.esb.ie
Flogas	www.flogas.ie
Kilronan Windfarm	www.kilronanwindfarm.com
Northern Ireland Electricity	www.nie.co.uk
Phoenix Natural Gas	www.phoenix-natural-gas.com

children

- clubs & activities
- computer games
- days out
- film & television
- games
- magazines, books & authors
- toys
- websites

children

clubs and activities

An Óige	www.irelandyha.org
Astronomy Ireland	www.astronomy.ie
Boys and Girls Clubs of Northern Ireland	www.boysandgirlsclubs-ni.org.uk
Boys' Brigade	www.boys-brigade.org.uk
Challenge For Youth	www.cinni.org/challenge/cfy
Chess Ireland	http://ireland.iol.ie/jghurley
Co-operation Ireland	www.co-operation-ireland.ie
Cork Local Voluntary Youth Council	http://homepage.eircom.net/~clvyc/home.html
Exchange House Travellers Service	www.exchangehouse.ie
Girl Guides Association	www.guides.org.uk
Girls Brigade	www.girlsbrigadeni.com
Irish Association for Young People in Care	http://homepage.tinet.ie/~iaypic
Irish Girl Guides	www.irishgirlguides.ie
Irish Red Cross	www.redcross.ie
Leargas	www.leargas.ie
Macra na Feirme	http://indigo.ie/~macra
National Association of Youth Drama	www.youthdrama.ie
National Youth Agency (UK)	www.nya.org.uk
National Youth Council of Ireland	www.connect.ie/tribli/nyci.htmwww.youth.ie
National Youth Federation	www.iol.ie/~nyf
National Youth Theatre of the Deaf	www.nytd.connect.ie
NIyouth	www.niyouth.com
Oasis Family Centre	www.oasis-ni.org
Ocean Youth Trust	www.oytni.org.uk
Ógra Chorcaí	http://welcome.to/ogra
Omagh Youth & Community Workshop	www.omagh.gov.uk
President's Award/Gaisce	www.gaisce.net
Scout Association (NI)	www.scouts-ni.org.uk
Scouts	www.scout.ie
Table Tennis Ireland	http://homepage.eircom.net/~ojk/tti.html
YMCA Ireland	www.ymca-ireland.org
Young Christian Workers	www.iol.ie/~ycw
Youth Action (NI)	www.youthaction.org
Youth Council for Northern Ireland	www.youthcouncil-ni.org.uk
Youthreach	www.youthreach.org

computer games

GamesWorld	www.gamesworld.ie
GameZone	www.gamezone.ie
Irish Player	www.irishplayer.com
Nintendo	www.nintendo.co.uk
PlanIt4Kids.com	www.planit4kids.com
PlayStation	www.playstation-europe.com
PlayStation 2	www.playstation2.com
Sega	www.sega.com
Sega Dreamcast	www.dreamcast-europe.com

days out

Adventure Activities Irl	www.adventure-activities-ireland.com
Baboro	www.baboro.ie
Belfast Zoo	www.belfastzoo.co.uk
Birr Castle	www.birrcastle.com
Castleshane Adventures	www.letsgoawol.com
Celtic Adventures	www.activity-ireland.com
Cobh - The Queenstown Story	www.cohbhheritage.com
Countryside Access & Activities Network (NI)	www.countrysiderecreation.com
Crossfire Paintball Games	www.crossfire.ie
Dreamworld Family Entertainment Centre	www.dreamworld.co.uk
Dublin Bay Sea Thrill	www.seathrill.ie
Dublin Zoo	www.dublinzoo.ie
Dunmore East Adventure Centre	www.dunmoreadventure.com
East Coast Adventure Centre	www.eastcoastadventure.com
Enfo	www.enfo.ie
F1 Karting	www.f1karting.com
Flutters Amusements	www.flutters-portrush.com
Fota Wildlife Park	www.cork-guide.ie/fota.htm
Funderland	www.funfair.ie
Gartan Outdoor Education Centre	www.gartan.com
Glenans Sailing	www.glenans-ireland.com
Heritage Council	www.heritagecouncil.ie
Irish Tourist Board	www.ireland.travel.ie/thingstodo
Kart City	www.kartcity.net
Kilkenny International Air Rally	www.kinair.com
Killarney National Park	http://homepage.tinet.ie/~knp
Killary Adventure Company	www.killary.com
Lambert Puppet Theatre	www.lambertpuppettheatre.com
Lisnavagh Gardens	www.lisnavagh.com
Mosney Holiday Centre	www.mosney.ie

Northern Ireland Tourist Board	www.discovernorthernireland.com
Phil's Amusements	www.portrush.co.uk/phils
Predator Paintball	www.paintballireland.com
RailTours Ireland	www.railtours.ie
Rally School Irl	www.rallyschoolireland.ie
Skirmish Paintball	www.skirmish.ie
Splatoon	www.skirmish.ie
The Adventure Agency	www.adventure.ie
The Ark	www.ark.ie
Twilight Zone	www.avaleisure.co.uk
W5	www.w5online.co.uk
West Cork Model Railway Village	www.clon.ie/mvillage.html

film & television

Animal Zone	www.bbc.co.uk/animalzone
Antz	www.antz.com
Art Attack	www.artattack.co.uk
Barney	www.barneyonline.com
Batman & Robin	www.batman-robin.com
BBC Schools	www.bbc.co.uk/education/schools
Bill Nye the Science Guy	www.disney.com/disneytelevision/billnye
Blue Peter	www.bbc.co.uk/bluepeter
Bob the Builder	www.bobthebuilder.org
Bug's Life	www.abugslife.com
Cartoon Network	www.cartoon-network.co.uk
CBBC	www.bbc.co.uk/cbbc
Channel 4 Schools	www.schools.channel4.com
CITV	www.citv.co.uk/citv
Clangers	www.clangers.co.uk
Den2	www.rte.ie/tv/den2/index.html www.rte.ie/den2
Dennis the Menace	www.kingfeatures.com/features/comics/dennis/about.htm
Digimon - The Movie	www.foxkids.com/tvshows/digimon/digimonmovie
Discovery Channel	www.discovery.com
Disney Channel	www.disneychannel.co.uk
Dr Dolittle 2	www.drdolittle2.com
Dungeons And Dragons	www.seednd.com
Fairy Tale	www.fairytalemovie.com
Flash Gordon	www.kingfeatures.com/features/comics/fgordon/about.htm
Fox Kids	www.foxkids.co.uk
Garfield	www.garfield.com
Hercules	www.herc.co.uk

Hyperlinks	www.bbc.co.uk/hyperlinks
Kid's Channel	www.kids-channel.co.uk
Little Mermaid	www.thelittlemermaid.com
Live & Kicking	www.bbc.co.uk/kicking
Mighty Morphin Power Rangers	www.foxkids.com/power_rangers
Mórbegs	www.rte.ie/morbegs
Mulan	www.mulan.com
Munsters	www.munsters.com
Muppets	www.muppets.com
Muppets from Space	www.muppetsfromspace.com
Newsround	www.bbc.co.uk/newsround
Nickelodeon	www.nicktv.co.uk
PlanIt4Kids.com	www.planit4kids.com
Pokémon the First Movie	www.pokemonthemovie.com
Popeye	www.kingfeatures.com/comics/popeye
Rugrats	www.cooltoons.com/shows/rugrats
Rugrats in Paris	www.nick.com/all_nick/movies/rugrats_paris
Rugrats the Movie	www.nick.com/rugrats.tin
Sabrina the Teenage Witch	www.paramount.com/tvsabrina
Sesame Street	www.sesamestreet.com
Shrek	www.shrek.com
Simpsons	www.thesimpsons.com
SpyKids	www.spykids.com
Star Trek	www.startrek.com
Star Wars	www.starwars.com
Stuart Little	www.stuartlittle.com
Tarzan	www.tarzan.co.uk
Teletubbies	www.teletubbies.com
TG4	www.tg4.ie/english/children
The Emperor's New Groove	http://disney.go.com/disneypictures/emperorsnewgroove
Thunderbirds	www.thunderbirdsonline.co.uk
Tomb Raider	www.tombraidermovie.com
Top of the Pops	www.totp.beeb.com
Toy Story	www.toystory.com
Tweenies	www.bbc.co.uk/education/tweenies
Universal Studios	www.universalstudios.com
Walking with dinosaurs	www.bbc.co.uk/dinosaurs
Wallace & Gromit	www.aardman.com
Warner Bros	www.kids.warnerbros.com
X-Men	www.x-men-the-movie.com
Xena Warrior Princess	www.mca.com/tv/xena

games

Chess Ireland	http://ireland.iol.ie/jghurley
Community Games	www.communitygames.ie
Monopoly	www.monopoly.com
Pokémon	www.pokemon.com
Scrabble	www.scrabble.com

magazines, books & authors

Anne Fine	www.annefine.co.uk
Beano	www.beano.co.uk
Beatrix Potter	www.peterrabbit.co.uk
British Arthur Ransome Society	www.arthur-ransome.org
Children's Book Council	www.cbcbooks.org
DC Comics	www.dccomics.com
Dorling Kindersley	www.dk.com
Dr Seuss	www.seussville.com
Enid Blyton	www.blyton.com
Eric Carle	www.eric-carle.com
Flash Gordon	www.kingfeatures.com/features/comics/fgordon/about.htm
Girl's World	www.agirlsworld.com
Goosebumps	www.scholastic.com/goosebumps
Hagar the Horrible	www.kingfeatures.com/features/comics/hagar/about
HarperCollins Children's Books	www.harperchildrens.com
Harry Potter	www.harrypotter.com
Judy Blume	www.judyblume.com
Ladybird Books	www.ladybird.co.uk
Marvel Comics	www.marvelcomics.com
Miffy	www.miffy.co.uk
Mr Men	www.mrmen.net
National Geographic for Kids	www.nationalgeographic.com/kids
Paddington Bear	www.paddingtonbear.co.uk
PlanIt4Kids.com	www.planit4kids.com
Right Start	www.rightstartmagazine.co.uk
Roald Dahl	www.roalddahl.org
Snoopy	www.snoopy.com
Spider Man	www.kingfeatures.com/features/comics/spidermn/about.htm
Thomas the Tank Engine	www.thomasthetankengine.com
Tintin	www.tintin.be
Watership Down	www.watershipdown.net
Willie Wonka	www.wonka.com
Winnie the Pooh	www.winniethepooh.co.uk

toys

Action Man	www.actionman.co.uk
Barbie	www.barbie.com
Beanie Babies	www.ty.com
Brio	www.brio.co.uk
Cabbage Patch Kids	www.cabbagepatchkids.com
Cluedo	www.cluedo.com
Corgi	www.corgi.co.uk
Crayola	www.crayola.com
Etch-a-sketch	www.etch-a-sketch.com
Fisher Price	www.fisher-price.com
Furbys	www.furbys.co.uk
Hasbro	www.hasbro.com
Hornby	www.hornby.co.uk
Knex	www.knex.co.uk
Lego	www.lego.com
Little Tikes	www.rubbermaid.com/littletikes
Matchbox	www.matchboxtoys.com
Mattel	www.mattel.com
Meccano	www.meccano.com
Mr Potato Head	www.mrpotatohead.com
Panini	www.panini.co.uk
PlanIt4Kids.com	www.planit4kids.com
Playmobil	www.playmobil.de
Pokémon	www.pokemon.com
Scalextric	www.scalextric.co.uk
Si-O(fada)g	www.siogdolls.com
Silly Putty	www.sillyputty.com
Slinky	www.slinkytoys.com
Smyths Toys	www.toys.ie
Tomy	www.tomy.co.uk
Toys-n-Ireland	www.ireland-now.com/toys/index.html
Toys.com	www.etoys.com
Toyzone	www.toyzone.co.uk

websites

Alfy	www.alfy.co.uk
AOL UK Kids' Channel	www.aol.co.uk/channels/kids
Ask Jeeves for Kids	www.ajkids.com
Big Idea	www.bigidea.com
Bonus.com	www.bonus.com
Brain Teaser	www.brain-teaser.com
Carnegie Museum Discovery Room	www.clpgh.org/cmnh/discovery
Citizens Information Database	www.cidb.ie
Compuserve Kids	www.compuserve.com/gateway/kids

Cooking for Kids	www.learnfree.co.uk/cookingforkids/html
Disney	www.disney.com
EcoKids	www.bytesize.com/ecokids
eoincostello.com	www.eoincostello.com
Eplay	www.eplay.co.ukm
European Youth Observatory	www.diba.es/eyo/index.html
Freeserve Revision	www.freeserve.net/education/examrevision
Galaxy Kids	www.galaxykids.co.uk
Get Net Wise	www.getnetwise.org
Homework Elephant	www.homeworkelephant.free-online.co.uk
How Stuff Works	www.howstuffworks.com
IOL Kidz	home.iol.ie
Kids' Almanac	www.kids.infoplease.com
Kids' Crosswords	www.kidcrosswords.com
Kids' Domain	www.kidsdomain.com
Kids' Jokes	www.kidsjokes.com
KidsCom	www.kidscom.com
KidsNet	www.kidsnet.ie
Microsoft Kids	www.microsoft.com/kids
Northern Ireland for Kids	www.ni4kids.com
Oxygen	www.oxygen.ie
Polly Pocket	www.pollypocket.co.uk
Puzzle Up	www.puzzleup.com
Rollercoaster.ie	www.rollercoaster.ie
RSPCA Kids. Stuff	www.rspca.org.uk/content/kids_stuff.html
Smart as Kids	www.smartazzkids.com
Soccer Central	www.soccercentral.ie
Solo Parenting	www.solo.ie
The Big Busy House	www.harperchildrens.com
The Freezone Network	www.freezone.com
The Park	www.oceanfree.net/thepark/flash.html
Theodore's Tugboat	www.cochran.com/theodore
Thunk	www.thunk.com
UTV - Kidzone	www.utv.co.uk/kidzone
Warner Bros Kids' Page	www.kids.warnerbros.com
Yahoo! Games	http://games.yahoo.com
Yahooligans!	www.yahooligans.com
Youth Information	www.youthinformation.ie
YouthInformation.com	www.youthinformation.com
YouthOrg UK	www.youth.org.uk

websites – educational

Bitesize Revision	www.bbc.co.uk/education/revision
Education Ireland	www.educationireland.ie

EduNet	www.edunet.ie
Eircom Learning	www.eircomlearning.ie
Enchanted Learning	www.enchantedlearning.com
Esat Young Scientist and Technology Exhibition	www.esatys.com
European Schoolnet	www.eun.org
Examteacher.com	http://examteacher.com
Freeserve Revision	www.freeserve.net/education/examrevision
Golden Vale Young Entrepreneurs Scheme	www.yes.ie
Higher Education Authority	www.hea.ie
Homework Elephant	www.homeworkelephant.co.uk
Irish Centre for Talented Youth	www.dcu.ie/ctyi
IrishKnowledge.com	www.irishknowledge.com
Junior Cert.Net	www.juniorcert.net
Language Centre of Ireland	www.lci.ie
Learning Store	www.learningstore.co.uk
Leaving Cert.net	www.leavingcert.net
Line One Learning	www.lineone.net/learning
National Concert Hall Education	www.nch.ie/education.htm
National Parents Council – Post Primary	www.npcpp.ie
National Parents Council – Primary	http://indigo.ie/~npcp/index1.html
PassTheLeaving.com	www.passtheleaving.com
RTÉ - Irish Education Links	www.rte.ie/tv/education/edulinks.html
Schools Online (Science)	www.shu.ac.uk/schools/sci/sol/contents.htm
Scoilnet	www.scoilnet.ie
Teachers.ie	www.teachers.ie
Technology Awareness Programme in Schools	www.it-tallaght.ie/taps
TopStudy	www.topstudy.com
Viking Irish Network	www.ncte.ie/viking
Youth Pathways Project	www.15up.com/15

education, training and research

- adult education
- agriculture
- ballet, drama & music
- books, magazines & websites
- catering & hospitality
- colleges of further education
- colleges of higher education
- computer training
- distance & part-time learning
- educational organisations
- institutes of technology
- private third-level colleges
- schools
- students
- universities
- vocational colleges

education, training and research

adult education

Adult Learning Information Centre Europe	www.clingendael.nl/alice/ewwwiris.htm
Aontas	www.aontas.com
Cork Adult Education	www.corkadulteducation.ie
DeLLTTi (Lifelong Learning Online)	www.ucd.ie/~delltti
Dublin Adult Learning Centre	www.dalc.ie
International Council for Adult Education	www.web.net/icae
National Adult Literacy Agency	www.nala.ie
National Training & Development Institute	www.rehab.ie/ntdi
Nightcourses.com	www.nightcourses.com
Web Guide to Lifelong Learning, Cork	http://homepage.tinet.ie/~adulteducation/sl.htm

agriculture

BIM	www.bim.ie
Enniskillen College of Agriculture	www.enniskillencollege.ac.uk
Greenmount College of Agriculture & Horticulture	www.greenmount.ac.uk
Pallaskenry Agricultural College	www.pallaskenry.com
Royal Agricultural College	www.royagcol.ac.uk
TEAGASC	www.teagasc.ie

ballet, drama & music

Gaiety School of Acting	www.gaietyschool.com
Music for Youth	www.mfy.org.uk
National Performing Arts School	www.npas.ie
Royal Irish Academy	www.ria.ie
Set Dance	www.setdance.com
Sound Training Centre	www.soundtraining.com
Youth Drama	www.youthdrama.ie

books, magazines & websites

CareerNet	www.iol.ie/careernet
Careers World	www.careersworld.com
Colleges Web	www.collegesweb.com
Education Depot	www.education-depot.com
Education Magazine	www.educationmagazine.ie
Eirestudent.com	www.eirestudent.com
Elements Magazine	www.ul.ie/~childsp/elements
Faith In Schools	www.faithinschools.org
Flunknet - Student Wide Web	www.flunk.net
Guide to Grants, Scholarships & Disability Benefits	www.ahead.ie/grants/grants.html

Higher Education Ireland	www.highereducationireland.com
Ireland's Online Education Guide	www.absoluted.com/education
Irish Student-web	www.an-lar.com
Irish Times - Education & Living	www.ireland.com/education/el
Nudge Student Information Centre	www.nudge.co.uk
Oxygen	www.oxygen.ie
RTE Educational Television	www.rte.ie/tv/education
ScoilNet	www.scoilnet.ie
StudyWeb	www.studyweb.com
Teachers.ie	www.teachers.ie
TES Times Educational Supplement	www.tes.co.uk
WildIreland	www.wildireland.ie

catering & hospitality

Ballymaloe Cookery School	www.ballymaloe-cookery-school.ie
Berry Lodge	www.berrylodge.com
CERT Tourism Training	www.cert.ie
Food & Drink Training Council	www.fdtc.co.uk
Northern Ireland Hotel & Catering College	www.nihcc.ac.uk
Shannon College of Hotel Management	www.shannoncollege.com

colleges of further education

Ballsbridge College of Business Studies	www.iol.ie/~bbcoll
Belfast College of Training and Education	www.belfast-college.com
Belfast Institute of Further and Higher Education	www.belfastinstitute.ac.uk
Bray Institute of Further Education	www.iol.ie/~bife
Castlereagh College of Further and Higher Education	www.castlereagh.ac.uk
Colaiste Dhulaigh, Coolock	www.colaistedhulaigh.ie
Colaiste Stiofain Naofa, Cork	www.csn.ie
Crumlin College of Further Education	www.iol.ie/~crumlin
East Antrim Institute of Further and Higher Education	www.eaifhe.ac.uk
East Down Institute of Further and Higher Education	www.eastdowninstitute.ac.uk
Fermanagh College of Further Education	www.fermanaghcoll.ac.uk
Inchicore College of Further Education	www.iol.ie/~inchvec
Institute of Lifelong Learning	www.qub.ac.uk/ill

Lisburn College of Further and Higher Education	www.liscol.ac.uk
Loughry College	www.nics.gov.uk/dani/loughry
Newry and Kilkeel Institute of Further and Higher Education	www.newry-kilkeel.ac.uk
North East Institute of Further and Higher Education	www.nei.ac.uk
North West Institute of Further and Higher Education	www.nwifhe.ac.uk
Northern Ireland Open College Network	www.niocn.co.uk
Omagh College of Further Education	www.omagh.ac.uk
Senior College, Ballyfermot	www.scb.ie
Senior College, Dun Laoghaire	www.scd.ie
Senior College, Sallynoggin	www.scs.dife.ie
St. John's College, Cork	www.stjohnscollege.com
The Causeway Institute of Further and Higher Education	www.causeway.ac.uk
The Distance Learning College of Ireland	www.dlci.fsnet.co.uk
Upper Bann Institute of Further and Higher Education	www.ubi.ac.uk
Whitehall College of Further Education	www.iol.ie/~whitehal/listing2.html

colleges of higher education

All Hallows College Dublin	www.allhallows.ie
Burren College of Art	www.iol.ie/~burren
Castlereagh College	www.castlereagh.ac.uk
Froebel College	http://indigo.ie/~froebel
Greenmount Agricultural College	www.greenmount.ac.uk
Mary Immaculate College Limerick	www.mic.ul.ie
Mater Dei Institute of Education	www.materdei.ie
Michael Smurfit Graduate School of Business	www.smurfitschool.com
Milltown Institute	www.milltown-institute.ie
National College of Ireland	www.ncirl.ie
Newry & Killkeel Institute	www.newry-kilkeel.ac.uk
Royal College of General Practitioners	www.rcgp.org.uk
St. Louise's School of Nursing	http://homepage.tinet.ie/~stlou/
St. Mary's College Belfast	www.stmarys-belfast.ac.uk
Stranmillis College	www.stran-ni.ac.uk
Tipperary Rural & Business Developement Institute	www.trbdi.ie
Waterford School of Nursing	www.iol.ie/~ronniest

computer training

Bua Training	www.buatraining.com
Cyber House Computer Training	www.cyberhouse.ie
DMA Computers	www.dmacomputers.ie
Interactive Avenue	www.interactive-avenue.ie
Irish Times Training	www.irish-times.com/training
Kayser's Computing	www.kayserscomputing.com
Ossidian	www.ossidian.com
Searc	www.searc.ie
Teambuild	www.teambuild.ie
Technology Productions Limited	www.iol.ie/~tpl
WBT Systems	www.wbtsystems.com

distance & part-time learning

Deis	www.deis.cit.ie
DeLLTTi (Lifelong Learning Online)	www.ucd.ie/~delltti
DMA Computers	www.dmacomputers.ie
Future School	www.futureschool.ie
Ireland's Online Guide to Day & Evening Courses	www.absoluted.com/education
Nightcourses.com	www.nightcourses.com
Open University	www.open.ac.uk
Oscail - National Distance Education Centre	www.oscail.ie
Wolfhound Press Guide to Evening Courses	www.wolfhound.ie/eveningclasses

educational organisations

general

AIESEC	www.ie.aiesec.org
Association for Higher Education and Disability	www.ahead.ie
Association of NI Colleges	www.anic.ac.uk
Central Applications Office	http://indigo-ie/~cao
Class North Eastern Centre	www.class-ni.org.uk
Community Relations Training Learning Consortium	www.crtlc.org
Conservation & Education Unit	www.belfastcity.gov.uk
Diversity 21	www.diversity21.co.uk
Education Service Of Leargas	www.leargas.ie/education
Educational Guidance Service For Adults	www.egsa.org.uk
FÁS	www.fas.ie
Forest Education Centre	www.dardni.gov.uk/forestry
Institute of Guidance Counsellors	www.igc-edu.ie
Learning Store	www.learningstore.co.uk
National Centre for Guidance in Education	www.ncge.ie

National Centre for Technology in Education	www.ncte.ie
National Parents Council – Post Primary	www.npcpp.ie
National Parents Council – Primary	http://indigo.ie/~npcp/index1.html
Northern Ireland Business Education Partnership	www.nibep.com
Northern Ireland Council for Integrated Education	www.nicie.org.uk
Northern Ireland Council for Postgraduate Medical & Dental Education	www.nicpmde.com
Northern Ireland Higher Education Council	www.nihec.ac.uk
Northern Ireland Network for Education	www.nine.org.uk
Select Education	www.selecteducation.co.uk
Youth Pathways Project	www.15up.com
Youthreach	www.youthreach.org

governing bodies

Belfast Education and Library Board	www.belb.co.uk
British Council, Ireland	www.britishcouncil.org/ireland
Central Applications Office	www.cao.ie
Conference of Heads of Irish Universities	www.chiu.ie
Department of Education	www.irlgov.ie/educ
Department of Education, Northern Ireland	www.deni.gov.uk
Ecctis UK Colleges	www.ecctis.co.uk
Higher Education & Training Awards Council	www.hetac.ie
Higher Education Authority	www.hea.ie
International Education Board Ireland (IEBI)	www.educationireland.ie
Irish Council for International Students	www.icosirl.ie
National Council for Curriculum Assesment	www.ncca.ie
National Council for Vocational Awards (NCVA)	www.ncva.ie
National University of Ireland (NUI)	www.nui.ie
NI Council for the Curriculum Examination	www.ccea.org.uk
North Eastern Education and Library Board	www.neelb.org.uk
Northern Ireland Student Centre	www.nistudents.com
Qualifax	http://kola.dcu.ie/~qualifax

South Eastern Education and Library Board	www.seelb.org.uk
Southern Education and Library Board	www.selb.org
Staff Commission for Education and Library Boards	www.staffcom.org.uk
UCAS (Universities and College Admissions Service)	www.ucas.ac.uk
Western Education and Library Board	www.welbni.org

institutes of technology

Athlone Institute of Technology	www.ait.ie
Belfast Institute	www.belfastinstitute.ac.uk
Causeway Institute	www.causeway.ac.uk
Dublin Institute of Advanced Studies	www.dias.ie
Dublin Institute of Technology	www.dit.ie
Dun Laoghaire Institute	www.iadt-dl.ie
Dundalk Institute of Technology	www.dkit.ie
Galway-Mayo Institute of Technology	www.gmit.ie
Institute of Technology, Blanchardstown	www.itb.ie
Institute of Technology, Carlow	www.itcarlow.ie
Institute of Technology, Cork	www.cit.ie
Institute of Technology, Limerick	www.lit.ie
Institute of Technology, Sligo	www.itsligo.ie
Institute of Technology, Tallaght	www.it-tallaght.ie
Institute of Technology, Tralee	www.ittralee.ie
Letterkenny Institute of Technology	www.lyit.ie
Limerick Institute of Technology	www.lit.ie
Mountcollyer Technology Centre	www.mountcollyer.ac.uk
Teemore Learning Centre	www.teemorelearning.moonfruit.com
Upper Bann Institute	www.ubifhe.ac.uk
Waterford Institute of Technology	www.wit.ie

private third-level colleges

American College Dublin	www.amcd.ie
Griffith College Dublin	www.gcd.ie
LSB College	www.indigo.ie/lsb
Portobello College	www.portobello.ie
Royal College of Surgeons	www.rcsi.ie

schools

List of Irish Primary Schools	http://ireland.iol.ie/ednet/schools/primary.html
List of Irish Secondary Schools	http://ireland.iol.ie/ednet/schools/second.html

Schools in Northern Ireland	www.deni.gov.uk/schoolmap/schoolsmap.htm

summer schools

Achill Archaeological Field School	www.achill-fieldschool.com
Bard Summer School	www.bard.ie
CelticSummer.com	www.celticsummer.com
Dublin Language Centre and Camp Ireland	www.dlc.ie
Irish School of Landscape Painting	http://indigo.ie/~swebb
Yeats International Summer School	www.yeats-sligo.com/html/summer.html

students

Éire Student	www.eirestudent.com
NUS-USI	www.nus-usi.org.uk
Oxygen	www.oxygen.ie
Queens University Student Union	www.qubsu.org
Union of Students Ireland	www.usi.ie
USIT	www.usit.ie

universities

Dublin City University	www.dcu.ie
Free University of Ireland	http://homepage.tinet.ie/~saorollscoil
National University of Ireland, Maynooth	www.may.ie
Queen's University	www.qub.ac.uk
The Open University	www.open.ac.uk
Trinity College Dublin	www.tcd.ie
University College Cork	www.ucc.ie
University College Dublin	www.ucd.ie
University College Galway	www.ucg.ie
University of Limerick	www.ul.ie
University of Ulster, Coleraine	www.infc.ulst.ac.uk

vocational colleges

ABC First Aid Training	www.firstaidtraining.ni.fm
Arranmore Island Vocational School	http://homepage.tinet.ie/~mhicdiarmada
City of Dublin VEC	www.cdvec.ie
Coleraine Technical College	www.causeway.ac.uk
Institute of Technology Tallaght	www.it-tallaght.ie
Limerick VEC	www.lvec.org
Monaghan VEC	www.monaghanvec.ie
National College of Ireland	www.ncirl.ie
Waterford Institute of Technology	www.wit.ie

food and drink

- breweries
- chefs
- clubs & associations
- famous brands
- fast food
- food marketing
- irish foods
- magazines & websites
- restaurants
- state agencies
- trade associations
- whiskey
- wine

food and drink

breweries

international

Bass Ale	www.bassale.com
Beck's	www.becks-beer.com
Budweiser	www.budweiser.com
Carlsberg	www.carlsberg.com
Cobra	www.cobrabeer.com
Corona	www.corona.com
Foster's	www.fostersbeer.com
Grolsch	www.grolsch.com
Heineken	www.heineken.com
Holsten	www.holsten.de
Kronenbourg	www.kronenbourg1664.co.uk
Miller Lite	www.millerlite.com
Scrumpy Jack	www.scrumpyjack.com

irish

Beamish & Crawford	www.beamish.ie
Biddy Earlys	www.beb.ie
Breó	www.iol.ie/~ange/breo.htm
Bulmers	www.bulmers.ie
Caffrey's	www.caffreys.ie
Carlow Brewing Company	www.carlowbrewing.com
D'Arcy's Dublin Stout	www.dublinbrewing.com
Guinness	www.guinness.ie
Harp	www.iol.ie/~ange/harp.htm
Hilden Brewery	www.beerline.co.uk/brew0161.htm
Irish Brewing Company	www.breworld.com/ibc
Murphy's Beer	www.murphysbeers.com
Porter House Brewing Company	http://dublinpubs.com/themes/porterhouse/inside/html/index2.htm
Wexford Brewing Company	http://homepage.tinet.ie/~wexbrew
Whitewater Brewing Co.	www.beerline.co.uk/brew0332.htm

chefs

Albert Roux	www.albertroux.co.uk
Chefshop.ie	www.chefshop.ie
Conrad Gallagher	www.irishfood.com/peacockalley/welcome.html
Darina Allen	www.ballymaloe-cookery-school.ie/forms/book.htm
Delia Smith	www.deliaonline.com
Derry Clarke	www.lecrivain.com

Gary Rhodes	www.bbc.co.uk/rhodesclassics
Jamie Oliver	www.jamieoliver.net
Keith Floyd	www.keithfloyd.co.uk
Martin Dwyer	www.dwyersrestaurant.com
Neil McFadden	www.irishfood.com/old-dublin/welcome.html
Noel McHugh	www.cakebox.ie
Paul and Jean Rankin	www.gourmetireland.com
Sean O'Sullivan	http://youenjacob.com/chez_youen
StarChefs	www.starchefs.com

clubs & associations

Campaign for Real Ale (CAMRA)	www.camra.org.uk
Cork Free Choice Consumer Group	www.corkfreechoice.ie
Vegetarian Friends	www.vegetarianfriends.com
Vegetarian Society	www.vegsoc.org
VegIreland	http://homepage.tinet.ie/~vegireland

famous brands

international

Absolut Vodka	www.absolutvodka.com
Bacardi	www.bacardi.com
Ben & Jerry's	www.benjerry.co.uk
Birds Eye	www.birdseye.com
Blue Dragon	www.bluedragon.co.uk
Boost	www.boost.co.uk
Buitoni	www.buitoni.co.uk
Campbell's	www.campbellsoup.com
Capri-Sun	www.capri-sun.com
Cheerios	www.cheerios.com
Chiquita	www.chiquita.com
Coca-Cola	www.coca-cola.ie
Creme Egg	www.cremeegg.co.uk
Crunchie	www.crunchie.co.uk
Cuisine de France	www.cuisinedefrance.ie
Danepak	www.danepak.co.uk
Danone	www.danonegroup.com
Del Monte	www.delmonte.com
Delifrance	www.delifrance.com
Dolmio	www.dolmio.com
Douwe Egberts	www.douwe-egberts.co.uk
Dr Pepper	www.drpepper.com
Drambuie	www.drambuie.co.uk
Dunkin' Donuts	www.dunkindonuts.com
Dwan	www.asharte.freeserve.co.uk/dwan.htm
Evian	www.evian.com

Frosties	www.tonythetiger.com
Fyffes	www.fyffes.com
Gerber Foods	www.gerberfoods.com
Grand Marnier	www.grand-marnier.com
Häagen Dazs	www.haagen-dazs.com
Haribo	www.haribo.com
Havana Club	www.havana-club.com
Heinz	www.heinz.com
Hellmann's/Bestfoods	www.bestfoods.com
Hula Hoops	www.hulahoops.co.uk
Jack Daniel's	www.jackdaniels.co.uk
Jim Beam	www.jimbeam.com
Kellogg's	www.kelloggs.ie
Kenco	www.kencocoffee.co.uk
Kinder Surprise	www.kindersurprise.co.uk
KitKat	www.kitkat.ie
Knorr	www.knorr.ie
Kraft	www.kraftfoods.com
Lucozade	www.lucozade.com
M&Ms	www.m-ms.com
Mars	www.mars.com
Moët & Chandon	www.moet.com
Monini	www.monini.com
Müller	www.muller.co.uk
Nabisco	www.chipsahoy.com
Nestlé	www.nestle.com
Nutella	www.nutellausa.com
Nutrasweet	www.nutrasweet.com
Nutri-Grain	www.nutri-grain.com
Old El Paso	www.oldelpaso.com
Peperami	www.peperami.com
Pepsi	www.pepsi.com
Perrier	www.perrier.com
Pop Tarts	www.poptarts.com
Pringles	www.pringles.com
Provamel	www.provamel.co.uk
Quaker Oats	www.quakeroatmeal.com
Quorn	www.quorn.com
Ragu	www.ragu.com
Red Bull	www.redbull.com
Ryvita	www.ryvita.co.uk
Sara Lee	www.saraleebakery.com
Schwartz Herbs	www.schwartz.co.uk
Schweppes	www.cadburyschweppes.com
Sharwood's	www.sharwoods.com
Silver Spoon	www.silverspoon.co.uk
Smirnoff	www.smirnoff.com
Snapple	www.snapple.com
Snickers	www.snickers.com
Southern Comfort	www.southerncomfort.com

St Ivel	www.st-ivel.co.uk
Sunny Delight	www.sunnyd.com
Sweet'N Low	www.sweetnlow.com
Thorntons	www.thorntons.co.uk
Tropicana	www.tropicana.com
Twix	www.twix.com
Uncle Ben's	www.unclebens.com
Vegimite	www.vegemite.com.au
Walkers	www.walkers.co.uk
Weetabix	www.weetabix.co.uk
Whole Earth	www.earthfoods.co.uk
Wrigley's	www.wrigley.com
Yogz	www.yogz.com

irish

Avonmore	www.glanbia.com
Baileys	www.baileys.com
Ballyfree	www.kerry.ie
Ballygowan	www.ballygowan.ie
Barry's Tea	www.barrystea.com
Bewley's	www.bewleys.com
Boru	www.boruirishvodka.com
Budweiser	www.budweiser.com
Butlers Handmade Irish Chocolates	www.butlers-chocolates.com
Cadbury Ireland	www.cadbury.ie
Chivers	www.chivers.ie
Clonakilty Food Company	www.clonakiltyblackpudding.ie
Club Mixers	www.miwadi.ie/clubmixer.htm
Club Orange	www.club.ie
Dairygold	www.dairygold.ie
Dawn	www.kerry.ie
Denny	www.kerry.ie
Dubliner	www.kerrygold.ie
Flahavans	www.flahavans.com
Galtee	www.galtee.ie
HB Ice-Cream	www.hbicecream.ie
Irish Pride	www.irishpride.ie
Kerry Spring	www.kerry.ie
Kerrygold	www.kerrygold.ie
Kilmeaden	www.glanbia.com
Lily O'Briens	www.lilyobriens.ie
Low-Low	www.kerry.ie
McCambridge Fine Irish Food	www.mccambridge.ie
Mi Wadi	www.miwadi.ie
Mitchelstown	www.galtee.ie
O'Kane Foods	www.okanefoods.com
Odlums	www.odlums.ie
Ormo	www.ormo-bakery.com
Premier Dairies	www.glanbia.com
Shamrock Foods	www.shamrockfoods.ie

Shaws	www.galtee.ie
Siúcra	www.irish-sugar.ie
Sno	www.galtee.ie
Tayto	www.taytocrisps.ie
Tipperary Irish Water	www.tipperary-water.ie
Volvic	www.miwadi.ie/volvic.htm
Yoplait	www.glanbia.com

fast food

Abrakebabra	www.abrakebabra.net
Apache Pizza	www.dialapizza.net
Around Noon	www.aroundnoonsandwiches.com
Burger King	www.burgerking.co.uk
Dunkin Donuts	www.dunkindonuts.com
Flash in the Pan	www.flashinthepan-ltd.com
Flout Power	www.flourpower.mcmail.com
Four Star Pizza	www.fourstarpizza.ie
Giulios	www.giuliostakeaway.com
Herrons Country Fried Chicken	www.herronscfc.com
KFC	www.kfc.co.uk
Kingfisher Dublin	www.kingfisherdublin.com
Little Chef	www.little-chef.co.uk
McDonald's	www.mcdonalds.com
Miss Sushi	www.misssushi.com
Niagara	www.niagara.co.uk
O'Briens Irish Sandwich Bar	www.obriens.ie
Pizza Hut	www.pizzahut.com
Subway	www.subway.com
Supermac's	www.supermacs.ie

food marketing

Bord Bia	www.bordbia.ie
Bord Glas	www.bordglas.ie
Bord Iascaigh Mhara - Irish Sea Fisheries Board	www.bim.ie
British Meat	www.britishmeat.org.uk
Irish Dairy Board	www.idb.ie
National Dairy Council (UK)	www.milk.co.uk
Northern Ireland Growth Challenge	www.nigc.org.uk
Ostlan	www.ostlan.net
Oz Clarke	www.ozclarke.com
Pub Guide	www.william-reed.co.uk/magazines/s_publife.html
Real Beer	http://realbeer.com
Shelf Life	www.shelflife.ie
Taste of Ireland	www.tasteofireland.com
The Food Island	www.foodisland.com
VegDining	www.vegdining.com

Vegetarian and Vegan Guide to Ireland	www.bealtaine.ie/vegguide
Wine Today	www.winetoday.com

irish foods

cheese

Gubbeen Cheese	www.westcorkweb.ie/gubbeen
Lavistown Cheese & Sausages	www.lavistownhouse.ie
Sheridans Cheesemongers	www.irishcheese.com
The Organic Centre	www.theorganiccentre.ie
West Cork Natural Cheese Ltd	www.wcnc.ie

chocolate

Butlers	www.butlerschocolates.com
Druid Chocolate	www.druidchocolate.ie
Lily O'Briens	www.lilyobriens.ie
Lir Chocolates	www.lirchocolates.ie

dairy

Dale Farm	www.dalefarm.co.uk
Dromona Quality Foods	www.dqf.co.uk
Foyle Food Group	www.foylefoodgroup.com
Glanbia	www.glanbia.ie
Linden Foods	www.lindenfoods.com
Mourne Country Meats	www.mournecountry.com
Rooney Fish	www.rooneyfish.com
Strathroy Dairy	www.strathroydairy.com

hampers

Bewleys Hampers	www.bewleys-hampers.ie
Celtic Hampers	www.celtichampers.ie
Doherty Gray	www.dohertygray.com

magazines & websites

Adlib	www.adlib.ie
Checkout Ireland	www.checkout.ie
Classicwhiskey.com	www.classicwhiskey.com
Consumers' Association of Ireland	www.consumerassociation.ie
Decanter.com	www.decanter.com
Drinkwine.com	www.drinkwine.com
Dublin Drinking	www.dublindrinking.com
Eat@Home	www.eatathome.ie
Epicurious	www.epicurious.com
Fifth Sense	www.fifthsense.com
Food and Wine	www.foodandwine.ie
Food and Wine.net	www.foodandwine.net
Gourmet Ireland	www.gourmetireland.com
Grocer	www.foodanddrink.co.uk
Ireland Guide	www.ireland-guide.com
Irish Pub Guide	www.irishpubguide.ie
IrishFood.com	www.irishfood.com

JustFood.com	www.justfood.com

restaurants

belfast

Deanes Brasserie/Restaurant	www.deanesbelfast.com
Edge, The	www.at-the-edge.co.uk
Nick's Warehouse	www.nickswarehouse.co.uk
Opus One	www.opusone.co.uk
Shu	www.shu-restaurant.com
The Square	www.thesquarebelfast.com

dublin

Aya	www.aya.ie
Ayumi-Ya	www.ayumia.ie
Bewley's	www.bewleys.ie
Caviston's Seafood Restaurant	www.cavistons.com
Cooke's Café	www.cookescafe.com
Dish	www.dish@indigo.ie
King Sitric	www.kingsitric.ie
Le Coq Hardi	www.tasteofireland.com/ restaurants/coqhardi
L'Ecrivain	www.lecrivain.com
Halo @ Morrison Hotel	www.morrisonhotel.ie
Moe's	moesdublin.com
Red Bank	www.guesthouseireland.com
Roly's Bistro	www.tasteofireland.com/ restuarants/rolys
Tea Rooms @ The Clarence	www.theclarence.ie

rest of ireland

Adare Manor, Co Limerick	www.adaremanor.ie
Aherne's Seafood Restaurant, Cork	www.ahernes.com
Avoca Handweavers, Co Wicklow	www.avoca.ie
Ballinalacken Castle, Co Clare	www.ballalackencastle.com
Ballymaloe House, Co Cork	www.ballymaloe.com
Buggy's Glencairn Inn, Co Waterford	www.buggys.net
Cromleach Lodge, Co Sligo	www.cromleach.com
Cuan, Co Down	www.thecuan.co.uk
D'Arcy's, Co Kerry	www.darcys-kenmare.com
Gregan's Castle, Co Clare	www.gregans.ie
Harvey's Point	www.commerce.ie/harveys-pt
Henley's Stone House, Co Down	www.henleysstonehouse.co.uk
La Cascade @ Sheen Falls, Co Kerry	www.sheenfallslodge.ie
Left Bank Bistro, Co Westmeath	www.leftbankbistro.com
Longueville House, Co Cork	www.longuevillehouse.ie
Marfield House, Co Wexford	www.marlfieldhouse.com
Marquis of Downshire, Co Down	www.marquisofdownshire.com
Richmond House, Co Waterford	www.richmondhouse.net
The Tannery, Co Waterford	www.tannery.ie
Strawbery Tree, Co Wicklow	www.brooklodge.com
Wineport Restaurant, Co Westmeath	www.wineport.ie

state agencies

An Bord Glas(Horticultural Board)	www.bordglas.ie
Bord Iascaigh Mhara	www.bim.ie
BSE Inquiry	www.bse.org.uk
Department of Agriculture, Food and Rural Development	www.irlgov.ie/daff
Department of Agriculture for Northern Ireland	www.dani.gov.uk
Emergency Nutrition Network	www.ennonline.net
European Consumer Centre	www.ecic.ie
Food Safety Authority of Ireland	www.fsai.ie
Guaranteed Irish	www.guaranteed-irish.ie
Hygienemark	www.hygienemark.com
Northern Ireland Centre for Diet and Health	www.science.ulst.ac.uk/niche
Teagasc	www.teagasc.ie

trade associations

Brewers and Licensed Retailers Association	www.blra.co.uk
Brewers' and Maltsters' Guild of Ireland	www.dublinbrewing.com/excise.html
British Potato Council	www.potato.org.uk
Dairy Council for Northern Ireland	www.dairycouncil.co.uk
Food & Drink Federation	www.fdf.org.uk
Guaranteed Irish	www.guaranteed-irish.ie
Hygiene Mark	www.hygienemark.com
International Association of Culinary Professionals	www.iacp-online.org
International Brewers' Guild	www.breworld.com/brewersguild
International Food Information Council	http://ificinfo.health.org
Irish Creamery and Milk Suppliers Association	www.icmsa.ie
Irish Fish Producers' Organisation	homepage.eircom.net/~ifpo
Irish Nutrition & Dietetic Institute	http://indigo.ie/~indicom/indi.htm
Irish Organic Farmers and Growers Association	www.irishorganic.ie
National Off-Licence Association	www.noffla.ie
NI Meat Exporters Association	www.nimea.co.uk
Northern Ireland Food & Drink Association Ltd	www.nifda.co.uk
Northern Ireland Seafood	www.niseafood.co.uk
Restaurant Association	www.ragb.co.uk
The Irish Farmer's Association	www.ifa.ie
Vintners Federation of Ireland	www.pubireland.com/aboutus.htm

Wine & Spirit Association of Ireland www.wineboard.com

whiskey

Bushmills	www.bushmills.com
Cooley	www.cooleywhiskey.com
Famous Grouse	www.famousgrouse.com
Glenfiddich	www.glenfiddich.com
Glenmorangie	www.glenmorangie.com
Green Spot	www.mitchellandson.com/features/greenspt.htm
J&B	www.jbscotch.com
Jack Daniels	www.jackdaniels.com
Jameson	www.jameson.ie
Laphroaig	www.laphroaig.com
Midleton	www.classicwhiskey.com/distilleries/midleton.htm
Seagram	www.seagram.com
Southern Comfort	www.southerncomfort.com
Tullamore Dew	www.tullamore-dew.org
Whiskey Magazine	www.whiskymag.com
Whisky Shop	www.whiskyshop.com

wine

Artistic Wines	www.artisticwines.ie
Berry Bros. & Rudd	www.berry-bros.ie
Bubble Brothers	www.bubblebrothers.com
Bunratty Mead	www.bunrattywinery iegateway.net
Burgundy Direct	www.burgundydirect.ie
Cellar Wines	www.cellarwines.ie
Dalton Wines	www.daltonwines.com
Drink Express	www.drinkexpress.ie
Drink Store	www.drinkstore.ie
e-Wine	www.ewine.ie
Ecock Wines	www.ecockwines.ie
Findlaters	www.findlaters.com
Front Page Wines	www.frontpagewines.com
Grants of Ireland	www.grantsofireland.ie
James Nicholson Wine Merchant	www.jnwine.ie
Karwig Wines Ltd	www.karwig-wines.ie
Le Caveau	www.lecaveau.ie
Leinster Merchant Wines	www.merchantwines.com
McCabes	www.telematix.ie/mccabes
Mill Wine Cellar	www.millwinecellar.ie
Mitchell & Son	www.mitchellandson.com
Moldova Wines	www.moldovawines.ie
Molloy's Liquor Stores	www.liquorstore.ie
Oddbins	www.oddbins.com
On The Grapevine	www.onthegrapevine.ie

Orgasmic Wines	www.orgasmicwines.com
Soleway Wines	www.soleway-wines.ie
The Wine Room	www.thewineroom.ie
TopWines	www.topwines.ie
Waterford Wine Vault	http://waterfordwinevault.com
Wine Development Board of Ireland	www.wineboard.com
Wine Ireland	www.wineireland.ie
Wine Online	www.wineonline.ie
Wine Works	www.wineworks.ie
Wines Direct	www.wines-direct.com

government

cross-border bodies
defence forces
embassies
foreign governments
international organisations
law
local, district & county councils
northern ireland
political parties
post offices
pressure groups
republic of ireland

government

cross-border bodies

Foyle, Carlingford & Irish Lights Commission	www.loughs-agency.org
Irish Language	www.bnag.ie
Trade & Business Development Body	www.intertradeireland.com
Tha Boord O Ulster Scotch	www.ulsterscotsagency.com

defence forces

Aircorps	www.military.ie/aircorps
An Garda Síochána	www.garda.ie
Army	www.military.ie/army
Army (UK)	www.army.mod.uk
Department of Defence	www.irlgov.ie/defence
Irish Defence Forces	www.military.ie
Ministry of Defence (UK)	www.mod.uk
Naval Service	www.military.ie/navy
Overseas Service	www.military.ie/overseas
RAF	www.raf.mod.uk
Reserve Forces	www.military.ie/reserve
Royal Navy	www.royal-navy.mod.uk

embassies

foreign embassies & consulates in ireland

Australia	www.australianembassy.ie
Belgium	www.diplobel.org
Denmark	www.denmark.ie
France	www.ambafrance.ie
Netherlands	http://indigo.ie/~nethemb
Sweden	www.swedishembassy.ie
United Kingdom	www.britishembassy.ie
USA	www.usembassy.ie

irish embassies abroad

Foreign Affairs, Department of (List of Irish Embassies Abroad)	www.irlgov.ie/iveagh
USA	www.irelandemb.org

foreign governments

Andorra	www.andorra.ad/govern
Argentina	www.senado.gov.ar
Armenia	www.gov.am
Australia	www.fed.gov.au
Austria	www.parlinkom.gv.at
Bangladesh	www.bangladeshgov.org
Belarus	www.belarus.net/parliame
Belgium	www.belgium.fgov.be
Belize	www.belize.gov.bz
Bolivia	www.congreso.gov.bo

Brazil	www.senado.gov.br
Brunei	www.brunei.gov.bn
Bulgaria	www.government.bg
Canada	www.canada.gc.ca
Chile	www.camara.cl
China	http://govinfo.cei.gov.cn
Costa Rica	www.casapres.go.cr
Croatia	www.sabor.hr
Cyprus	www.pio.gov.cy
Czech Republic	www.vlada.cz
Denmark	www.folketinget.dk
Egypt	www.shoura.gov.eg
El Salvador	www.sv/
Estonia	www.riik.ee/et
Fiji	www.fiji.gov.fj
Finland	www.eduskunta.fi
France	www.assemblee-nat.fr
German Parliament	www.bundesregierung.de
Germany	www.government.de
Ghana	www.ghana.gov.gh
Greece	www.mpa.gr
Hungary	www.mkogy.hu
Iceland	www.althingi.is
India	http://cabsec.nic.in
Indonesia	www.dpr.go.id
Israel	www.info.gov.il
Israel (Foreign Affairs)	www.israel.org
Italy	http://english.camera.it
Korea	www.assembly.go.kr
Latvia	www.saeima.lv
Lithuania	http://rc.lrs.lt
Luxembourg	www.chd.lu
Malaysia	www.parlimen.gov.my
Malta	www.magnet.mt
Mexico	www.senado.gob.mx
Netherlands	www.parlement.nl
New Zealand	www.govt.nz
Norway	www.stortinget.no
Oman	www.omanet.com
Pakistan	www.pak.gov.pk
Poland	www.poland.pl
Portugal	www.parlamento.pt
Romania	www.guv.ro
Russia	www.gov.ru
Russian Parliament	www.duma.ru
Singapore	www.gov.sg
South Africa	www.polity.org.za
Spain	www.la-moncloa.es
Sweden	www.royalcourt.se/eng
Switzerland	www.admin.ch

Thailand	www.parliament.go.th
Trinidad & Tobago	www.ttparliament.org
Turkey	www.tbmm.gov.tr
Turkish Cypriot	www.cm.gov.nc.tr
Ukraine	www.rada.kiev.ua
United Kingdom	www.ukonline.gov.uk
Uruguay	www.parlamento.gub.uy
USA (CIA)	www.cia.gov
USA (Congress)	www.congress.org
USA (FBI)	www.fbi.gov
USA (House of Representatives)	www.house.gov
USA (Senate)	www.senate.gov
USA (Supreme Court)	www.uscourts.gov
USA (White House)	www.whitehouse.gov
Vietnam	www.na.gov.vn
Yahoo's Government List	www.yahoo.com/government/countries
Yugoslavia	www.gov.yu

international bodies

International Red Cross	www.icrc.org
International Rescue Committee	www.theirc.org
Latin American Parliament	www.parlatino.org.br
NATO	www.nato.int
Organisation for Economic Co-operation & Development (OECD)	www.oecd.org
Organisation of Petroleum Exporting Countries (OPEC)	www.opec.org
Smithsonian Institution	www.si.edu
UNESCO	www.unesco.org
United Nations	www.un.org
United Nations International Children's Fund (UNICEF)	www.unicef.org
World Bank	www.worldbank.org
World Food Programme	www.wfp.org
World Health Organisation	www.who.int
World Meteorological Organisation	www.wmo.ch
World Trade Organisation	www.wto.org

international organisations

european

Commonwealth	www.comparlhq.org.uk
Council of Europe	www.coe.fr
European Central Bank	www.ecb.int
European Commission	www.europa.eu.int
European Court of Human Rights	www.dhcour.coe.fr
European Court of Justice	www.curia.eu.int/en
European Investment Bank	http://eib.eu.int

European Monetary Union	www.europeanmovement.ie/emu.htm
European Parliament	www.europarl.eu.int
European Trade Union Confederation	www.etuc.org
European Union	www.europa.eu.int

other

Bank for International Settlements	www.bis.org
G8	www.genoa-g8.it
International Albert Schweitzer Foundation	www.schweitzer.org
International Atomic Agency	www.icao.int
International Court of Justice	www.icj-cij.org
International Crisis Group	www.intl-crisis-group.org
International Labour Organisation	www.ilo.org
International Maritime Organisation	www.imo.org
International Monetary Fund	www.imf.org

law

Bar Council	www.lawlibrary-ie/barcouncil
Bar Council (UK)	www.barcouncil.org.uk
Bunreacht na hÉireann/ Constitution of Ireland	www.irlgov.ie/taoiseach/publication/constitution/intro.htm
Courts Service	www.courts.ie
Employment Equality Agency	www.equality.ie
European Court of Human Rights	www.echr.coe.int
European Court of Justice	http://europa.eu.int/cj/en
International Court of Justice	www.icj-cij.org
Irish Council for Civil Liberties	www.iccl.ie
Irish Law	www.irish-law.org
Law Library of Ireland	www.lawlibrary.ie
Law Lounge	http://lawlounge.com/main.htm
Law Society of England & Wales	www.lawsoc.org.uk
Law Society of Ireland	www.lawsociety.ie
Law Society of Northern Ireland	www.lawsoc-ni.org
Law.com	www.law.com
Northern Ireland Executive	www.nics.gov.uk
Northern Ireland Legal Aid Department	www.nilad.org
Northern Ireland Ombudsman	www.ni-ombudsman.org.uk
Ombudsman	www.irlgov.ie/ombudsman/pub.htm
Web Journal of Current Legal Issues	http://webjcli.ncl.ac.uk

local, district & county councils

northern ireland

Antrim	www.antrim.gov.uk
Ards	www.ards-council.gov.uk

Armagh	www.armagh.gov.uk
Ballymena	www.ballymena.gov.uk
Ballymoney	www.ballymoney.gov.uk
Banbridge	www.banbridgedc.gov.uk
Belfast	www.belfastcity.gov.uk
Carrickfergus	www.carrickfergus.org
Castlereagh	www.castlereagh.gov.uk
Coleraine	www.colerainebc.gov.uk
Cookstown	www.cookstown.gov.uk
Craigavon	www.craigavon.gov.uk
Derry	www.derrycity.gov.uk
Down	www.downdc.gov.uk
Dungannon & South Tyrone	www.dungannon.gov.uk
Fermanagh	www.fermanagh.gov.uk
Larne	www.larne.com/borough_council
Lisburn	www.lisburn.gov.uk
Magherafelt	www.magherafelt.gov.uk
Moyle	www.moyle-council.org
Newry & Mourne	www.newry.org/nmdc.htm
Newtownabbey	www.newtownabbey.gov.uk
North Down	www.northdown.gov.uk
Omagh	www.omagh.gov.uk
Strabane	www.strabanedc.co.uk

republic of ireland

Cavan (UDC)	www.cavanudc.ie
Cork	www.corkcoco.com
Donegal	www.donegal.ie/dcc
Dun Laoghaire-Rathdown	www.dlrcoco.ie
Fingal	www.fingalcoco.ie
Galway	www.galway.ie
Kerry	www.kerrycoco.ie
Kildare	www.kildare.ie/countycouncil
Kilkenny	www.kilkennycoco.ie
Laois	www.laois.ie
Leitrim	www.leitrimcoco.ie
Limerick	www.limerickcorp.ie
Longford	www.longford.ie
Louth	www.louthcoco.ie
Mayo	www.mayococo.ie
Meath	www.meath.ie
Monaghan	homepage.tinet.ie/~monaghan
Offaly	www.offaly.ie
Roscommon	www.roscommon.ie
Sligo	www.sligo.ie
South Dublin	www.sdcc.ie
Tipperary	www.tipperary.ie
Waterford	www.waterfordcoco.ie
Wexford	www.wexford.ie
Wicklow	www.wicklow.ie

northern ireland

agencies

Belfast Harbour Commissioners	www.belfast-harbour.co.uk
Central Services Agency	www.csa.n-i.nhs.uk
Child Support Agency	www.dhssni.gov.uk/child-support
Commission for Racial Equality	www.cre.gov.uk
Communications Unit	www.dani.gov.uk
Community Aid Ltd	www.comaid2000.co.uk
Companies Registry	www.idbni.co.uk
Compensation Agency	www.compensationni.gov.uk
Connswater Housing Association Ltd	www.connswater.org.uk
Customs & Excise	www.hmce.gov.uk
Driver & Vehicle Testing Agency	www.doeni.gov.uk/dvta
Eastern Health & Social Services Board	www.ehssb.n-i.nhs.uk
Environment & Heritage Service	www.doeni.gov.uk
Foyle Basin Council	www.sustainableireland.com
Foyle Fisheries Commission	www.locks-agency.org
Health & Safety Executive	www.hseni.gov.uk
Housing Executive	www.nihe.gov.uk
Immigration Office	www.homeoffice.gov.uk
Industrial Development Board for Northern Ireland	www.idbni.com
Industrial Therapy Organisation	www.actionmentalhealth.org.uk
Laganside Corporation	www.laganside.com
Londonderry Port & Harbours Commissioners	www.londonderryport.com
Maritime & Coastguard Agency	www.mcga.gov.uk
NI Certification Office for Trade Unions & Employment	www.nicertoffice.com
North Down Development Organisation Ltd	www.nddo.u-net.com
Northern Ireland Advisory Committee on Telecommunications	www.acts.org.uk
Northern Ireland Council for the Curriculum Examinations & Assessment	www.ccea.org.uk
Northern Ireland Human Rights Commission	www.nihrc.org
Parades Commission	www.paradescommission.org
Planning Appeals Commission	www.pacni.gov.uk
Public Record Office	www.nics.gov.uk/pro_home.htm
Southern Health & Social Services Board	www.shssb.org
Trading Standards Service	www.tssni.gov.uk
Transport Advisory Committee	www.nitrans.org.uk
Warrenpoint Harbour Authority	www.warrenpointharbour.co.uk

departments

Department for Regional Development	www.nics.gov.uk/rd.htm
Department for Social Development	www.dsdni.gov.uk
Department of Agriculture	www.doani.gov.uk
Department of Culture, Arts & Leisure	www.dcalni.gov.uk
Department of Economic Development	www.dedni.gov.uk
Department of Education	www.deni.gov.uk
Department of Employment & Learning	www.nics.gov.uk/el.htm
Department of Enterprise, Trade & Investment	www.detini.gov.uk
Department of Environment	www.doeni.gov.uk
Department of Finance	www.dfpni.gov.uk
Department of Health, Social Services & Public Safety	www.dhsspsni.gov.uk
Northern Ireland Assembly	www.ni-assembly.gov.uk
Northern Ireland Office	www.nics.gov.uk
Office of the First Minister & Deputy First Minister	www.ofmdfmni.gov.uk

political parties

Alliance Party	www.allianceparty.org
Fianna Fáil	www.fiannafail.ie
Fine Gael	www.finegael.ie
Green Party	www.greenparty.ie
Labour Party	www.labour.ie
Northern Ireland Labour Party	www.labourni.org
Northern Ireland Women's Coalition	www.niwc.org
Ógra Fianna Fáil	www.ogra.ie
Progressive Democrats	www.progressivedemocrats.ie
Sinn Féin	www.sinnfein.ie
Social Democratic & Labour Party	www.sdlp.ie
Socialist Party	www.dojo.ie/socialist
Socialist Workers Party	www.clubi.ie/swp
Ulster Democratic Unionist Party	www.dup.org.uk
Ulster Unionist Party	www.uup.org
Workers Party	www.workers-party.org

post offices

An Post	www.anpost.ie
Royal Mail	www.royalmail.co.uk

pressure groups

Amnesty International	www.amnesty.ie
Ash	www.ash.ie

Campaign for Nuclear Disarmament	http://indigo.ie/-goodwill/icnd.html
Fair Trade Foundation	www.fairtrade.org.uk
Friends of the Earth	www.foe.co.uk
Greenpeace International	www.greenpeace.org
Learn and Live	http://members.aol.com/learnanliv
Women's Solidarity	www.womensolidarity.com

republic of ireland

agencies

Arts Council	www.artscouncil.ie
Bord Bia	www.bordbia.ie
Bord Fáilte	www.ireland.travel.ie/home
Bord Glas	www.bordglas.ie
Bord Iascaigh Mhara	www.bim.ie
Bord Pleanála	www.pleanala.ie
Central Statistics Office (CSO)	www.cso.ie
CERT	www.cert.ie
Comhairle	www.comhairle.ie
Commissioners of Irish Lights	www.cil.ie
Consumer Affairs	www.odca.ie
Employment Equality Agency	www.equality.ie
Enterprise Ireland	www.enterprise-ireland.com
Environmental Information Service	www.enfo.ie
Environmental Protection Agency	www.epa.ie
Euro Changeover Board of Ireland	www.irlgov.ie/ecbi-euro
Fás	www.fas.ie
Forfás	www.forfas.ie
Health and Safety Authority	www.hsa.ie/osh
Heritage Council, The	www.heritagecouncil.ie
Heritage Ireland	www.heritageireland.ie
Houses of the Oireachtas	www.irlgov.ie/oireachtas/frame.htm
IDA Ireland	www.idaireland.com
Irish Dairy Board	www.idb.ie
Irish Film Board	http://ireland.iol.ie/filmboard
Irish Government	www.irlgov.ie
Irish Marine Institute	www.marine.ie
Irish Radio and Television Commission	www.irtc.ie
Irish Sports Council	www.irishsportscouncil.ie
National Archives of Ireland	www.nationalarchives.ie
National Centre for Guidance in Education	www.iol.ie/ncge
National Gallery of Ireland	www.nationalgallery.ie
National Library of Ireland	www.heanet.ie/natlib
National Treasury Management Agency	www.ntma.ie

Office of Public Works (OPW)	www.opw.ie
Office of the Ombudsman	www.irlgov.ie/ombudsman
Ordnance Survey	www.irlgov.ie/osi
Public Offices Commission	www.irlgov.ie/poc
Revenue Commissioners	www.revenue.ie
State Laboratory	www.statelab.ie
Teagasc	www.teagasc.ie
Údarás na Gaeltachta	www.gaeltacht.ie
Valuation Office	www.valoff.ie

healthcare

advice & support
ancillary services
animal health
complementary
dentistry
government agencies
health board/trusts
hospitals & clinics
journals, magazines & websites
medicine & surgery
nursing & midwifery
pharmacy
psychiatry, psychology & psychotherapy
research
vision

healthcare

advice & support

Acne Advice	www.medinfo.co.uk/conditions/acne.html
Action Cancer	www.actioncancer.org
Action for Blind People	www.afbp.org
Action Mental Health	www.actionmentalhealth.org.uk
ADD Contact	www.addcontact.org.uk
Advice on Children's Problems	www.medical-legal.co.uk/patient_info/children.htm
Age Action Ireland	http://indigo.ie/~ageact/age_indx.html
Age Concern	www.ageconcern.ni.btinternet
Aids Ireland	www.aidsireland.com
Alcoholics Anonymous Ireland	www.alcoweb.com
Alone	www.alone.ie
Alzheimer Society of Ireland	www.alzheimer.ie
Alzheimer's Association	www.alz.org
American Cancer Society	www.cancer.org
Anthony Nolan Bone Marrow Trust	www.anthonynolan.com
Arthritis Care	www.arthritiscare.org.uk
Arthritis Foundation of Ireland	www.arthritis-foundation.com
Ash Ireland	www.ash.ie
Asthma and Allergy Information and Research	www.users.globalnet.co.uk/~aair
Asthma Help	www.asthma-help.co.uk
Asthma Society of Ireland	www.asthmasociety.ie
Aware	www.aware.ie
Back Care	www.backpain.org
Back Up Trust	www.backuptrust.org.uk
Barnardos	www.barnardos.ie
Brainwave	www.brainwave.org.uk
Bray Cancer Support & Information Centre	www.iol.ie/~bcsc
Breast Cancer Care	www.breastcancercare.org.uk
British Dyslexics	www.dyslexia.uk.com
British Epilepsy Association	www.epilepsy.org.uk
British Heart Foundation	www.bhf.org.uk
British Liver Trust	www.britishlivertrust.org.uk
British Lung Foundation	www.lunguk.org
British Vascular Foundation	www.bvf.org.uk
Brook Advisory Centre	www.brook.org.uk
Cairde	www.cairde.org
Cancer and Leukaemia in Childhood	www.clic.uk.com
Cancer BACUP	www.cancerbacup.org.uk
Cancer UK	www.cancerhelp.org.uk

Centre for Recovery from Drug & Alcohol Abuse	www.recovery.org.uk
Cerebral Palsy Action	www.cpaction.org.uk
Children with Leukaemia	www.leukaemia.org
Cleft Lip and Palate Association	www.clapa.mcmail.com
Coeliac Society of Ireland	www.coeliac.ie
Colon Cancer Concern	www.coloncancer.org.uk
Cruse Bereavement Care	www.crusebereavementcare.org.uk
Cystic Fibrosis Association of Ireland	www.internet-ireland.ie/horizon/cfireland
Deaf Blind (UK)	www.deafblinduk.org.uk
Depression Alliance	www.depressionalliance.org
Diabetes (UK)	www.diabetes.org.uk
Digestive Disorders Foundation	www.digestivedisorders.org.uk
Disability Action	www.disabilityaction.org
Disability Federation of Ireland	www.iol.ie/~dfi
Donegal Cheshire Apartments	www.infowing.ie/dochap
Doorway To Life	www.doorwaytolife.com
Down Syndrome WWW Page	www.nas.com/downsyn
Downs Syndrome Association	www.dsa-uk.com
Dream Flight	www.dreamflight.org
Dublin Rape Crisis Centre	www.drcc.ie
Dyspraxia Association	http://indigo.ie/~dyspraxi
Eating Disorders Association	www.edauk.com
Ectopic Pregnancy	www.ectopic.org
Employment Health Advisers	www.eha.ie
Enable Ireland	www.enableireland.ie
Epilepsy Association	www.epilepsy.org.uk
European Infertility Network	www.ein.org
Everyman – Action Against Male Cancer	www.icr.ac.uk/everyman
Eye UK	www.eyeuk.com
Family Planning Association	www.fpa.org.uk
Gingerbread	www.gingerbread.ie
Give Hope Brain Tumour Support	www.givehope-btmr.org.uk
Haemophilia Society	www.haemophilia.org.uk
Information Centre for Individuals with Disabilities	www.disability.net
International Spinal Research Trust	www.spinalresearch.org
Irish Cancer Society	www.irishcancersociety.ie
Irish Diabetic Association	www.iol.ie/diabetes
Irish Family Planning Association	www.ifpa.ie
Irish Heart Foundation	www.irishheart.ie
Irish Kidney Association	www.ika.ie
Irish Motor Neurone Disease Association	www.iol.ie/~killeen/stevemnd/imndawar.htm
Irish Society for Autism	http://ireland.iol.ie/~dary/isa

Irish Sudden Infant Death Association	www.iol.ie/~isidansr/home.htm
Irish Wheelchair Association	www.iwa.ie
ISPCC	www.ispcc.ie
Jennifer Trust for Spinal Muscular Atrophy	www.jtsma.org.uk
La Leche League of Ireland	http://homepage.tinet.ie/~lalecheleague
Lymphoma Association	www.lymphoma.org.uk
Macmillan Relief	www.macmillan.org.uk
Marfan Association	www.marfan.org.uk
Medinfo	www.medinfo.co.uk
Mencap	www.mencap.org.uk
Meningitis Research Foundation	www.meningitis.org.uk
Mental Health Association of Ireland	http://mhai.healthyirish.com
Migraine Association of Ireland	www.migraine.ie
Migraine Trust	www.migrainetrust.org
Mind	www.mind.org.uk
Miscarriage Association	www.the-ma.org.uk
Miscarriage Association of Ireland	www.coombe.ie/mai
MS Ireland	www.ms-society.ie
Multiple Sclerosis Society NI	www.mssocietyni.co.uk
Muscular Dystrophy Ireland	www.mdi.ie
Myasthenia Gravis Association	www.mgauk.org
National Back Pain Association	www.backpain.org
National Endometriosis Society	www.endo.org.uk
National Fertility Association	www.issue.co.uk
National Institute of Mental Health	www.nimh.nih.gov
National Menigitis Trust	www.meningitis-trust.org
National Osteoporosis Society	www.nos.org.uk
Northern Ireland Chest Heart & Stroke Association	www.nichsa.com
Northern Ireland Childminding Association	www.nicma.org
Northern Ireland Pre School Playgroup Association	www.nippa.org
Ovacome	www.ovacome.org.uk
Paralinks	www.paralinks.net
ParentLine	www.parentline.ie
Parents Advice Centre	www.pachelp.org
Parents and Professionals & Autism	www.ulst.ac.uk/papa
Parkinson's Association of Ireland	www.officeobjects.com/parkinsons
Patient UK	www.patient.org.uk
Post Polio Support Group	http://homepage.eircom.net/~ppsg
Psoriatic Arthropathy Alliance	www.paalliance.org
Repetitive Strain Injury (UK)	www.rsi-uk.org.uk
Roller Coaster	www.rollercoaster.ie

Roy Castle Cause for Hope Foundation	www.roycastle.org
Schizophrenia Ireland	www.ireland.iol.ie/lucia
Shared Parenting	www.sharedparenting.org
Solo	www.solo.ie
Spinal Injuries Foundation	www.spinal.co.uk
Stroke Association	www.stroke.org.uk
Treoir	http://indigo.ie/~treoir
Turner Syndrome	www.tss.org.uk
Twins & Multiple Birth Association	www.tambani.org
Ulster Cancer Foundation	www.ulstercancer.co.uk
VHI Healthe.com	www.vhihealthe.com
Victim Support Ireland	www.victimsupport.ie
Women's Aid	www.womensaid.ie

ancillary services

Age-Related Health Care	http://indigo.ie/~arhc
Anthony Nolan Bone Marrow Trust	www.anthonynolan.com
Association of Ambulance Personnel	http://ireland.iol.ie/~emtpro
Association of Professional Ambulance Personnel	www.apap.org.uk
Beeches Management Centre	www.beeches-mc.co.uk
Blood Transfusion Service	www.n-i.nhs.uk/niblood
Bone Marrow Transplant Information and Support	www.bmtsupport.ie
British Blood Transfusion Service	www.bbts.org.uk
British Organ Donor Society	www.argonet.co.uk/body
Carers Ireland	www.carersireland.com
Clearing House on Health Outcomes	www.ich.ie
DDA Care Services Ltd	www.ddacareservices.com
Federation of Voluntary Bodies	www.fed-vol.com
Forum on Water Flouridation in Ireland	www.fluoridationforum.ie
Health and Safety Authority	www.hsa.ie
Health Education Authority	www.hea.org.uk
Health Promotion Unit	www.healthpromotion.ie
Institute of Food Science and Technology	www.ifst.org
Institute of Public Health of Ireland	www.publichealth.ie
Irish Association of Social Workers	http://iasw.eire.org
Irish Blood Transfusion Board	www.ibts.ie
Irish Donor Network	www.ika.ie/irishdonornetwork
Medical Advisory Services for Travellers Abroad (MASTA)	www.masta.org
National Association of Authorities & Trusts	www.nahat.net
National Breast Screening Programme	www.nbsp.ie
National Cancer Registry of Ireland	www.ncri.ie

National Disease Surveillance Centre	www.ncnm.ie
National Medicines Information Centre	www.stjames.ie/nmic/nmicinde.html
Northern Ireland Ambulance Service	www.n-i.nhs.uk/nias/welcome.htm
Northern Ireland Hospice	www.nihospice.com
Nursing Homes Registry	www.nursinghomes.co.uk
Office for Health Gain	www.ofhg.com
Office for Health Management	www.tohm.ie
Pain Management Group	http://painclinic.netfirms.com
Radiological Protection Institute of Ireland	www.rpii.ie
Rehab Group	www.rehab.ie
Royal Institute of Public Health and Hygiene	www.riphh.org.uk
Specialist Health	www.specialisthealth.co.uk

animal health

Bray Vet Animal Hospital	www.brayvet.com
British Small Animal Veterinary Association	www.bsava.com
Dublin Society for the Prevention of Cruelty to Animals	www.dspca.ie
Gilabbey Veterinary Hospital	www.vetscork.ie
Irish Animals on the Web	www.irishanimals.com
Irish Companion Animal Veterinary Association	http://homepages.iol.ie/~ivahq/icava1.htm
Peoples Animal Welfare Society	www.paws.dna.ie
Veterinary Council of Ireland	www.vci.ie
Veterinary Ireland	www.vetinaryireland.com

complementary

Accredited Bowen Therapists in Ireland	www.homestead.com/bowenireland
Acupuncture Foundation	www.acupuncturefoundation.com
Alexander Technique	www.alexandertechnique.com
Aromatherap.ie	www.aromatherap.ie
British Acupuncture Council	www.acupuncture.org.uk
British Dietetic Association	www.bda.uk.com
British Homoeopathic Library	www.hom-inform.org
British Osteopathic Association	www.osteopathy.org
British School of Homeopathy	www.homoeopathy.co.uk
Catalase	www.catalase.com
Chartered Society of Physiotherapy	www.csphysio.org.uk
Chiropractic Association of Ireland	www.chiropractic.ie

College of Integrated Chinese Complimentary Health & Treatment Clinic	www.healthclinic.freeuk.com
Complementary House	www.complementaryhouse.com
Custom Orthotics	www.customorthotics.net
Dr Edward Bach Centre	www.bachcentre.com
Drugless Psychiatrist	www.druglesspsychiatrist.com
Foundation for Traditional Chinese Medicine	www.demon.co.uk/acupuncture
Harvest Moon Centre	www.harvestmoon.ie
Helen Coe Health Care	www.health-care-ireland.com
Holistic Ireland	www.holistic.ie
Institute of Physical Therapy	www.iptas.ie
Irish Aromatherapy	www.webnow.com/irisharomatherapy
Irish Institute of Counselling & Hypnotherapy	www.iol.ie/~therapy
Irish Nutrition & Dietetic Institute	http://indigo.ie/~indicom/indi.htm
Irish Reflexologist's Institute	www.reflexology.ie
Kinesiology	www.kinesiology.ie
Medicine	www.cicm.org.uk
Professional Homeopaths in Europe	www.homeopathy-ecch.org
Register of Chinese Herbal Medicine	www.rchm.co.uk
Reiki.ie	www.reiki.ie
Royal College of Speech & Language Therapists	www.rcslt.org
Society of Teachers of the Alexander Technique (STAT)	www.stat.org.uk
Stresscare	www.stresscare.ie
Transcendental Meditation Cork	www.tmcork.org
Transcendental Meditation in Ireland	www.tm-ireland.org
Ultimate Health Ireland	www.ultimatehealthireland.com
World Federation Chiropractic	www.wfc.org

dentistry

American Dental Association	www.ada.org
British Dental Association	www.bda-dentistry.org.uk
British Society of Dentistry for the Handicapped	www.bsdh.org.uk
Century Dental	www.centurydental.ie
Colgate	www.colgate.com
Dental Anxiety & Phobia Association	www.healthyteeth.com
Dental Health Foundation	www.dentalhealth.ie
Dental Practice Board	www.dentanet.org.uk
Dr. PG O'Reachtagain	www.my-teeth.com
Dublin Dentist School	www.tcd.ie/dental_school

Fiacla	www.fiacla.ie
Fixodent	www.keep-on-smiling.com
National Dentists Directory	www.nationaldirectories.net
Oral-B	www.oral-b.com
Sensodyne	www.sensodyne.ie
University Dental School & Hospital, Cork	www.ucc.ie/ucc/denthosp

government agencies

Chief Medical Officer (NI)	www.dhsspsni.gov.uk
Department of Health & Children	www.doh.ie
Department of Health & Social Services (NI)	www.dhsspsni.gov.uk
Institute of Health Management	www.ihm.org.uk
National Rehabilitation Board	www.nrb.ie

health boards/trusts

Department of Health & Children	www.doh.ie
Eastern Health Board	www.ehb.ie
Eastern Regional Health Authority	www.erha.ie
EU Health & Consumer Protection	www.europa.eu.int/comm/dgs/health_consumer/index_en.htm
Foyle Health & Social Services Trust	www.foyletrust.org
Mid Western Health Board	www.mwhb.ie
Midland Health Board	www.mhb.ie
North Eastern Health Board	www.nehb.ie
North Western Health Board	www.nwhb.ie
South & East Belfast Health and Social Services Trust	www.sebt.org.uk
South Eastern Health Board	www.sehb.ie
Southern Health Board	www.shb.ie
Western Health Board	www.mayo-cs.ie

hospitals & clinics

complementary

Hale Clinic	www.haleclinic.com
Harvest Moon Holistic Healing Centre	www.harvestmoon.ie
Helen Coe Health Care	www.health-care-ireland.com

private

Blackrock Clinic	www.blackrock-clinic.ie
BMI Healthcare	www.bmihealth.co.uk
Bon Secours Ireland	www.bonsecours.org/ie
Bray Women's Health Centre	www.braywomenshealthcentre.ie
Breast Feeding Clinic	www.breastfeeding-clinic.com
Bristol Cancer Help Centre	www.bristolcancerhelp.org
BUPA	www.bupa.co.uk

BUPA Ireland	www.bupaireland.ie
Galway Private Hospital	http://indigo.ie/~galvia
Glenashling Nursing Home	www.glenashling.com
Laser Centre	www.lasercentre.ie
Leopardstown Park Hospital	www.lph.ie
Marie Stopes Health Clinics	www.mariestopes.org.uk
Mater Private Hospital	www.materprivate.ie
Mayo Clinic	www.mayo.edu
Moyglare Nursing Home	www.moyglarenursinghome.ie
PPP Healthcare	www.ppphealthcare.co.uk
Priory Clinic	www.prioryclinic.com
Quarrybanks Nursing Home	www.quarrybanksnursinghome.com
San Remo Nursing & Convalescence Home	www.sanremonursinghome.com
Sancta Maria Nursing Home	www.irishnursinghomes.net
Simms Fertility Clinic	www.sims.ie
St John of God Hospital	www.iol.ie/~stjog
VHI Health	www.vhihealthe.com

public

Adelaide and Meath Hospital	www.amnch.ie
Beaumont Hospital	www.beaumont.ie
Belfast Royal	www.royalhospitals.ac.uk
Cappagh Orthopaedic Hospital	www.cappagh.ie
Central Remedial Clinic	www.crc.ie
Children's Hospital, Temple Street	www.childrenshospital.ie
Coombe Women's Hospital	www.coombe.ie
Galway Regional Hospitals	www.grh.ie
Incorporated Orthopaedic Hospital of Ireland	www.ioh.ie
Mater Misericordiae Hospital	www.mater.ie
Mayo General Hospital	www.mgh.ie
Monaghan General Hospital	www.monaghanhospital.com
National Maternity Hospital	www.nmh.ie
Our Lady's Hospice	www.ourladyshospice.com
Peamount Hospital	www.iol.ie/~peamount/peamount.htm
Rotunda Hospital	www.rotunda.ie
Royal Hospital Donnybrook	www.rhd.ie
St. James's Hospital	www.stjames.ie
St. Vincent's University Hospital	www.ucd.ie/~svh-erc/main.htm

journals, magazines & websites

Allen Carr's Easy Way to Stop Smoking	www.allencarrseasyway.com
American Journal of Health Promotion	www.healthpromotionjournal.com

Baby Directory, The	www.babydirectory.com
Baby2Kids	www.baby2kids.ie
British Medical Journal	www.bmj.com
British Nursing News	www.nurse-nurses-nursing.com/bnno.html
Citizens Information Centres	www.nssb.ie
Dr Koop	www.drkoop.com
Good Health Directory for Alternative Medicine	www.goodhealthdirectory.com
Health A to Z	www.healthatoz.com
Hub - Northern Ireland Youth Forum Information Point	www.the-hub-ni.com
Irish Journal of Medical Science	www.rami.ie/ijms
Irish Medical Directory	www.imd.ie
Irish Medical Journal	www.imj.ie
Irish Medical Times	www.imt.ie
Irishdocs.com	www.irishdocs.com
Irishhealth.com	www.irishhealth.com
Journal of Public Health Medicine	www.oup.co.uk/pubmed
KidsHealth	www.kidshealth.org
Lancet	www.thelancet.com
Male Health Center	www.malehealthcenter.com
Mayo Clinic Health Oasis	www.mayohealth.org
Medicine Weekly	www.eireannpublications.ie
Medinet	www.medinet.ie
NHS Direct	www.nhsdirect.nhs.uk
Nursing Times	www.nursingtimes.net
Positive Health	www.positivehealth.com
Pulse	www.epulse.co.uk
React	www.react.ie
ThirdAge	www.thirdage.com
ThriveOnline	www.thriveonline.com
VHI Health	www.vhihealthe.ie
Women's Health Interactive	www.womens-health.com

medicine & surgery

Anatomical Society	www.anatsoc.org.uk
Association of Anaesthetists of Great Britain & Ireland	www.aagbi.org
Association of Clinical Pathologists	www.pathologists.org.uk
British Association of Plastic Surgeons	www.baps.co.uk
British Medical Association	www.bma.org.uk
British Psychological Society	www.bps.org.uk
General Medical Council (UK)	www.gmc-uk.org
Health Service Employers Agency	www.hsea.ie
Human Assisted Reproduction Ireland (HARI)	www.hari.ie
Irish College of General Practitioners	www.icgp.ie

Irish Medical Council	www.medicalcouncil.ie
Irish Medical News	www.irishmedicalnews.ie
Irish Medical Organisation	www.imo.ie
Irish Medicines Board	www.imb.ie
Irish Nutrition and Dietetic Institute	www.indi.ie
Irish Society of Chartered Physiotherapists	www.iscp.ie
Irish Society of Occupational Medicine	www.iol.ie/~isom
Medical Defence Union	www.the-mdu.com
Medical Research Council	www.mrc.ac.uk
National Sports Medicine Institute of the UK	www.nsmi.org.uk
Northern Ireland Surgical Training	www.nisurgery.org
Orthodontic Society of Ireland	http://orthodontics.ie
Royal Academy of Medicine in Ireland	www.rami.ie
Royal College of Physicians of Ireland	www.rcpi.ie
Royal College of Surgeons in Ireland	www.rcsi.ie
Royal College of Surgeons, England	www.rcseng.ac.uk
Tropical Medical Bureau	www.tmb.ie
World Health Organisation	www.who.int

nursing & midwifery

Active Birth Centre	www.activebirthcentre.com
An Bord Altranais (Irish Nursing Board)	www.nursingboard.ie
Association for Improvements in Maternity Services	www.aims.org.uk
British Nursing Association	www.bna.co.uk
English National Board for Nursing, Midwifery & Health Visiting	www.enb.org.uk
Florence Nightingale Foundation	www.florence-nightingale-foundation.org.uk
Home Birth Association of Ireland	www.iol.ie/~hba
Irish Nurses Organisation	www.ino.ie
National Board for Nursing, Midwifery & Health Visiting, Northern Ireland	www.n-i.nhs.uk/nbni
National Council for the Professional Development of Nursing & Midwifery	www.ncnm.ie
National HIV Nurses Association	www.nhivna.org.uk
Royal College of Nursing	www.rcn.org.uk

School of Nursing Waterford Regional Hospital	www.iol.ie/~ronniest
UCD Department of Nursing Studies	www.ucd.ie/~nursings/nshpage.htm
UK Central Council for Nursing, Midwifery & Health Visiting	www.ukcc.org.uk

pharmacy

Brodericks Pharmacy	www.broderickspharmacy.com
CH Chemists	www.chtralee.com
Dolan's Pharmacy	www.irishpharmacist.com
Food and Drug Administration	www.fda.gov
Irish Pharmaceutical Healthcare Association	www.ipha.ie
McCabes Pharmacy	www.mccabespharmacy.com
National Pharmaceutical Association	www.npa.co.uk
Nish Pharmacies	www.iol.ie/nishpharmacy
Nolan's Pharmacy	http://thenet.ie/nolanspharmacy
O'Sullivan's Pharmacy	www.osullivanspharmacy.com
Pharmaceutical Society of Ireland	www.pharmaceuticalsociety.ie
Royal Pharmaceutical Society of Great Britain	www.rpsgb.org.uk
Ryan's Pharmacy	www.ryanpharm.com
Staunton's Pharmacy	www.stauntons.ie
Uniphar	www.uniphar.ie

psychiatry, psychology & psychotherapy

BodyWatch	www.bodywatch.ie
British Psychological Society	www.bps.org.uk
Cluain Mhuire Service	www.iol.ie/~stjog/cluain_mhuire.htm
Cork Clinic	www.corkclinic.com
Department of Pyschology, TCD	www.tcd.ie/psychology
Drugless Psychiatrist	www.druglesspsychiatrist.com
Dublin County Stress Clinic	www.iol.ie/~stjog/stress.htm
Hanuman Strategies	www.hanumanstrategies.com
Ian Epstein	www.ianepstein.com
Institute of Clinical Hypnotherapy & Psychotherapy	www.hypnosiseire.com
Institute of Mental Health	www.imhl.com
Irish Association for Counselling and Therapy	www.irish-counselling.ie
John Crimmins	www.addiction.ie
Pearn Kandola	www.pearnkandola.com
Psychological Assessment & Consulting	www.psyassess.com
Royal College of Psychiatrists (Irish Division)	http://homepage.tinet.ie/~irishrcpsych/psymain.html

School of Psychology (Queen's University Belfast)	www.psych.qub.ac.uk
UK Council for Psychotherapy	www.psychotherapy.org.uk

research

Committee for Public Management Research	www.irlgov.ie/cpmr
Health Economics Research Unit	www.abdn.ac.uk/heru
Health Research Board Ireland	www.hrb.ie
Institute of Public Administration	www.ipa.ie
Medical Research Council	www.mrc.ac.uk
Proclear	www.proclear.com
RAFT Institute	www.raft.ac.uk
School of Health & Related Research	www.shef.ac.uk/~scharr
Society for the Study of Fertility	www.ssf.org.uk

vision

Allergan	www.allergan.com
Bausch & Lomb	www.bausch.com
Boots Opticians	www.bootsopticians.co.uk
British Ophthalmic Anaesthesia Society	www.boas.org
Ciba Vision	www.cibavision.com
College of Optometrists	www.college-optometrists.org
Cooper Vision	www.coopervision.com
Dixon Hempenstall Opticians	www.dixonhempenstall.com
EyeCon	www.eyecon.ie
Eyes Online	www.eyesonline.co.uk
Getlenses.com	www.getlenses.com
Insight Opticians	www.insightopticians.ie
Lizars Opticians Ltd	www.blackandlizars.com
McGivneys	www.mcgivneys.com
Opticians Online	www.opticiansonline.ie
Specsavers	www.specsavers.com
Stauntons	www.stauntons.ie
SuperSpecs	www.superspecs.net
Vision Care	www.visioncare.ie
Vision Express	www.visionexpress.co.uk
Wesley Jessen	www.wesley-jessen.com
World Council of Optometry	www.worldoptometry.org

help!

- advice
- breakdown services
- charities
- community
- consumer organisations & ombudsmen
- developing world
- education
- emergency services
- health

advice

Action Mental Health	www.actionmentalhealth.org.uk
Adopted People's Association	www.connect.ie/~apa
Adoption Board	www.adoptionboard.ie
Adoption Information Line	www.adoption.org.uk
Adoption Ireland	www.adoptionireland.com
Age Concern	www.ace.org.uk
Alcoholics-Anonymous	www.alcoholics-anonymous.org
Alliance for Choice	http://members.aol.com/~choiceni
Alone	www.alone.ie
Anapsys Counselling Services	www.anapsys.co.uk
Anti-Bullying Campaign	www.ourworld.compuserve.com/homepages/anti_bullying
Association of Independent Advice Centres	www.aica.net
Asthma Society	www.asthmasociety.ie
Chest, Heart & Stroke N I	www.nichsa.com
Citizen's Information Database	www.cidb.ie
Combat Poverty Agency	www.cpa.ie
Cura	www.cura.ie
Cystic Fibrosis Association	www.cfireland.ie
Dublin Rape Crisis Centre	www.drcc.ie
Edith Wilkins Hope Foundation	www.edithwilkins.com
Emigrant Advice	http://indigo.ie/~emigrant
EUMom	www.eumom.com
European Consumer Centre	www.ecic.ie
Fighting Blindness Ireland	www.fightingblindness.ie
Gingerbread	www.gingerbread.ie
Irish Family Planning Association	www.ifpa.ie
Just the Facts	www.justthefacts.org
Life Pregnancy Care Service	www.life.ie
Migraine Association of Ireland	www.migraine.ie
National Council for the Blind	www.ncbi.ie
Northern Ireland Human Rights Commission	www.nihrc.org
Parental Equality	www.parentalequality.ie
Parents Advice Centre	www.pachelp.org
Parkinson's Active Liaison and Support	http://gofree.indigo.ie/~pdpals
Rollercoaster	www.rollercoaster.ie
Samaritans	www.samaritans.org
Solo	www.solo.ie
Tall Person's Club of GB & Ireland	www.tallclub.co.uk
Threshold	www.threshold.ie

Wider Circle (Troubles Stress Help)	www.widercircle.org
Women's Aid	www.womensaid.ie

breakdown services

Automobile Association	www.theaa.com
Automobile Association Ireland	www.aaireland.ie
Green Flag	www.greenflag.co.uk
RAC	www.rac.co.uk
RAC Ireland	www.rac.ie

charities

animals

Cruelty to Irish Animals	www.irishanimals.com
Donkey Sanctuary	www.thedonkeysanctuary.org.uk
Dublin Society for Prevention of Cruelty to Animals	www.dspca.ie
Friends of the Sea Otters	www.seaotters.org
Information League for the Protection of Horses	www.ilph.org
Irish Seal Sanctuary	www.irishsealsanctuary.com
ISPCA	www.ispca.ie
PAWS	www.go.to/paws
Royal Society For the Prevention of Cruelty to Animals	www.rspca.org.uk
Wild Ireland	www.wildireland.ie
World Wide Fund for Nature	www.panda.org
WWF UK	www.wwf-uk.org

children

Barnardos	www.barnardos.ie
Barretstown Gang Camp	www.barretstowngc.ie
Chernobyl Children's Project	www.adiccp.org
Children In Need	www.bbc.co.uk/cin
Children's Research Centre	www.tcd.ie/childrens_centre
Cradle	www.cradle-bosnia.org
Friends of the Children of Chernobyl	www.children-of-chernobyl.org
Health Action Overseas	www.iol.ie/~hao
International Famine Centre	www.ucc.ie/famine
Irish Youth Foundation	www.iyf.org.uk
National Society for the Prevention of Cruelty to Children	www.nspcc.org.uk
Sporting Proud	www.sportingproud.org
The Hope Project	www.hopeireland.com
To Russia With Love	www.torussiawithlove.ie
Youth Council for NI	www.youthcouncil-ni.org.uk

community

Blazing Saddles	www.blazingsaddles.ie
Cancer Research Campaign NI	www.crc.org.uk
Christian Aid Ireland	www.christian-aid.org
Combat Poverty Agency	www.cpa.ie
Comic Relief	www.comicrelief.org.uk
Community Relations Council	www.community-relations.org.uk
Cooperation Ireland	www.cooperationireland.org
Diana Memorial Fund	www.theworkcontinues.org
Dirty Dublin	www.dirtydublin.com
Dublin Simon Community	www.iol.ie/~dubsimon
Focus Ireland	www.focusireland.ie
Neighbourhood Watch	www.nwatch.org.uk
Rotary International	www.rotary.org
Salvation Army	www.salvationarmy.ie
Samaritans	www.samaritans.co.uk
Threshold	www.threshold.ie

consumer organisations & ombudsmen

Advertising Standards Authority for Ireland	www.asai.ie
Association of Independent Advice Centres (NI)	www.aiac.net
Citizens Advice Bureau (NI)	www.niacab.org
Consumer Advice	www.consumerline.org
Consumers' Association of Ireland	www.consumerassociation.ie
Consumerworld	www.consumerworld.org
European Consumer Information Centre	www.ecic.ie
General Consumer Council of NI	www.gccni.org.uk
NI Ombudsman	www.ni-ombudsman.org.uk
(Irish) Office of the Ombudsman	www.irlgov.ie/ombudsman
(Irish) Office of the Director of Consumer Affairs	www.odca.ie
Trading Standards Service	www.tssni.gov.uk

developing world

Action Aid	www.oneworld.org/actionaid
Agency for Personal Service Overseas	www.apso.ie
Amnesty International	www.amnesty.org
Concern	www.concern.ie
Goal	www.goal.ie
Muc Concern For Kosovo	www.mucoink.com
Oxfam Ireland	www.oxfamireland.org
The Village	www.thevillage.ie
Trocaire	www.trocaire.ie
World Vision Ireland	http://wvireland.org

education

Self Help Development International	www.selfhelpintl.ie

emergency services

Garda Siochana	www.garda.ie
Irish Ambulance Services	ambulance.eire.org
Irish Fire Services	irishfireservices.com
NI Ambulance Services	www.n-i.nhs.uk

health

Action Cancer	www.actioncancer.org
Aids Ireland	www.aidsireland.com
Anthony Nolan Bone Marrow Trust	www.anthonynolan.com
Breast Cancer Campaign	www.bcc-uk.org
British Heart Foundation	www.bhf.org.uk
Cairde	www.cairde.org
Coeliac Society of Ireland	www.coeliac.ie
Daniel Woods Memorial Fund	www.blast-it.com
Dental Health Foundation	www.dentalhealth.ie
Diabetes Federation of Ireland	www.diabetesireland.ie
Irish Brain Research Foundation	www.ibrf.ie
Irish Cancer Society	www.irishcancersociety.ie
Irish Heart Foundation	www.irishheart.ie
Irish Society for Autism	www.iol.ie/~isal
Irish Society of Quality in Healthcare	www.isqh.net
Mater Hospital Foundation	www.mater-foundation.ie
Meningitis C Immunisation Program	www.meningitis.ie
Meningitis Research Foundation	www.meningitis.org
MS Society	www.ms-society.ie
Multiple Sclerosis Society NI	www.mssocietyni.co.uk
St. John Of God	www.sjog.ie
Sue Ryder Foundation	http://homepage.eircom.net/~sueryderfoundation
The Myasthenia Gravis Association	www.mgauk.org
Ulster Cancer Foundation	www.ulstercancer.co.uk
Western Alzheimers Association	http://pollennet.com/waf
World Federation of Haemophilia	www.wfh.org

hobbies and leisure

astrology
ballooning
bird watching
boating
chess
cookery
fishing
flying
football
gambling
games
gardening
genealogy
handicrafts
horseriding
miscellaneous clubs & associations
models
motorbikes
music
outdoor pursuits
pets
photography
stamps
ten pin bowling

hobbies and leisure

astrology

About Astrology	http://astrology.about.com
Astrologer's Perspective	www.anastrologers perspective.com
Astrology Association of Great Britain	www.astrologer.com/aanet
Astrology Online	www.astrology-online.com
Astrology Online Ireland	http://anamspirit.com/links/astrology.html
Astrology World	www.astrology-world.com
Chinese Astrology	www.chinese-astrology.com
Faculty of Astrology Studies	www.astrology.org.uk
Irish Astronomical Society	www.indigo.ie/~stepryan/ias.htm
Irish Psychics Live	www.realm.ie
Johnathan Cainer	www.cainer.com
Paul Wade	www.astrologywizard.com
Russell Grant	www.russellgrant.com

ballooning

British Association of Balloon Operators	www.babo.org.uk
Hot Air Ballooning	www.launch.net
Irish Balloon Flights	www.balloons.ie

bird watching

Bird Trip and Tours	www.birdwatch.co.uk
Bird Watching in Northern Ireland	www.interknowledge.com/northern-ireland/ukibrd01.htm
Birds Ireland	www.birdsireland.com
BirdWatch Ireland	www.birdwatchireland.ie
Birdwatch.net	www.birdwatch.net
RSPB	www.rspb.org.uk
Wildfowl & Wetlands Trust	www.wwt.org.uk

boating

Association of Waterways Cruising Clubs	www.penpont.demon.co.uk/awcchp.htm
British Canoe Union	www.bcu.org.uk
Clontarf Yacht and Boat Club	www.cybc.itgo.com
Dublin University Sailing Club	www.tcd.ie/clubs/sailing
Glenan's Sailing Club	www.glenans-ireland.com
Inland Waterways Association (UK)	www.waterways.org.uk
Inland Waterways Association of Ireland	www.iwai.ie
Ireland Afloat	www.afloat.ie
Irish Amateur Rowing Union	www.ul.ie/~rowing/iaru.html

Irish Boat Shop	www.irishboatshop.com
Irish Canoe Union	www.irishcanoeunion.com
Irish Catamaran	www.catamaran.ie
Irish Sailing Association	www.sailing.ie
Irish Voyageurs	www.voyageurs.co.uk
National Association of Boat Owners	www.nabo.org.uk
National Yacht Club	www.nyc.ie
Sailing in Ireland	www.celticventures.com
Ulster Cruising	www.ulstercruising.freeserve.co.uk
Waterway Holidays	www.waterwayholidays.com
Yachtfinder	www.yachtfinder.ie
Yachting and Boating World	www.ybw.com

chess

British Chess Federation	www.bcf.ndirect.co.uk
British Chess Magazine	www.bcmchess.co.uk
Chess Ireland	www.irishchess.com
Chess Master	www.chessmaster.com
Garry Kasparov	www.clubkasparov.ru
Internet Chess Club	www.chessclub.com
Irish Chess Union	http://homepage.tinet.ie/~acad/
London Chess Centre	www.chesscentre.com
Prince August	www.princeaugust.ie
This Week in Chess	www.chess.co.uk
Ulster Chess Union	www.rct26.dial.pipex.com/ucu_index.htm
World Chess Federation	www.fide.com

cookery

Allrecipes.com	www.allrecipes.com
Ballymaloe Cookery School	www.ballymaloe-cookery-school.ie
BBC Food & Drink	www.bbc.co.uk/foodanddrink
Gourmet Ireland	www.gourmetireland.com
Irish Cookery School, Pontoon	www.pontoon.mayo-ireland.ie/cookschl/cookschl.htm
Leith's School of Food & Wine	www.leiths.com
Limerick Good Food	www.limerickgoodfood.com
Mosiman Academy	www.mosiman.com
Total Ireland Cookbook	www.totalireland.com/interact/cooking

fishing

Angling Ireland	www.angling.travel.ie
Countryside Alliance	www.countryside-alliance.net
Fish Ireland	www.fishireland.com
Fishing in Ireland	www.fishingireland.com

Fishing in Nothern Ireland	www.interknowledge.com/northern-ireland/ukifish1.htm
Fishing Ireland	www.fishingireland.net
Fishing Works	www.fishingworks.com
Fishing World	www.fishing.org
Ireland Fly Fishing	www.irelandflyfishing.com
Irish Federation of Sea Anglers	www.ifsa.ie
Shannon Fishery Board	www.shannon-fishery-board.ie
UK Angling Guide	http://uk-fishing.com
UK Fly Fishing & Tyers Federation	www.fly-fisherman.org.uk
Where to Fish:Ireland	www.where-to-fish.com/4.html

flying

Aviation Society of Ireland	http://ireland.iol.ie/~asire
Belfast Flying Club	www.belfast-flying-club.com
British Aerobatics Association	www.aerobatics.org.uk
British Disabled Flying Club	www.fly.to/bdfc
British Gliding Association	www.gliding.co.uk
Civil Aviation Authority	www.caa.co.uk
Commisioner for Aviation Regulation	www.aviationreg.ie
Connaught Aero Club	http://homepage.tinet.ie/~connaughtaeroclub
Dublin Gliding Club	www.kildare.ie/dublinglidingclub
Flyer	www.flyer.co.uk
Irish Aviation	www.irishaviation.net
Irish Aviation Authority	www.iaa.ie
Kite Flying in Ireland	www.kites.org/dmr
Ormond Flying Club	www.ormandflyingclub.com
PC Pilots of Ireland	www.pcpilotsireland.com
Red Arrows	www.raf.mod.uk/reds/index.html
Royal Aeronautical Society	www.raes.org.uk
Salthill Airshow	http://airshow.topcities.com
Ulster Aviation Society	http://dnausers.d-n-a.net/dnetrazq
Ulster Flying Club	www.ulsterflyingclub.co.uk

football

Amateur Football League	www.soccerbot.com/afl
Football Associations of Ireland	www.fai.ie
GAA Online	www.gaa.ie
Irish Football Association	www.irishfa.com
Irish Football Page	www.clubi.ie/fpage/
Irish Soccer Website	www.tomsoc.cx
Junior Irish Soccer	www.jririshsoccer.org
Soccer Central	www.soccercentral.ie
Sunday Football League Directory	www.sunday-football.co.uk

Umbro International Football Festival	www.worldwidesoccer.co.uk
World Football@ireland.com	www.ireland.com/sports/soccer

gambling

Bet.ie	www.bet.ie
Celtic Bookmakers	www.celticbookmakers.com
City Index	www.cityindex.co.uk
Complete Casino Gaming and Gambling Directory	www.casinocity.com
Curragh	www.curragh.ie
Eirbet	www.eirbet.com
Greyhound Racing Board	www.thedogs.co.uk
Irish Greyhound Board	www.igb.ie
Irish Horse Racing	www.irish-horse-racing.com
Irish Horseracing Authority	www.iha.ie
Irish Lottery Syndicates	www.irishlotto.net
Irish Racing	www.irish-racing.com
Irish-racing.com	www.irish-racing.com
Ladbrokes	www.ladbrokes.co.uk
Littlewoods Bet247	www.bet247.co.uk
Mauci	www.mauci.com
Mecca Bingo Online	www.meccabingo.com
National Lottery	www.lotto.ie
National Lottery (UK)	www.national-lottery.co.uk
Paddy Power	www.paddypower.com
Professional Sports Betting Advisory	www.probetadvisory.com
Sean Graham	www.seangraham.com
Sporting Index	www.sportingindex.com
Stanley Racing	www.stanleyleisure.com
Toals Bookmakers	www.toals.co.uk
Tote	www.tote.co.uk
Tote Ireland	www.tote.ie
Turf Club	www.turfclub.ie
UK Betting	www.ukbetting.com
VIP Casino	http://vipireland.com/casino
William Hill	www.williamhill.co.uk

games

About Board Games	http://boardgames.about.com/mbody.htm
Contract Bridge Association of Ireland	http://indigo.ie/~irebridg
Games Workshop	www.games-workshop.com
Loquax	www.loquax.co.uk
Monopoly	www.monopoly.com
Northern Ireland Bridge Union	www.nibu.co.uk
Scrabble	www.scrabble.com

Trivial Pursuit	www.trivialpursuit.com

gardening

Barnsdale Gardens (Geoff Hamilton)	www.barnsdalegardens.co.uk
BBC Ground Force	www.bbc.co.uk/groundforce
Black & Decker	www.blackanddecker-europe.com/ireland
Chelsea Flower Show	www.rhs.org.uk/chelsea
Flower & Plant Association	www.flowers.org.uk
Flymo	www.flymo.co.uk
Garden Heaven	www.rte.ie/tv/gardenheaven
Gardeners' World	www.gardenersworld.beeb.com
Gardening-uk	www.gardening-uk.com
Gardening.com	http://gardening.sierrahome.com
Greenfingers.com	www.greenfingers.com
Hampton Court Palace Flower Show	www.rhs.org.uk/hamptoncourt
Hayter	www.hayter.co.uk
Herb Society	www.herbsociety.co.uk
Heritage Seed Library	www.hdra.org.uk
Hirequip	www.hirequip.ie
Irish Garden Magazine	www.theirishgarden.com
Irish Gardening Online	www.irishgardeningonline.com
Irish Wildflowers	www.kerryweb.ie/destination-kerry/dingle/wildflower.html
Levington	www.levington.co.uk
Miracle-Gro	www.miraclegro.com
Mulvey's	www.mulveys.com
National Garden Exhibition Centre	www.clubi.ie/calumet
New Eden	www.neweden.co.uk
Organic Gardening	www.organicgardening.com
Permaculture Association	www.permaculture.co.uk
Qualcast	www.qualcast.co.uk
Royal Horticultural Society	www.rhs.org.uk
Spear & Jackson	www.spear-and-jackson.com
The Irish Garden	www.theirishgarden.com
The Organic Centre	www.theorganiccentre.ie
Windowbox.com	www.windowbox.com

genealogy

A to Z of Irish Genealogy	www.irish-insight.com/a2z-genealog
Adopted Peoples Association	www.adoptionireland.com
Ancestors@Ireland.com	www.ireland.com/ancestor
Ancestry Research	www.ancestors.co.uk
Association of Professional Genealogists in Ireland	http://indigo.ie/~apgi
British Heraldic Archive	www.kwtelecom.com/heraldry

Council of Irish Genealogical Organisations	http://indigo.ie/~gorry/cigo.html
Family Records Centre	www.pro.gov.uk/about/frc
Federation of Family History Societies	www.ffhs.org.uk
FlyLeaf Press	www.flyleaf.ie
Gendex Genealogical Index	www.gendex.com
Genealogical Society of Ireland	www.dun-laoghaire.com/genealogy/main.html
Genealogy	www.genealogy.org
Genealogy Resources	www.distantcousin.com
Genealogy.ie	www.genealogy.ie
Genealogy@GoIreland.com	www.goireland.com/genealogy
General Register Office, Ireland	www.groireland.ie
GENUKI, UK & Ireland Genealogy	www.genuki.org.uk
Institute of Heraldic & Genealogical Studies	www.ihgs.ac.uk
Ireland Information	www.ireland-information.com
Irish Ancestral Research Association	www.tiara.ie
Irish Family History Foundation	www.irishroots.net
Irish Family History Society	www.mayo-ireland.ie/Geneal/IFHisSoc.htm
Irish Genealogical Congress	www.ancestordetective.com/igc.htm
Irish Genealogical Project	www.irishgenealogy.ie
Irish Genealogy	www.irishgenealogy.com
Local Ireland Genealogy	www.local.ie/genealogy
Mormons Family Search	www.familysearch.org
Names UK	www.namesuk.com
National Archives of Ireland	www.nationalarchives.ie
National Library of Ireland	www.heanet.ie/natlib
North of Ireland Family History Society	www.nifhs.org
Northern Ireland Statistics and Research Agency	www.nisra.gov.uk
Public Record Office	www.pro.gov.uk
Public Record Office of Northern Ireland	http://proni.nics.gov.uk
RootsWeb	www.rootsweb.com
Society of Genealogists	www.sog.org.uk
Ulster Historical Foundation	www.ancestryireland.com

handicrafts

Celtic Crafts	www.celtic-crafts.com
Ceramics Monthly	www.ceramicsmonthly.org
Craft Granary	www.craftgranary.com
Crafts Council of Ireland	www.craftscouncil-of-ireland.ie
Donegal Crafts	www.donegalcrafts.com
Husqvarna	www.husqvarnastudio.co.uk
Needlecraft	www.ils.ie/needlecraft

horseriding

Bantry Horseriding	http://homepage.eircom.net/~wehrli
British Horse Society	www.bhs.org.uk
British Show Jumping Association	www.bsja.co.uk
Connemara & Coast Trail	www.aille-cross.com
Dingle Horse Riding	www.dinglehorseriding.com
El Rancho	www.dingleweb.com/elrancho
Equestrian Holidays Ireland	www.ehi.ie
Equestrian Travel	www.equestrian.travel.ie
Greystones Equestrian Centre	www.greystones-ireland.com
Hazelwood Guesthouse and Riding Stables	http://homepage.tinet.ie/~hazelwood
Horse Holiday Farm	www.horseholidayfarm.net
Horse Riding Ireland	www.horseridingireland.net
Irish Horses	www.irish-horses.com
Irish Racing	www.irish-racing.com
Killarney Riding Stables	www.killarney-reeks-trail.com
Long's Horseriding & Ponytrekking	www.irishcrafts.com/horses
Mount Pleasant Pony Trekking & Horse Riding Centre	www.mountpleasantcentre.com
Pony Club	www.pony-club.org.uk
Willie Daly Horse Riding	www.williedaly.com
World of Horses	www.worldofhorses.co.uk

miscellaneous clubs and associations

An Óige	www.irelandyha.org
Boys' Brigade	www.boys-brigade.org.uk
Catholic Guides of Ireland	www.iol.ie/~cgil
Chess Ireland	http://ireland.iol.ie/jghurley
Crossfire Paintball Games	www.crossfire.ie
Foróige	www.foroige.ie
Irish Girl Guides	www.irishgirlguides.ie
Irish Radio Transmitter Society (IRTS)	www.irts.ie
Irish Red Cross	www.redcross.ie
Macra na Feirme	www.macra.ie
Mensa	www.mensa.org
National Women's Council of Ireland	www.nwci.ie
National Youth Council of Ireland	www.connect.ie/tribli/nyci.htm
President's Award/Gaisce	www.gaisce.net
Skirmish Paintball	www.skirmish.ie
Youth Council for Northerin Ireland	www.youthcouncil-ni.org.uk
Youthnet NI	www.youthnetni.org.uk

models

Airfix	www.airfix.co.uk
Corgi	www.corgi.co.uk
Heir Island Model Boats	www.heirisland.com

Hornby	www.hornby.co.uk
Irish Air Corp Aircraft	http://www.geocities.com/maxdecal
Irish Air Corps Aircraft Models	www.geocities.com/capecanaveral/launchpad/6787
Mamod	www.mamod.co.uk
Meitheal mara	www.mmara.com
Model Planes@about.com	http://miniatures.about.com
Scalextric	www.scalextric.co.uk
Tamiya	www.tamiya.com
Wild Geese Wargames Club	www.iol.ie/~oconnor
Wilesco	www.wilesco.de

motorbikes

Aprilla	www.aprilla.com
BikeWorld	www.bikeworld.ie
BMW	www.bmw.co.uk
British Motor Racing Circuits	www.bmrc.co.uk
British Motorcycle Club	www.bemsee.co.uk
Coleraine & District Motor Club	www.irishroadracing.co.uk
Donegal Kawasaki Team	http://homepage.eircom.net/~hondas
Freelancers Club	www.freelancers.f2s.com
Harley Riders Ireland	http://homepage.eircom.net/~rockedge/hri
Harley-Davidson	www.harley-davidson.co.uk
Honda	www.honda.co.uk
Irish Garda Motorcycle Club	www.ipagmc.com
Irish Motorcyclists' Action Group	www.iol.ie/~maglink
Maddock Motorcycles	www.maddockonline.com
Moto Guzzi	www.motoguzzi.it
Motor Cycle Industry Association	www.mcia.co.uk
Motor Cycle News	www.motorcyclenews.com
Motor Cycle Union of Ireland	www.mcui.ie
Motor Cycle West	http://homepage.tinet.ie/~motorbike/
Motor Cycle World Magazine	www.motorcycleworld.co.uk
Motor Sport Ireland	www.motorsportireland.com
Motor Sports Association	www.msauk.org
Motorcycle Enthusiasts Club	www.stepaside.net/mec
Nightbreed MCC	www.nightbreed-mcc.co.uk
Northern Ireland Motorsport	www.nimotorsport.co.uk
Piaggio	www.piaggio.com
Quad Racing Ireland	www.quadracingireland.com
Rubber Side Down	www.elementary.ie/exup.ireland.html
Suzuki	www.suzuki.co.uk
Triumph	www.triumph.co.uk
TVR	www.tvr-eng.co.uk

Vespa	www.vespa.com
Yamaha	www.yamaha-motor.co.uk

music

Akai	www.akai.com
Belfast Music Supplies	www.belfastmusic.com
Blüthners	www.bluthers.co.uk
Boosey & Hawkes	www.boosey.com
CelticTV	www.celtictv.com
Chappell	www.uk-piano.org/chappell
Classical Piano	www.classicalpiano.com
Comhaltas Ceoltóirí Éireann	www.comhaltas.com
Fender	www.fender.com
Gibson	www.gibson.com
Guitar Tabs Universe	www.guitartabs.cc
Harmony Central	www.harmony-central.com
Harp.net	www.harp.net
HMV	www.hmv.com
Irish Music Mail	www.irishmusicmail.com
Irish Music Rights Organisaton	www.imro.ie
Irish Music Warehouse	www.irishmusicwarehouse.ie
Irish Traditional Music Archive	www.itma.ie
Kemble Pianos	www.uk-piano.org/kemble
Marshall Amplification	www.marshallamps.com
Matchetts Music	www.matchettsmusic.com
Music Maker	www.musicmaker.ie
Musician	www.musician.com
Musician Inc	www.musicianinc.ie
Musician's Guide	www.musiciansguide.com
Openear	www.openear.ie
Premier Percussion	www.premier-percussion.com
Steinway	www.steinway.com
Walton's Music	www.waltonsirishmusic.com
WM Rees Instruments	www.traditionalharps.com
Yamaha	www.yamaha.co.uk

outdoor pursuits

9feet	www.9feet.com
Altberg Boots	www.altberg.co.uk
Association for Adventure Sports	www.adventuresports.ie
Blacks	www.blacks.co.uk
Cappanalea Outdoor Pursuits Centre	www.iol.ie/kerry-insight/cappanalea
Caving	www.cavingireland.org
Delphi Adventure Centre	www.delphiadventureholidays.ie
Dingle Mountaineering Club	www.iol.ie/~dunquin/mountain.html
Doolin Activity Lodge	www.doolinlodge.com
Great Outdoor Recreation Pages	www.gorp.com

Ireland Afloat	www.afloat.ie
Irish Climbing Online	www.climbing.ie
Irish Girl Guides	www.irishgirlguides.ie
Irish Orienteering	www.orienteering.ie
Irish Parachute Club	www.skydive.ie
Lowe Alpine Shop	www.thealpineshop.ie
Monaghan Outdoors	www.monaghan-outdoors.com
Mountain Biking Association of Dublin	www.geocities.com/yosemite/1092
Mountaineering Council of Ireland	www.mountaineering.ie
National Diving School Ireland	www.nds.ie
Ordnance Survey Ireland	www.irlgov.ie/osi
Orienteering Maps in Northern Ireland	www.askip.demon.co.uk/nioa/where.html
Outdoor Adventure Store	www.outdooradventurestore.ie.
Parachute Association of Ireland	http://indigo.ie/~pai
President's Award/Gaisce	www.gaisce.net
Shoecare-Clothescare-Equipcare	www.shoecare-eu.com
UL Outdoor Persuits Club	www.ul.ie/~opc

pets

AcmePet	http://acmepet.petsmart.com
Birdwatch Ireland	www.birdwatchireland.ie
Bray Vet	www.brayvet.com
Crufts	www.crufts.org.uk
Donkey Sanctuary	www.thedonkeysanctuary.org.uk
Dublin Society for Prevention of Cruelty to Animals	www.dspca.ie
Electronic Zoo	http://netvet.wustl.edu/e-zoo.htm
Irish Animals on the Web	www.irishanimals.com
Irish Society for the Prevention of Cruelty to Animals (ISPCA)	www.ispca.ie
Kennel Club	www.the-kennel-club.org.uk
NewPet.com	www.newpet.com
Pedigree Petfoods	www.petcat.co.uk
Peoples Animal Welfare Society (PAWS)	www.paws.dna.ie
Pet Bookshop	www.petbookshop.com
Pet-Net	www.pet-net.net
Petmad	www.petmad.com
Pets At Home	www.petsathome.com
Pets Direct UK	www.petsdirectuk.com
Pets on Holiday	www.pets-on-holiday.com
Pets: Part of the Family	www.petspartofthefamily.com
RSPCA	www.rspca.org.uk
Vet Info	www.vetinfo.com
Whiskas Cat Food	www.petsource.com/whiskas

Yahoo! Pets	http://pets.yahoo.com

photography

Agfa	www.agfa.com
Canon	www.canon.co.uk
Casio	www.casio.co.uk
Cheese Magazine	www.cheesemagazine.com
Contax	www.contax.com
Cork Camera Repair Services	www.camerarepairs.ie
Digital Photography Review	www.dpreview.com
Dublin Camera Exchange	www.cameraexchange.ie
Dublin In Bits	http://gallery.adnet.ie
Epson	www.epson.com
Fuji Film	www.fujifilm.com
Gallery of Photography	www.irish-photography.com
Ireland: Light, Body and Soul	http://ireland.aov.com
Kodak	www.kodak.co.uk
Konica	www.konica.com
Minolta	www.minolta.co.uk
Monaghan Photographic Society	www.county-monaghan.net/mps
Nikon	www.nikon.co.uk
Olympus	www.olympus-europa.com
Panasonic	www.panasonic.com
Photographics Repair Services	www.prs.ie
PhotoLogic	www.photologic.ie
Polaroid	www.polaroid.com
Samson	www.samson.com
Sigma	www.sigma-aldrich.com
Source Magazine	www.sourcemagazine.demon.co.uk
Staunton's Camera Centre	www.stauntons.ie
The Camera Shop	www.thecamerashop.ie
Which Camera	www.whichcamera.co.uk

stamps

An Post Philatelic Serviwes	www.anpost.ie/philatelic
Éire Philatelic Association	www.eirephilatelicassoc.org
Ireland Stamps	www.irelandstamps.com
Irish Airmail Society	http://members.aol.com/karlfranzw/AirmailSociety.html
Irish Stamp Gifts	www.irishnation.com/irishstamps.htm
National Philatelic Society	www.ukphilately.org.uk/nps
Philatelic Traders' Society	www.philatelic-traders-society.co.uk
Quality Company	www.clubi.ie/qualitycompany/ireland
Royal Mail	www.royalmail.com

Royal Philatelic Society London, The	www.rpsl.org.uk
The Great Britain Philatelic Society	www.gbps.org.uk

ten pin bowling

Bowlers Web	www.bowlersweb.com
Bowling.org.uk	www.bowling.org.uk
British Tenpin Bowling Association	www.btba.org.uk
East Cork Superbowl	www.perksfunfair.com
Go-TenPin	www.gotenpin.co.uk
Irish Tenpin Bowling Association	www.tenpin-ireland.com
LeisurePlex	www.leisureplex.ie
Tallaght Tenpin Bowling School	www.iol.ie/~flange
The Network Club	www.networkclub.ie
Universities and Colleges Tenpin Bowling Association	www.dataweb.co.uk/uctba

information sources

- encyclopaedias
- libraries
- maps
- museums
- news agencies
- newspapers
- opinion polls
- phone numbers
- professional bodies
- reference
- weather

information sources

encyclopaedias

Britannica	www.britannica.co.uk
Catholic Encyclopaedia	www.newadvent.org/cathen/
Encarta	www.encarta.msn.com
Encyclopedia	www.encyclopedia.com
Grolier	www.grolier.com
Hutchinson	www.bt-ern.co.uk/helicon
Probert	www.probert-encyclopaedia.co.uk

libraries

national institutions

An Chomhairle Leabharlanna	www.iol.ie/~libcounc
British Library	www.bl.uk
Chester Beatty Library	www.cbl.ie
Libraries Online	www.lolipop.ie
Library Association of Ireland	www.iol.ie/~lai
Marsh's Library, Dublin	www.marshlibrary.ie
National Archives of Ireland	www.nationalarchives.ie
National Library of Ireland	www.heanet.ie/natlib

public libraries

Ballyfermot Public Library	www.lolipop.ie
Clare County Libraries	www.clarelibrary.ie
Cork City Libraries	www.corkcorp.ie/services/index_library.html
Cork County Council Libraries	www.corkcoco.com/cccmm/services/library
Dublin City Public Library	www.iol.ie/dublincitylibrary
Dún Laoghaire-Rathdown Public Libraries	www.dlrcoco.ie/library
Fingal County Libraries	www.iol.ie/~fincolib
Galway Public Libraries	www.galwaylibrary.ie
Kildare County Libraries	www.kildare.ie/library
Longford County Library	http://longford.local.ie/content/9837.shtml
Mayo County Library	www.mayo-ireland.ie
Roscommon County Libraries	http://ireland.iol.ie/~roslib
Tipperary Libraries	www.iol.ie/~tipplibs

university libraries

Dublin City University Library	www.dcu.ie/library
National University of Ireland, Maynooth	www.may.ie/library
Queens University, Belfast	www.qub.ac.uk/lib
Trinity College, Dublin	www.tcd.ie/Library
University College Cork, Boole Library	http://booleweb.ucc.ie

University College Galway, Hardiman Library	www.library.nuigalway.ie
University College, Dublin	www.ucd.ie/~library
University of Limerick, Library	www.ul.ie/~library
University of Ulster	www.ulst.ac.uk/library
Waterford Institute of Technology Libraries	www.wit.ie/library/newpage2.htm
Western Education & Library Board	www.welbni.demon.co.uk
Wexford County Libraries	www.wexford.ie/library.htm

maps

3D Atlas Online	www.3datlas.com
Active Maps of Ireland	http://slarti.ucd.ie/maps/ireland.html
Association for Geographic Information (UK)	www.agi.org.uk
Australian National Mapping Agency	www.auslig.gov.au
British Cartographic Society	www.cartography.org.uk
British Geological Survey	www.bgs.ac.uk
Committee of the National Mapping Agencies of Europe	www.cerco.org
Geography Network	www.geographynetwork.com
Geomatics Canada	www.geocan.nrcan.gc.ca
Harvey	www.harveymaps.co.uk
Land Information New Zealand	www.linz.govt.nz
Mapblast	www.mapblast.com
Multi-purpose European Ground-Related Information Network	www.megrin.org
Multimap	www.multimap.com
National Map Centre (Irish)	www.mapcentre.ie
National Map Centre (UK)	www.mapstore.co.uk
Ordnance Survey Ireland	www.irlgov.ie/osi
Ordnance Survey of Northern Ireland	www.nics.gov.uk/doe/ordnance
Ordnance Survey (UK)	www.ordsvy.gov.uk
Shell Geostar	www.shellgeostar.com
Society of Cartographers	www.soc.org.uk
Stanfords	www.stanfords.co.uk
Street Map	www.streetmap.co.uk
US Geological Survey	www.usgs.gov

museums

Cavan County Museum	http://homepage.tinet.ie/~ccm
Chester Beatty Library	www.cbl.ie
Collins Barracks	www.ireland-withpatpreston.com/collinsbarracks.htm
Down County Museum	www.downdc.gov.uk
Dublinia	www.school-trip.com/ireland/dublinia
Dungarvan Museum Society Online	www.dungarvanmuseum.org

Garda Síochána Historical Society Museum	www.geocities.com/CapitolHill/7900/museum.html.
Heritage Ireland	www.heritageireland.ie
HMS Belfast	www.iwm.org.uk/belfast
Hotpress Irish Music Hall of Fame	www.imhf.com
Hunt Museum	www.ul.ie/~hunt/
Irish Museum of Modern Art	www.modernart.ie
James Joyce Centre	www.jamesjoyce.ie
Kehoes Pub and Maritime Museum	www.kehoes.com
Kennedy Homestead	http://indigo.ie/~wexweb
Kilmainham Gaol	www.irelandseye.com/aarticles/travel/attractions/museums/kilmain.shtm
MuseumNet	www.museums.co.uk
Museums and Galleries Commission	www.museums.gov.uk
National Gallery of Ireland	www.nationalgallery.ie
National History Museum	www.nhm.ac.uk
North Down Heritage Centre	www.north-down.gov.uk/heritage
Royal Ulster Constabulary Museum, Belfast	www.ruc.police.uk
Sheelin Irish Lace Museum	www.irish-lace.com
Strokestown Park House and The Irish Famine Museum	www.strokestownpark.ie
Trinity College	www.tcd.ie/Secretary/visitor.html
Ulster American Folk Park	www.folkpark.com
Ulster History Park	www.omagh.gov.uk/uhpindex.htm
Ulster Museum	www.ulstermuseum.org.uk
Upperlands Eco-Museum	www.upperlands.com
VisitDublin	www.visitdublin.ie
Wicklow Gaol	www.wicklow.ie.gaol

news agencies

AFP Asia	www.asia.dailynews.yahoo.com
AP World	www.newsday.com
CNN	www.cnn.com
Emerald News Media	www.btinternet.com/~emeraldnews
IRN	www.irn.co.uk
ITN	www.itn.co.uk
News Unlimited	www.newsunlimited.co.uk
Newshound	www.nuzhound.com
NewsNow	www.newsnow.co.uk
PA News	www.pa.press.net
PR Newswire	www.prnewswire.com
Reuters	www.reuters.com
Sky	www.sky.com/news
Tass	www.tass.ru/english

Teletext	www.teletext.co.uk
Universal Press Syndicate	www.uexpress.com
UPI/AFP	www.drudgereport.com

newspapers

Athlone Observer	http://ireland.iol.ie/littlebug/athobs
Ballyclare Gazette	www.ulsternet-ni.co.uk
Belfast Telegraph	www.belfasttelegraph.co.uk
Carrickfergus Advertiser	www.ulsternet-ni.co.uk
Clare Champion	www.clarechampion.ie
Connaught Telegraph	www.mayo-ireland.ie
Daily Express	www.express.co.uk
Daily Telegraph	www.telegraph.co.uk
Derry Journal	www.derryjournal.com
Derry People and Donegal News	www.donegalnews.com
Examiner, The	www.examiner.ie
Financial Times	www.ft.com
Foinse	www.foinse.ie
Galway Advertiser	www.galwayadvertiser.ie
Guardian	www.guardian.co.uk
Ireland On Sunday	www.irelandonsunday.com
Ireland Today	www.ireland-today.ie
Irish Chronicle	www.irishchronicle.com
Irish Examiner	www.irishexaminer.ie
Irish Independent	www.independent.ie
Irish News	www.irishnews.com
Irish Times	www.ireland.com
Irish Voice	www.irishvoice.com
Irish World	www.theirishworld.com
Kerry's Eye	www.kerryseye.com
Kingdom, The	www.kingdompaper.com
Limerick Leader	www.limerick-leader.ie
Limerick Post	www.limerickpost.ie
Marine Times	www.marinetimes.ie
Mayo Gazette	www.mayogazette.com
Mayo News	www.mayonews.ie
Mirror	www.mirror.co.uk
Morton Newspapers	www.mortonnewspapers.com
Munster Express	www.munster-express.ie
New York Times	www.nytimes.com
Northside People	www.northsidepeople.ie
Observer	www.observer.co.uk
People Newspapers	www.peoplenews.ie
Racing Post	www.racingpost.co.uk
Southside People	www.southsidepeople.ie
Sun	www.currantbun.com
Sunday Business Post	www.sbpost.ie
Sunday Times	www.sunday-times.co.uk
Sunday Tribune	www.tribune.ie

Sunday World	www.sundayworld.com
Telegraph	www.telegraph.co.uk
The Times	www.the-times.co.uk
Tyrone Courier	www.ulsternet-ni.co.uk
Ulster Gazette	www.ulsternet-ni.co.uk
Ulster Herald	www.ulsterherald.com
Unison	www.unison.ie
USA Today	www.usatoday.com
Wall Street Journal	www.wsj.com
Washington Post	www.washingtonpost.com
Waterford News and Star	www.waterford-news.com
Waterford Today	www.waterford-today.ie
Week, The	www.theweek.co.uk

opinion polls

Audit Bureau of Circulation	www.abc.org.uk
British Market Research Association	www.bmra.org.uk
Gallup	www.gallup.com
ICM	www.icmresearch.co.uk
Irish Marketing Surveys	www.imsl.ie
Mintel.com	www.mintel.com
Mori	www.mori.com
MRBI	www.esomar.ni/directory/110222.html-new
NOP	www.nop.co.ik

phone numbers

BT Online Phonebook	www.bt.com/phonenetuk
Eircom	www.eircom.ie-new
Golden Pages	www.goldenpages.ie
Independent Directory	www.independent-directory.ie
Kompass Business Directory	www.kompass.ie
Phonenumbers.net	www.phonenumbers.net
Telephone Code Changes	www.numberchange.org
Telephone Directories on the Web	www.teldir.com
Thomson Directories	www.thomweb.co.uk
UK PhoneBook	www.ukphonebook.com
Yellow Pages	www.yell.co.uk

professional bodies

European Newspaper Publishers Association	www.enpa.be
Press Association	www.pa.press.net
Regional Newspaper Advertising Network	www.rnan.ie
Regional Newspapers Associations of Ireland	www.rnan.ie
Society of Editors	www.ukeditors.com

reference

3D Atlas Online	www.3datlas.com
Active Maps of Ireland	http://slarti.ucd.ie/maps/ireland.html
An Post	www.anpost.ie
Arts, Heritage, Gaeltacht & the Islands	www.irlgov.ie/ealga
Citizens Information Database	www.cidb.ie
Duchas, The Heritage Services	www.heritageireland.ie
ENFO - Information of the Environment	www.enfo.ie
FTSE	www.ftse.com
Geological Survey of Ireland	www.gsi.ie
Information Society Commission	www.isc.ie
Irish Central Statistics Office	www.cso.ie
Irish Toasts	http://islandireland.com/Pages/folk/sets/toasts.html
Irish Tourist Board	www.ireland.travel.ie
Jane's	www.janes.com
Kelly's Guide	www.kellysonline.net
Northern Ireland.net	www.northernireland.net
Northern Irish Tourist Board	www.discovernorthernireland.com
Online.ie	www.online.ie
Oxford English Dictionary	www.oed.com
Roget's Thesaurus	www.thesaurus.com
The Irish Genealogical Project	www.irishgenealogy.ie
Ulster Historical Foundation	www.uhf.org.uk

weather

BBC Weather Centre	www.bbc.co.uk/weather
Belgium	www.meteo.oma.be
France	www.meteo.fr
Germany	www.dwd.de
Irish Internet Weather Centre	www.geocities.com/Vienna/1340/iw.html
ITN	www.itn.co.uk/weather
ITV Weather	www.itv-weather.co.uk
Local.ie Weather	www.local.ie/general/weather
Met Eireann	www.met.ie
Met Office	www.metoffice.com
Netherlands	www.knmi.nl
Northern Ireland Weather	www.northernireland.net/ni/weather.htm
Online Weather	www.onlineweather.com
USA	www.nws.noaa.gov
Very Useful UK Weather Page, The	www.uk-weather.co.uk
Weather Call	www.weathercall.co.uk
Weather Channel UK	www.weather.co.uk

World Meteorological Organisation	www.wmo.ch
Yahoo Uk & Ireland Weather	http://uk.weather.yahoo.com

living

dating agencies
driving schools
family support
hairdressers, beauty salons & image consultants
health & fitness
home improvements
magazines & websites
professional bodies & trade associations
religion
utilities
weddings

living

dating agencies

121 Fusion	www.121fusion.com
Another Friend	www.anotherfriend.com
Circles Club	www.circlesclub.ie
Elite Introductions	www.elite.ie
Gay Ireland	www.gay.ie
Gay Ireland Online	www.gaire.com
Introsearch	www.introsearch.com
Ireland For Singles	www.ireland.forsingles.com
Irish Penpals	www.irishpenpals.com
Irish Personals	www.west-point.org/users/usma1989/46586/irish-personals.htm
Irish Singles Directory	www.irishsinglesdirectory.com
Irish Singles Online	www.irishsinglesonline.ie
Lisdoonvarna Match Maker	www.matchmakerireland.com
NI Dating Service	www.nidating.com
Proposals	www.proposalsireland.com
Sure Date	www.suredate.ie
Who's Who for the Unattached	www.irishdating.com

driving schools

'Agood' Driving School	www.agood.co.uk
ABBA Driving School	www.abbadrivingschool.com
Acclaim Driving Academy	www.acclaimdrivingacademy.co.uk
Astral School of Motoring	www.astralmotoring.ie
Defensive Driver Training	www.defensivedriver.ie
Doak Driver Training	www.doak.co.uk
Driving Instructor Register of Ireland	www.dir.ie
Driving Test Information	www.drivingtest.ie
IMS	www.ims-driver-rider-training.co.uk
Irish School of Motoring	www.ism.ie
John A Ryan Driving School	www.johnaryandriving.com
Loyola Driving School	www.loyoladrivingschool.com
Motor Schools Association of Ireland	http://website.lineone.net/~msainews
Northern Ireland Driving Schools	www.drivingschoolsni.com
Rally School Ireland	www.rallyschoolireland.ie
Transport Training Services Ltd	www.transport-training.co.uk

family support

Adoption Board	www.adoptionboard.ie
European Child Care Professionals, Dublin	www.eccpd.com

Family Life Services	www.thefamilycentre.com
Gingerbread	www.gingerbreadni.org
Irish Adoption Contact Register	www.adoptionireland.com
Irish Countrywomen's Association	www.icwa.ie
Irish Family Planning Association	www.ifpa.ie
Irish Foster Care Association	www.ifca.ie
parentalequality.ie	www.parentalequality.ie
Rollercoaster.ie	www.rollercoaster.ie
Solo.ie	www.solo.ie
The Children's Research Centre	www.tcd.ie/childrens_centre

hairdressers, beauty salons & image consultants

Alex Mekki Hair Salon	www.alexmekki.com
Beauty Bath	www.beautybath.ie
Bellissimo Hair Health Beauty Complex	www.bellissimo.ie
Bliss	www.bliss.ie
Bodicare.com	www.bodicare.com
Celtic Milled Beauty Products	www.celticmilledbeauty.com
Color Me Beautiful	www.cmbireland.com
Company Haircutters	www.company.group.tm
Cork Academy of Hairdressing	www.corkacademy hairdressing.com
Health Farms of Ireland	www.healthfarmsofireland.com
Ian McCullough Hair Design	www.ianmcculloughhair.co.uk
Lipstick Ireland	www.lipstick-ireland.com
Paul Shappiro	www.paulshappiro.com
Peter Mark	www.petermark.ie
Samara	www.finditbusiness.net/samara
Scruples	www.scruplesonline.com
The Hair Room	www.thehairroomni.co.uk
Toni & Guy	www.toniandguy.co.uk
Vidal Sassoon	www.vidalsassoon.co.uk

health & fitness

A – Z Fitness Links	www.atozfitness.com/links
Arena Health & Fitness Belfast Ltd	www.arenaclub.co.uk
Bodyfirm	www.bodyfirmpilates.com
Cloona Health Centre	www.cloona.ie
Diet Information	www.diet-i.com
Elysium at the Culloden	www.hastingshotels.com
Fit 4 Anything	www.fit4anything.net
Fitness First	www.fitnessfirst.com
Fitness Ireland	www.fitnessireland.com
Fitness Jumpsite	http://primusweb.com/fitnesspartner
Gobbins Lodge	www.gobbins.lodge.com
Gyms Dublin	www.ireland.com/dublin/living/sport/gymslist.htm

Herbal Health For You	www.limerickbiz.com/herbalhealth
Personal Training Northern Ireland	www.ptni.co.uk
REACT	www.react.ie
Sports Coach	www.athleticscoach.co.uk
Unislim	www.unislim.com
Weightwatchers	www.weightwatchers.com
West Wood Health & Fitness Clubs	www.westwood.ie
YMCA	www.ymca.ie
Yoga Ireland	http://indigo.ie/~cmouze/

home improvements

design

2cooldesign	www.2cooldesign.ie

kitchens & appliances

AEG	www.aeg-direct.com
Aga & Rayburn	www.aga-rayburn.co.uk
Baumatic	www.baumatic.co.uk
Belling	www.belling.co.uk
Bosch	www.bosch.co.uk
Cannon	www.cannongas.co.uk
Cash & Carry Kitchens	www.cashandcarrykitchens.com
Creda	www.creda.co.uk
Cucina Direct	www.cucinadirect.co.uk
De Dietrich	www.dedietrich.co.uk
Divertimenti	www.divertimenti.co.uk
Drumms Kitchen Accessories	www.drumms.ie
Dyson	www.dyson.com
Electrolux	www.electrolux.co.uk
Gaggia	www.gaggia.it
GEC	www.gec.co.uk
Hoover	www.hoover.co.uk
Hotpoint	www.hotpoint.co.uk
Huenna Kitchens	www.huennakitchens.ie
Indesit	www.indesit.co.uk
Intoto	www.intoto.co.uk
Keuro Kitchens of Kilkenny	www.keurokitchens.com
Le Creuset	www.lecreuset.com
Linn	www.linn.co.uk
Magnet	www.magnet.co.uk
Miele	www.miele.co.uk
Mission	www.mission.co.uk
Mitsubishi Electric	www.meuk.mee.com
Moben	www.moben.co.uk
Neff	www.neff.co.uk
Panasonic	www.panasonic.co.uk
Parkes Interiors	www.parkesinteriors.co.uk
Philips	www.philips.com

Redring	www.redring.co.uk
Russell Hobbs	www.russell-hobbs.com
Servis	www.servis.co.uk
Sharp	www.sharp.co.uk
Sheffield Steel	www.made-in-sheffield.com
Smeg	www.smeguk.com
Stoves	www.stoves.co.uk
Stylecraft Kitchens, Cork	www.stylecraft-kitchens.com
Technics	www.technics.co.uk
Tefal	www.tefal.co.uk
Toshiba	www.toshiba.co.uk
Ultimate Appliances & Kitchens	www.ultimateappliancesandkitchens.com
Village Kitchens	www.villkit.com
Whirlpool	www.whirlpool.co.uk
Zanussi	www.zanussi.co.uk

products

Arro – DIY online	www.arrodiy.ie
Atlantic Homecare	www.atlanticdiy.com
B&Q	www.diy.com
Homebase	www.homebase.co.uk
Irish Interiors	www.irishinteriors.ie
Noyeks	www.noyeks.ie
Woodies	www.woodiesdiy.ie

home life

Billpay	www.billpay.ie
Persil	www.persil.co.uk

magazines & websites

All About Parents	www.allaboutparents.com
Baby Directory	www.babydirectory.com
BBC Good Homes	www.goodhomes.beeb.com
Big Issue	www.bigissue.com
Charlotte Street	www.charlottestreet.com
Cosmopolitan	www.cosmomag.com
Country Life	www.countrylife.co.uk
Elle	www.ellemag.com
Esquire	www.esquiremag.com
FHM	www.fhm.co.uk
Good Housekeeping	www.goodhousekeeping.com
GQ	www.gq-magazine.co.uk
Hello!	www.hello-magazine.co.uk
House & Garden	www.houseandgarden.co.uk
IVenus.com	www.ivenus.com
Jewish.net	www.jewish.net
Life	www.pathfinder.com/life
Loaded	www.loaded.co.uk
Magazine Shop	www.magazineshop.co.uk

Maxim	www.maximmag.com
Men's Health	www.menshealth.com
National Enquirer	www.nationalenquirer.com
New Woman	www.newwomanonline.co.uk
Playboy	www.playboy.com
Private Eye	www.private-eye.co.uk
Reader's Digest	www.readersdigest.co.uk
Shout	www.dcthomson.co.uk/mags/shout
Spectator	www.spectator.co.uk
Tatler	www.tatler.co.uk
Vanity Fair	www.vanityfair.co.uk
Viz	www.viz.co.uk
Vogue	www.vogue.co.uk
World of Interiors	www.worldofinteriors.co.uk
Zoom	www.zoom.co.uk

professional bodies & trade associations

Irish Auctioneers & Valuers Institute	www.iavi.ie
John Sisk	www.sisk.ie
RECI	www.reci.ie
Tenders Ireland	www.tendersireland.com
Top 1000 Construction Companies in Ireland	www.itw.ie/top/construc.htm

religion

buddhism

Amida Trust	http://ai.iit.nrc.ca/~andre/amida/home.html
Aukana Trust	www.aukana.org.uk
Buddha Mind	www.abm.ndirect.co.uk
Buddhism	www.chezpaul.org.uk/buddhism/index.htm
Buddhist Society UK, The	www.thebuddhistsociety.org.uk
Buddhistnet	www.buddhistnet.co.uk
Cham Tse Ling	www.quietmountain.org/dharmacentres/ctl
Dechen Dharma Community	www.dechen.org
Glasgow Buddhist Centre	www.glasgowbuddhistcentre.com
Heritage Trust	www.members.aol.com/yeshiuk/index.html
Heruka Buddhist Centre	www.heruka.org
International Meditation Centres	www.webcom.com/~imcuk
International Zen Association	www.zen-izauk.org
Jampa Buddhist Centre	www.geocities.com/tokyo/dojo/8599
Kagyu Samyeling Monastry & Buddhist Centre	www.samyeling.org
Khedrupje Buddhist Centre	www.meditateinhull.org.uk

Lumbini Nepalese Buddha Dharma Society	www.buddhadharma.org.uk
UK Association for Buddhist Studies	www.sunderland.ac.uk/~os0dwe/bsa.shtml
Urthona	www.urthona.com
Western Ch'an Fellowship	www.w-c-f.org.uk

christianity

Africa Inland Mission	www.aim-us.org
All Hallows College	www.allhallows.ie
Alpha	www.alpha.org.uk
Archdiocese of Dublin	www.dublindiocese.ie
Belfast Bible College	www.belfastbiblecollege.com
Bible Society in Northern Ireland	www.bsni.co.uk
Callan Community	www.iol.ie/~callanpb/callan
Care for the Family	www.care-for-the-family.org.uk
Carmelite Sisters of Ireland	www.carmelitesisters.ie
Carrigaline Baptist Church	www.carrigalinebaptist.org
Christ Church Dublin	www.cccdub.ie
Christian End Time Ministries	http://homepages.iol.ie/~wilend
Christian Fellowship Church	www.cfc-net.org
Christian Radio	www.ucb.co.uk
Christian Renewal Centre	www.crc-rostrevor.org
Christian Union Society – University College Cork	www.ucc.ie/ucc/socs/ucccu
Church of Ireland	www.ireland-anglican.org
Crossfire Trust	www.crossfiretrust.net
Diocese of Limerick	www.limerick-diocese.org
Diocese of Waterford & Lismore	www.waterfordlismore.com
Discalced Carmelites	www.discalcedcarmelites.ie
Evangelical Presbyterian Church	www.epc.org
Faith Mission	www.faithmission.org
Fellowship Bible Church	www.fbc.ie
Gideons International	www.gideons.org
Interserve Ireland	www.isire.org
Irish Bible School	http://homepage.eircom.net/~ibs
Irish Council of Churches	www.unite.co.uk/customers/icpep
Jesuits	www.jesuit.ie/choice
Knights of Saint Columbanus	www.knightsofstcolumbanus.ie
L'Arche UK	www.larche.org.uk
Mercy International Centre	www.mercy-international.org
Methodist Church in Ireland	www.irishmethodist.org
Monastry of St. Alphonsus	http://homepages.iol.ie/~gfox
Mother's Ireland – Ireland	www.mothersunion.ie
Mother's Union	www.themothersunion.org
New Life Baptist Fellowship	http://indigo.ie/~newlife/index.htm

Newry Cathedral	www.newrycathedral.org
Presbyterian Church	www.presbyterianireland.org
Presbyterian Herald	www.presbyterianireland.org
Quakers	www.quakers.org.uk
Roman Catholic Church (Bishops Conference of Ireland)	www.catholiccommunication.ie
Order of St. Augustine	www.augustinians.ie
Salvation Army	www.salvationarmy.co.uk
Seventh-day Adventist Church	www.adventist.org.uk
Sisters of Sion	www.bellinter.net
Soapbox Expeditions	www.soapboxexpeditions.com
St. Patrick's Cathedral	www.stpatrickscathedral.ie
The Christian Union Movement	www.uccf.org.uk
Traidcraft	www.traidcraft.co.uk
Trinity Presbyterian Church	http://homepage.eircom.net/~stephenmurray
Whitewell Metropolitan Tabernacle	www.whitewell.com
Worldvision	www.worldvision.org.uk
Worldvision Ireland	www.wvireland.org
Youth Alive	www.geocities.com/athens/2235
Youth for Christ (NI)	www.yfc-ireland.com

hinduism

Institute for Applied Spiritual Technology	www.ifast.net
International Society for Krishna Consciousness	www.iskcon.org.uk
ISKCONI Leicester UK	www.gauranga.org
Jay Swaminarayan	www.shreeswaminarayan.org.uk
National Hindu Students Forum	www.nhsf.org.uk
Vivekananda Centre London	www.vivekananda.btinternet.co.uk
Yoga Village UK	www.yogauk.com

islam

Association of Muslim Researchers	www.amrnet.demon.co.uk
Centre of Islamic & Middle Eastern Law	www.soas.ac.uk/centres/islamiclaw
Investigating Islam	www.islamic.org.uk
Islamic Research Academy	www.isra.org.uk
Jamia Al-Karam	www.btinternet.com/~alkaram
Muslim Directory	www.muslimdirectory.co.uk
SI Education Society	http://siedu.com
Teachings of Islam	www.shirazi.org.uk
UK Islamic Education Waqf	www.ukiew.org

judaism

Ajb Online	http://users.charity.vfree.com/a/ajb

Beth Shalom Holocaust Centre	www.holocaustcentre.net
bnei akiva	www.bneiakiva.org/uk
European Association for Jewish Studies	http://nonuniv.ox.ac.uk/~eajs
Holocaust History	www.holocausthistory.net
Ilford 345	http://website.lineone.net/~robertleach/345.htm
Institute for Jewish Policy Research	www.jpr.org.uk
Irish-Jewish Museum, The	www.eecs.tufts.edu/~zblocked/ijm
Jewish Blind & Disabled	www.jbd.org
Jewish Museum London	www.jewmusm.ort.org
JLGB	www.jlgb.org
Liberal Jewish Synagogue, The	www.ljs.org
Limmud	www.limmud.org.uk
RSY – Netzer	http://welcome.to/rsy.netzer
Union of Liberal & Progressive Synagogues	www.ulps.org
Yakar	www.yakar.org.uk
Yoffi FZY	www.btinternet.com/~green.house/yoffi/imagemap.htm

others

An Fainne	http://indigo.ie/~imago/moot.html
Atheist, Agnostic & Humanist	www.abarnett.demon.co.uk/atheism/index.html
Baha'i Community of the United Kingdom	www.bahai.org.uk
Baha'i Council for Scotland	www.bci.org/scotland
Baha'i Information Office	www.iol.ie/~isp/
Beshara School of Intensive Esoteric Information	www.beshara.org
British Martinist Order	www.bmosite.org/intro.htm
Celtic Shamans Universe	www.peagreenboat.demon.co.uk
Centre for Alternative Technology	www.cat.org.uk
Church of Scientology UK	www.scientology.org.uk
Church of the Open Mind	www.hibbert.org.uk
Core Shamanism	www.users.dircon.co.uk/~snail
Dowsing – Shamanism	www.anamspirit.com
Feng Shui Association	www.fengshuiassociation.co.uk
Fountain International	www.fountain-international.org
Freedom Magazine (Scientology)	www.freedom.org.uk
International Centre for Reiki Training	www.reiki.org
International Shinto Foundation	http://shinto.org

Pagan Federation	www.paganfed.org
Pagan Ireland	www.synergy.ie/bevandel/
Sainthill College for Scientologists	http://sainthill.org.uk
Satanism UK	www.satanism-uk.com
Shamanism UK & Europe	www.shamanism.co.uk
Shinto	www.religioustolerance.org/shinto.htm
Spiritualist's National Union	www.snu.org.uk
Spiritualists Lyceum Union	www.thelyceum.org.uk
Spirituality 2000	www.spirituality2000.org
Transcendental Meditation	www.tmcork.org
Wicca	http://members.tripod.com/~leedouglas/wicca.html

sikhism

InfoSikh	www.infosikh.co.uk
Khalsa Human Rights	http://dspace.dial.pipex.com/town/square/ev90495
Maharajah Duleep Singh Centenary Trust	www.mdsct.org.uk
Sikh Information	www.info-sikh.com
Sikh Justice	www.sikhjustice.com
Sikh Spirit	www.sikhspirit.com
Sikhism in the United Kingdom	www.geocities.com/athens/1818/sikhhome.htm

utilities

Bord Gais Eireann	www.bordgais.com
Bord Na Móna	www.bnm.ie
Calor Gas	www.calorgas.ie
Eirtricity	www.eirtricity.ie
EPower	www.epower.ie
ESB	www.esb.ie
Flogas	www.flogas.ie
Kilronan Windfarm	www.kilronanwindfarm.com
Northern Ireland Electricity	www.nie.co.uk
Phoenix Natural Gas	www.phoenix-natural-gas.com
Texaco	www.texaco.com

weddings

Cratloe Weddings	www.cratloeweddings.com
Dana Bridal Footwear	www.weddingshoeworld.com
Direct Weddings	www.directweddings.co.uk
Irish Weddings	www.irish-weddings.com
Irish Weddings Online	www.irishweddingsonline.com
The Knot	www.theknot.com
Weddings Ireland	www.weddings-ireland.com
Weddings Online	www.weddingsonline.ie

personal finance

banks and building societies
credit cards
insurance
mortgages
other
professional bodies

with www.bankofireland.ie

Bank of Ireland's interactive website is the largest and most comprehensive of any Irish Bank. The online services we offer range from applying for your Credit Card, Motorloan, Personal Loan and Mortgage, to checking your accounts and paying your bills through Banking 365 Online, along with a whole host of other electronic banking options. **www.bankofireland.ie** truly does bring your bank into your home and office. And you don't even have to tidy up for us.

you can go to the bank just as you are

Bank of Ireland

personal finance

banks and building societies

24-hour Online (AIB)	www.24hour-online.ie
365 Online	www.365online.com
Abbey National	www.abbeynational.co.uk
ACC Bank	www.accbank.ie
Alliance & Leicester	www.alliance-leicester.co.uk
Allied Irish Bank	www.aib.ie

Anglo Irish Bank	www.angloirishbank.ie
Bank of Ireland	www.boi.ie
Bank of Scotland	www.bankofscotland.co.uk
Barclays	www.barclays.co.uk
Bradford & Bingley Building Society	www.themarketplace.com
Central Bank	www.centrealbank.ie
Corrib Finance	www.corribfinance.ie
Dundrum Credit Union	www.dundrumcu.ie
EBS	www.ebs.ie
Euro Finance Group	www.eurofinancegroup.ie
Finance Ireland	www.financeirl.ie
First Active	www.firstactive.ie
First Trust Bank	www.firsttrustonline.co.uk
Girobank (NI)	www.girobank.co.uk
Halifax	www.halifax.co.uk
HSBC Bank	www.hsbc.co.uk
ICC Bank	www.icc.ie
Irish League of Credit Unions	www.creditunions.ie
Irish Nationwide	www.irish-nationwide.com
Irish Permanent	www.irishpermanent.ie
Lombard & Ulster	www.lombard.ie
National Irish Bank	www.nib.ie
Nationwide Building Society	www.nationwide.co.uk
Northern Bank	www.nbonline.co.uk
Progressive Building Society	www.theprogressive.com
Standard Life Bank	www.standardlifebank.com
TSB Bank	www.tsbbank.ie
Ulster Bank	www.ulsterbank.com
Woolwich	www.thewoolwich.co.uk

credit cards

American Express	www.americanexpress.co.uk
Diner's Club	www.dinersclub.com
Master Card	www.mastercard.com
MBNA	www.mbna.ie
Visa	www.visa.com

insurance

123 Insurance	www.123.ie
A2Z	www.a2z.ie
Abbey National	www.abbey-online.co.uk
Accident General	www.accidentgeneral.ie
Adelaide Insurance Services	www.adelaidebank.com
Allianz	www.allianz.ie
Allied Dunbar	www.allieddunbar.co.uk
Alpha Claims Service	www.alphaclaims.ie
ARB	www.arb.ie
Autopoint	www.autopoint.ie
AXA	www.axa.ie
BUPA Ireland	www.bupaireland.ie
Canada Life	www.canadalife.com
Dublin Financial	www.dublinfinancial.com
E-Insurance Ireland	www.e-insuranceireland.com
Eagle Star	www.eaglestar.co.uk
Endsleigh Insurance	www.endsleigh.co.uk
First Call Direct	www.firstcalldirect.ie
First Rate Direct	www.first-rate-direct.co.uk
Friends First	www.friendsfirst.ie
Friends' Provident	www.friendsprovident.com
Get Cover	www.getcover.com
Hibernian	www.hibernian.ie
Insure.ie	www.insure.ie
LA Brokers	www.labrokers.ie
New Ireland	www.newireland.ie
Northern Ireland Insurance Brokers	www.northernireland-insurancebrokers.co.uk
Norwich Union	www.norwichunion.co.uk
One Direct	www.anpost.ie/one
Prudential	www.pru.co.uk
Royal Liver Assurance	www.royalliver.com
Royal Sun Alliance	www.royalsunalliance.ie
Scottish Equitable	www.scottishequitable.co.uk
St. Paul	www.stpaul.com
Standard Life	www.standardlife.com
Sun Life	www.sunlifeofcanada.co.uk
United Friendly	www.united-friendly.co.uk
VHI	www.vhi.ie
Yachtsman Marine Brokers	www.yachtsman.ie

mortgages

Friendly Mortgages	www.friendlymortgages.com
Home Loan Company	www.thehomeloancompany.co.uk
Irish Mortgage Corporation	www.irishmortgage.ie
Irish Permanent Mortgages	www.yourmortgage.net
Mortgage & Debt Services NI	www.mortgagebrokersni.com

Mortgage Advice Shop, The	www.mortgageadviceshop.com
Mortgage Intelligence	www.mortgage-intelligence.co.uk
Mortgage Interest Saving System	www.mortgageiss.com
National Mortgage Service	www.nms.ie
Rea Mortgage Service	www.rea.ie
The Independent Mortgage Shop	www.tims.co.uk
The Mortgage Door	www.themortgagedoor.co.uk
The Mortgage Shop	www.themortgageshop online.net
The Mortgage Store	www.mortgagestore.ie

other

an Bord Pinsear	www.pensionsboard.ie
AICS Debt Collection	www.eircollect.ie
Assett Management Trust	www.amt.ie
Credit Management Services	www.creditmanagement.ie
FBD Holdings	www.fbd.ie
Finfacts (portal)	www.finfacts.ie
PricewaterhouseCoopers	www.pwcglobal.com

professional bodies

Chartered Insurance Institute	www.cii.co.uk
Housing Finance Agency	www.hfa.ie
Irish Banks' Information Service	www.ibis.ie
Irish Bank Officials Ass.	www.iboa.ie
Irish Bankers' Federation	www.ibis.ie
Irish Insurance Federation	www.iif.ie
The Institute of Bankers in Ireland	www.institute-of-bankers.com

places

countries (government)
historic railways & museums
libraries
monuments and historic buildings
museums
parks & gardens
tourist attractions
tourist information
web cams

places

countries (government)

europe

Albania	www.parlament.al
Andorra	www.andorra.ad/govern/index.html
Armenia	www.gov.am/en
Austria	www.austria.gv.at/e
Belarus	www.belarus.net/parliame/
Belgium	www.belgium.fgov..be
Bosnia and Herzegovina	www.fbihvlada.gov.ba
Bulgaria	www.government.bg
Croatia	www.vlada.hr/english/contents.html
Cyprus	www.pio.gov.cy
Czech Republic	www.czech.cz
Denmark	www.ft.dk
Estonia	www.riik.ee/en
Finland	www.eduskunta.fi
France	www.service-public.fr/accueil/english.html
Germany	www.bundesregierung.de
Greece	www.parliament.gr
Iceland	http://brunnur.stjr.is/interpro/stjr/stjr.nsf/pages/english-index
Ireland	www.irlgov.ie
Italy	www.governo.it
Latvia	www.saeima.lv
Lithuania	http://rc.lrs.lt
Luxembourg	www.gouvernement.lu
Malta	www.magnet.mt
Monaco	www.gouv.mc
Norway	www.odin.dep.no/odin/engelsk/index-b-n-a.html
Poland	http://poland.pl
Portugal	www.presidenciarepublica.pt
Romania	http://domino.kappa.ro/guvern/ehome.nsf
Russia	www.government.gov.ru/english/
Slovakia	www.prezident.sk
Slovenia	www.sigov.si
Spain	www.admiweb.org
Sweden	www.riksdagen.se/index_en.asp
Switzerland	www.admin.ch
Turkey	www.mfa.gov.tr
UK	www.ukonline.gov.uk

rest of the world

Afghanistan	www.afghangovernment.org
Angola	www.angola.org/angola
Australia	www.access.gov.au
Azerbaijan	www.president.az
Bahamas	www.bahamas.com
Bahrain	www.bahrain.gov.bh
Bangladesh	www.bangladeshgov.org
Belize	www.belize.gov.bz
Bolivia	www.congreso.gov.bo
Brazil	www.brasil.gov.br
Brunei	www.brunei.gov.bn
Burkina Faso	www.primature.gov.bf
Cambodia	www.ocm.gov.kh
Cameroon	www.compufix.demon.co.uk/camweb
Canada	http://canada.gc.ca/howgoc/glance_e.html
Chile	www.congreso.cl
China	www.cei.gov.cn/govinfo/english/default1e.shtml
Colombia	www.presidencia.gov.co
Dominican Republic	www.presidencia.gov.do
Egypt	www.alhokoma.gov.eg
El Salvador	www.sv
Fiji	www.fiji.gov.fj
Gambia	www.gambia.com
Georgia	www.parliament.ge
Ghana	www.ghana.gov.gh
Haiti	www.haitifocus.com/haitie/gov.html
India	www.indiagov.org
Israel	www.info.gov.il/eng/mainpage.asp
Jamaica	www.cabinet.gov.jm
Japan	www.jwindow.net/GOV/gov.html
Jordan	www.kingabdullah.jo
Kazakhstan	www.president.kz
Korea, South	www.korea.net
Kuwait	www.moinfo.gov.kw
Kyrgyzstan	www.gov.kg
Liberia	www.liberia.net
Malaysia	www.parlimen.gov.my
Mauritius	http://ncb.intnet.mu/govt/
Mexico	www.presidencia.gob.mx/?NLang=en
Micronesia	www.fsmgov.org
Mongolia	www.parl.gov.mn

Morocco	www.mincom.gov.ma
Namibia	www.gmnet.gov.na
New Zealand	www.nz.com
Pakistan	www.pak.gov.pk
Rwanda	www.rwanda1.com/government/
Samoa	www.samoa.ws/govtsamoapress/
Singapore	www.gov.sg
South Africa	www.gov.za
Sri Lanka	www.priu.gov.lk
Thailand	www.thaigov.go.th
Tibet	www.tibet.com
Uganda	www.government.go.ug
USA	www.fedworld.gov
Uzbekistan	www.gov.uz
Vanuatu	www.vanuatugovernment.gov.vu
Yemen	www.gpc.org.ye
Yugoslavia	www.gov.yu

historic railways & museums

Bluebell Railway Preservation Society	www.bluebell-railway.co.uk
Cavan & Leitrim Railway	http://homepage.eircom.net/~yarpie/clr
Class 40 Preservation Society	www.cfps.co.uk
Corris Railway	www.corris.co.uk
Cumbria Steam Railways	www.visitcumbria.com/railway.htm
East Anglian Railway Museum	www.earm.co.uk
Ffestiniog	www.marketsite.co.uk/festrail
Flying Scotsman	www.flyingscotsman.com
Great Central	www.gcrailway.co.uk
Hackworth Victorian & Railway Museum	www.hackworthmuseum.co.uk
Keighley & Worth Valley Railway	www.kwvr.co.uk
Mid-Hants Watercress Line	www.watercressline.co.uk
National Railway Historical Society (UK)	www.siam.co.uk/nrhsuk
National Railway Museum (UK)	www.nrm.org.uk
Railway Preservation Society of Ireland	www.rpsi-online.org
Ravenglass & Eskdale Railway	www.ravenglass-railway.co.uk
Scottish Highland Railway Company	www.queenofscots.co.uk
Severn Valley Railway	www.svr.co.uk
Steeple Grange Light Railway	http://www-users.york.ac.uk/~ian100/sglr/
Talyllyn Railway	www.talyllyn.co.uk

UK Railways Online	www.geocities.com/rainforest/5665/
Welsh Highland Railway	www.whr.co.uk
Welsh Highland Railway Project	www.bangor.ac.uk/ml/whr/
Welshpool & Llanfair Light Railway	www.wllr.org.uk

libraries

Archbishop Marsh's Library, Dublin	www.marshlibrary.ie
Central Library Belfast	www.belb.org.uk
Chester Beatty Library, Dublin	www.cbl.ie
National Library of Ireland	www.nli.ie
Trinity College Dublin Library	www.tcd.ie

monuments and historic buildings

ireland

Bantry House, Co. Cork	www.cork-guide.ie/bnry_hse.htm
Belfast Castle	www.belfastcastle.co.uk
Belfast City Hall	www.belfastcity.gov.uk
Belvedere House, Co. Westmeath	www.belvedere-house.ie
Blarney Castle, Co. Cork	www.blarneycastle.ie
Bunratty Castle, Co. Clare	www.shannonheritagetrade.com
Christ Church Cathedral	www.cccdub.ie
City Hall, Dublin	www.dublincorp.ie/cityhall
Cregg Castle, Co. Galway	http://indigo.ie/~creggcas
Crown Liquor Saloon, Belfast	www.belfasttelegraph.co.uk/crown
Department of the Taoiseach	www.irlgov.ie/taoiseach/tour
Dunsany Castle, Co. Meath	www.dunsany.com
Grand Opera House, Belfast	www.goh.co.uk
Heritage Ireland	www.heritageireland.ie
Historic Irish Castles	www.historic.irishcastles.com
Irish Landmark Trust	www.irishlandmark.com
Irish National Heritage Park	www.inhp.com
Kennedy Homestead	http://indigo.ie/~wexweb
Kylemore Abbey	www.kylemoreabbey.com
Leinster House, Dublin	www.irlgov/oireachtas
Lismore Castle, Co. Waterford	www.lismorecastle.com
Longueville House	www.longuevillehouse.ie
Malahide Castle, Co. Dublin	www.visitdublin.com
Mansion House, Dublin	www.dublincorp.ie
National 1798 Visitor Centre	www.iol.ie/~98com
National Trust	www.nationaltrust.org.uk
Newgrange	www.stonepages.com
Quiet Man Heritage Cottage	www.quietman-cong.com
Sheelin Irish Lace Museum, Co. Fermanagh	www.irish-lace.com

St Patrick's Cathedral	www.stpatrickscathedral.ie
Stormont Castle	www.nics.gov.uk/castle/castle.htm
Trinity College, Dublin	www.tcd.ie
Yeats Memorial Building	www.yeats-sligo.com

rest of the world

10 Downing Street	www.number-10.gov.uk
Buckingham Palace	www.royal.gov.uk/palaces/bp.htm
Great Wall of China	www.chinavista.com/travel/greatwall/greatwall.html
Hadrian's Wall	www.northumbria-tourist-board.org.uk/hadrian
Houses of Parliament	www.parliament.uk
Palace of Versailles	www.smartweb.fr/versailles
Sistine Chapel	www.christusrex.org
St Paul's Cathedral	www.stpauls.co.uk
Stonehenge	www.stonepages.com
Tower of London	www.camelot-group.com/tower
Vatican	www.vatican.va
Westminster Abbey	www.westminster-abbey.org
Windsor Castle	www.royal.gov.uk/palaces/windsor.htm
World Heritage List	http://mirror-us.unesco.org/whc/heritage.htm

museums

ireland

Cobh Heritage Centre	www.cobhheritage.com
Derryglad Folk Museum	http://dha-/oncom/derryglad-folk-museum
Hunt Museum	www.ul.ie/~hunt
Inishowen Maritime Museum	www.homepage.eircom.net/~greencastlemaritime
Irish Museum of Modern Art	www.modernart.ie
Irish National Heritage Park, Co. Wexford	www.inhp.com
James Joyce Centre, Dublin	www.jamesjoyce.ie
National Gallery of Ireland	www.nationalgallery.ie
National Maritime Museum	www.dun-laoghaire.com/dir/maritime.html
National Print Museum, Dublin	http://ireland.iol.ie/~npmuseum/
Royal Ulster Rifles Museum, Belfast	http://rurmuseum.tripod.com
RUC Museum, Belfast	www.nics.gov.uk/ruc/museum/start.htm
Somme Heritage Centre, Newtownards	www.irishsoldier.org

Tower Museum, Londonderry	www.derrynet/tower
Ulster Folk & Transport Museum	www.nidex.com/uftm
Ulster History Park, Omagh	www.omagh.gov.uk/historypark.htm
Ulster Museum	www.ulstermuseum.org.uk

rest of the world

24-Hour Museum	www.24hourmuseum.org.uk
Germanisches National Museum	www.gnm.de
Guggenheim Bilbao	www.guggenheim-bilbao.es
Guggenheim, New York	www.guggenheim.org
J Paul Getty Museum, California	www.getty.edu
Library of Congress	www.loc.gov
Los Angeles Museum of Art	www.lacma.org
Louvre	www.louvre.fr
Metropolitan Museum of Art, New York	www.metmuseum.org
Museum of Modern Art, New York	www.moma.org
National Museum of American Art	www.nmaa.si.edu
Smithsonian Institution	www.si.edu
Uffizi Gallery, Florence	www.uffizi.firenze.it
Van Gogh Museum	www.vangoghmuseum.nl
Yad Vashem	www.yad-vashem.org.il

parks & gardens

Ballymaloe Cookery School Gardens, Co. Cork	www.ballymaloe-cookery-school.ie
Dillon Garden	http://dillongarden.com
Hilton Park Garden, Co. Monaghan	www.hiltonpark.ie
Irish National Stud Japanese Gardens & St Flachras Garden	www.irish-national-stud.ie
John F Kennedy Arboretum	www.wexfordirl.com
Kew Gardens, London	www.rbgkew.org.uk
Kilmokea Gardens, Co. Wexford	www.kilmokea.com
Knockcree Gardens, Dublin	www.dublingardens.com
Lisnavagh Gardens, Co. Carlow	www.lisnavagh.com
Mount Usher Gardens, Co. Wicklow	www.mount-usher-gardens.com
National Botanical Gardens	www.irelandseye.com/visit/IG/glasnevin.html
Phoenix Park	www.iol.ie/resource
Powerscourt Estate	www.powerscourt.ie
Royal Parks of London	www.open.gov.uk/rp
Strokestown Park Garden, Co. Roscommon	www.strokestownpark.ie
The Garden of Europe, Co. Kerry	www.kerryweb.ie/gardeneurope/schiller.html

tourist attractions

ireland

Aillwee Cave	www.aillweecave.ie
Armagh Planetarium	www.armagh-planetarium.co.uk
Belfast Zoo	www.belfastzoo.co.uk
Birr Castle Demesne	www.birrcastle.com
Book of Kells	www.tcd.ie/Library/kells.htm
Castle Espie Wildfowl & Wetlands Centre	www.wwt.org.uk
Clonmacnoise & West Offaly Railway Bog Tour	www.bnm.ie
Colin Glen Forest Park	www.colinglentrust.org
Crag Cave, Co. Kerry	www.cragcave.com
Dingle Oceanworld Mara Beo, Co. Cork	www.dingle-oceanworld.ie
Dolphin Watch	www.dolphinwatch.ie
Drogheda Heritage Centre, Co. Louth	www.trailblazer.ie/droghedaheritage
Dublin Viking Adventure & Feast	www.visit.ie/Dublin/dublin_viking_adv.html
Dublin Zoo	www.dublinzoo.ie
Dunsink Observatory, Dublin	www.Dunsink.dias.ie
Fota Wildlife Park	www.fotawildlife.ie
Glendeer Open Farm, Co. Roscommon	www.glendeer.com
Irish Famine Memorial	www.irishfaminefund.ie
Irish Music Hall of Fame	www.imhf.com
Killarney Model Railway	www.themodelshop-ireland.com
Lagan Lookout Centre	www.laganside.com
Lough Neagh Discovery Centre	www.craigavon.gov.uk/discovery.htm
Lullymore Heritage Park, Co. Kildare	www.kildare.ie/tourism/lullymore
Michael Coleman Heritage Centre, Co. Sligo	www.colemanirishmusic.com
Millstreet Country Park	http://mlcp.foundmark.com
Muckross Traditional Farms	www.muckrosshouse.ie
National 1798 Visitor Centre	www.1798centre.com
National Sealife Centre, Bray	www.sealife.ie
Newgrange Open Farm, Co. Meath	www.newgrangefarm.com
North Down Heritage Centre	www.northdown.gov.uk/heritage
Old Jameson Distillery, Dublin	www.irish-whiskey-trail.com
Palace Stables Heritage Centre, Co. Armagh	www.armagh-visit.com/palace_stables.htm
Royal Tara Visitor Centre, Co. Galway	www.royal-tara.com

Sligo Folk Park	www.sligofolkpark.com
St. Patrick's Trian, Co. Armagh	www.armagh-visit.com/st_patrick's_trian.htm
Streamvale Open Farm	www.streamvale.com
Ulster American Folk Park	www.folkpark.com
Ulster Folk & Transport Museum	www.nidex.com/uftm
Ulster Plantation Centre	www.theflightoftheearlsexperience.com
Visitor Attractions Association of Northern Ireland	www.vaani.com
W5, Belfast	www.w5online.co.uk
West Cork Model Railway Village	www.clon.ie

rest of the world

Disneyland Paris	www.2000.disneylandparis.com
Disneyland, California	www.disney.go.com/disneyland
Disneyworld, Florida	www.disney.go.com/disneyworld
Eiffel Tower	www.paris.org/Monuments/Eiffel
Seaworld, Florida	www.seaworld.org
South African National Parks	www.ecoafrica.com/saparks
Suez Canal	www.suezcanal.com
Sydney Opera House	www.soh.nsw.gov.au
Teatro alla Scala	www.lascala.milano.it

united kingdom

Deep Sea World, Scotland	www.deepseaworld.com
London Eye	www.londoneye.com
Madame Tussaud's	www.madame-tussauds.com
Cadbury World	www.cadburyworld.co.uk

tourist information

britain and ireland

Access Ireland	www.visunet.ie
Belfast Tourist Information	www.gotobelfast.com
Bord Fáilte – Irish Tourist Board	www.ireland.travel.ie
British Hotel Reservations Centre	www.bhrc.co.uk
Destination Ireland	www.foundmark.com/ireland.html
English Tourism Council	www.englishtourism.co.uk
Go Ireland	www.goireland.ie
Information Britain	www.information-britain.co.uk
Ireland	www.shamrock.org
Ireland Vacations	www.irelandvacations.com
Irelands Blue Book	www.irelands-blue-book.ie
IrelandsEye	www.irelandseye.com
Irishguide	http://theirishguide.com
Local Ireland	www.local.ie

Northern Ireland Tourist Board	www.discovernorthernireland.com
Scotland	www.holiday.scotland.net
Temple Bar	www.temple-bar.ie
Travel Ireland	www.travelireland.org
Visit	www.visit.ie
Wales Tourist Information	www.tourism.wales.gov.uk

counties in ireland

Antrim	www.northantrim.com
Armagh	www.countyarmagh.com
Carlow	www.carlowtourism.com
Cavan	www.countycavan.com
Clare	www.clarelive.com
Cork	www.cork-guide.ie
Derry	www.derry.net
Donegal	www.donegal.ie
Down	www.totalireland.com/down
Dublin	www.visitdublin.com
Fermanagh	www.interknowledge.com/northern-ireland
Galway	www.galwaytourism.ie
Kerry	www.kerry-tourism.com
Kildare	www.kildare.ie
Kilkenny	www.kilkenny.ie
Laois	www.laois.ie
Leitrim	www.countyleitrim.com
Limerick	www.limerick.com
Longford	http://longford.local.ie
Louth	www.ebookireland.com/louth.htm
Mayo	www.mayo-ireland.ie
Meath	www.meathtourism.ie
Monaghan	www.county-monaghan.net/links/html
Offaly	www.totalireland.com/offaly
Roscommon	www.roscommon.ie
Sligo	www.sligo.ie
Tipperary	www.tipp.ie
Tyrone	www.totalireland.com/tyrone
Waterford Tourism	www.waterfordtourism.org
Westmeath	www.iol.ie/wmeathtc
Wexford Tourism	www.wexfordtourism.com
Wicklow	www.wicklow.ie

europe

Austria	www.austria-tourism.at
Belgium	www.belgium-tourism.com
Cyprus	www.cyprustourism.org
Denmark	www.dt.dk
Europe	www.europeonline.com
Finland	www.mek.fi

France	www.franceguide.com
Germany	www.germany-tourism.de
Gibraltar	www.gibraltar.gi
Grenada	www.grenada.org
Guernsey	www.gtonline.net
Hungary	www.hungarytourism.hu
Iceland	www.icetourist.is
Ireland	www.ireland.travel.ie
Italy	www.enit.it
Jersey	www.jtourism.com
Liechtenstein	www.news.li/touri
Luxembourg	www.luxembourg.co.uk
Malta	www.tourism.org.mt
Monaco	www.monaco.mc
Netherlands	www.goholland.co.uk
Norway	www.norway.org.uk
Poland	www.europeonline.com/pol/index_gb.htm
Portugal	www.portugal.org
Romania	www.turism.ro
Serbia	www.serbia-info.com/ntos
Slovenia	www.slovenia-tourism.si
Spain	www.travel-library.com/europe/spain
Stockholm	www.gotostockholm.com
Sweden	www.swetourism.org.uk
Switzerland	www.myswitzerland.com
Turkey	www.turkey.org/turkey

rest of the world

Antigua & Barbuda	www.antigua-barbuda.com
Argentina	www.wam.co./ar/tourism
Armenia	www.tourismarmenia.com
Australia	www.aussie.net.au
Bahamas	www.gobahamas.com
Barbados	www.barbados.org
Belize	www.travelbelize.org
Bermuda	www.bermudatourism.com
Brazil	www.embratur.gov.br
Caribbean	www.caribbean-travel.com
Cayman Islands	www.caymanislands.ky
China	www.cnta.com
Dominican Republic	www.ios.uk.com/domrep
Dubai	http://dubaitourism.co.ae
Egypt	www.touregypt.net
Falkland Islands	www.tourism.org.fk
Ghana	www.ghanatourism.com
Greenland	www.greenland-guide.gl
Hong Kong	www.hkta.org
India	www.indiatouristoffice.org

Iran	www.itto.org
Israel	www.infotour.co.il
Jamaica	www.jamaicatravel.com
Japan	www.jnto.go.jp
Jordan	www.jordan-online.com
Kenya	www.kenyatourism.org
Korea	www.knto.or.kr
Lebanon	www.lebannon-tourism.gov.lb
Malaysia	www.tourism.gov.my
Maldives	www.visitmaldives.com
Mauritius	www.mauritius.net
Mexico	www.mexico-travel.com
Morocco	www.tourism-in-morocco.com
Nepal	www.welcomenepal.com
New Zealand	www.purenz.com
Orlando	www.go2orlando.com
Pakistan	www.tourism.gov.pk
Philippines	www.tourism.gov.ph
Puerto Rico	www.prtourism.com
Québec	www.tourisme.gouv.qc.ca/mag/en
Russia	www.russia-travel.com
Seychelles	www.seychelles.demon.co.uk
Singapore	www.stb.com.sg
South Africa	www.satour.com
St Kitts & Nevis	www.interknowledge.com/stkitts-nevis
St Vincent & The Grenadines	www.stvincentandgrenadines.com
Syria	www.syriatourism.org
Tahiti	www.tahiti-tourisme.com
Thailand	www.tourismthailand.org
Tunisia	www.tourismtunisia.co.uk
Uganda	www.ugandaweb.com
Uruguay	www.turismo.gub.uy
USA (Massachusetts)	www.mass-vacation.com
USA (Utah)	www.utah.com
USA (Virgin Islands)	www.usvi.net
Venezuela	www.venezuela.com

towns & cities

Belfast	www.tourism.belfastcity.gov.uk
Blackpool	www.blackpooltourism.com
Brighton	www.brighton.co.uk
Bristol	www.brisindex.co.uk/tourism
Cambridge	www.cambridge.gov.uk/leisure
Chinatown London	www.fresco-web.co.uk/chinatown
Cork	www.cork-guide.ie
Dublin	www.visitdublin.com

Galway	www.galwaytourism.ie
Limerick	www.limerick.com
London	www.tourist.co.uk
Manchester	www.manchesteronline.co.uk
Stratford	www.stratford.co.uk
Waterford	www.waterfordtourism.org

web cams

Australia	http://dreamwater.com/live/webcams.html
Camvista	www.camvista.com
Dublin	www.nci.ie/ispy
Earthcam	www.earthcam.com
Ireland	www.ireland.travel.ie
Live View of Dublin/Ireland.com	www.ireland.com/dublin
Loch Ness	www.lochness.scotland.net/index.cfm
Northern Ireland	www.niinternet.com/avcontent/webcams.html
Oxford Circus, London	www.fujiint.co.uk/street
Paris	http://www-compat.tf1.fr/livecam
Perth, Australia	http://perthcam.bankwest.com.au
Realtime Tokyo	http://info.nttls.co.jp/webcam/index.html
Statue of Liberty	www.sccorp.com/cam
Sydney	www.viewsydney.com.au
Webcam Central	www.camcentral.com
Worldcam	www.fat.co.uk/world/worldset10.html

science and nature

astronomy & space
conservation & nature
magazines & websites
places
societies and institutions
wildlife & animals
zoos, wildlife parks and aquaria

science and nature

astronomy & space

Armagh Observatory	http://star.arm.ac.uk
Armagh Planetarium	www.armagh-planetarium.co.uk
Astronomy	www.astronomy.com
Astronomy for Kids	www.dustbunny.com/afk/
Astronomy Ireland	www.astronomy.ie
Birr Castle Telescope	www.birrcastle.com/birr/astronomy
British Astronomical Association	www.cam.ac.uk/~baa
Campaign for Dark Skies	www.dark-skies.freeserve.co.uk
Cork Astronomy Club	http://indigo.ie/~chas/astronomy.html
Crawford Observatory	www.astro.ucc.ie/obs
Dunsink University	www.dunsink.dias.ie
Greenwich Mean Time	http://greenwichmeantime.com
Hubble Telescope	www.stsci.edu
Leicester University Astronomy Society	www.star.le.ac.uk/astrosoc/
NASA	www.nasa.gov
National Space Centre	http://nssc.star.le.ac.uk
Royal Astronomical Society	www.ras.org.uk
Sky at Night	www.bbc.co.uk/skyatnight
TCD Astronomy Society	www.csc.tcd.ie/~tass/
Virtual Solar System	www.solarsystem.12s.com

conservation & nature

Bord Iascaigh Mhara	www.bim.ie
Bord Na Mòna	www.bnm.ie
British Association of Nature Conservationists	www.greenchannel.com/banc/
British Trust for Conservation Volunteers	www.btcv.org
Coillte	www.coillte.ie
Countryside Agency	www.countryside.gov.uk
Crann	www.crann.ie
Earthwatch	www.uk.earthwatch.org
ENFO	www.enfo.ie
English Nature	www.english-nature.org.uk
Fauna & Flora International	www.fauna-flora.org
Flora Locale	www.floralocale.org
Friends of the Earth	www.foe.co.uk
Frontier Conservation	www.frontierprojects.ac.uk
Green Links	www.green-links.co.uk
Greenpeace	www.greenpeace.org
Hanson Environment Fund	www.hansonenvfund.org
International Conservation	

Awareness Network	www.ican21.org.uk
Irish African/Asian Conservation & Wildlife Trust	www.cyberhouse.ie/iaacwt
Irish Charr Conservation Group	www.charr.org
Irish Peatland Conservation Council	www.ipcc.ie
John Muir Trust	www.jmt.org
Joint Nature Conservation Committee	www.jncc.gov.uk
National Association of Regional Game Councils	www.nargc.ie
National Garden Exhibition Centre	www.clubi.ie/calumet
National Trust (UK)	www.ntenvironment.com
Native Woodland Trust	www.nativewoodtrust.ie
Natural Resources Institute	www.nri.org
Naturenet	www.naturenet.net
Open Spaces Society	www.oss.org.uk
Plant Life	www.plantlife.org.uk
Rainforest Action Network	www.ran.org
Royal Botanic Gardens	www.rbgkew.org.uk
Royal Society for Nature Conservation	www.rsnc.org
Society for Underwater Exploration	www.underwaterdiscovery.org
Soil Association	www.soilassociation.org
Tree Register	www.tree-register.org
United Kingdom Institute for Conservation	www.ukic.org.uk
Waterways Trust	www.thewaterwaystrust.com
Wildfowl & Wetlands Trust	www.wwt.org.uk
World Land Trust	www.worldlandtrust.org

magazines & websites

Irish Animals	www.irishanimals.com
Waterford Wildlife	www.waterfordwildlife.com
Wild Ireland	www.wildireland.ie

places

Aillwee Caves	www.aillweecave.ie
Birr Castle	www.birrcastle.com
Cliffs of Moher	www.shannonheritage.com/CliffsofMoher
Dingle Peninsula	www.dingle-peninsula.ie
The Burren	www.irelandmidwest.com/Theburren.htm

societies and institutions

British Antarctic Survey	www.antartica.ac.uk
British Geological Survey	www.bgs.ac.uk
British Horological Institute	www.bhi.co.uk
British Met Office	www.meto.gov.uk

British UFO Research Association	www.bufora.org.uk
Central Science Laboratory	www.csl.gov.uk
Cern	www.cern.ch
Council for Science & Technology	www.cst.gov.uk
Crann	www.crann.ie
Duchas	www.heritagedata.ie
Earthwatch	www.uk.earthwatch.org
ENFO	www.enfo.ie
Engineering & Physical Sciences Research Council	www.epsrc.ac.uk
English Nature	www.english-nature.org.uk
Environmental Protection Agency	www.epa.ie
Fauna & Flora International	www.ffi.org.uk
Field Studies Council	www.field-studies-council.org
Flora Locale	www.floralocale.org
Friends of the Earth	www.foe.co.uk
Geological Society	www.geolsoc.org.uk
Geological Survey of Ireland	www.gsi.ie
Greenpeace	www.greenpeace.org
Health & Safety Authority	www.hsa.ie
Information Society Commission	www.isc.ie
Institute of Broadcast Sound	www.ibs.org.uk
Institute of Hydrology	www.nwl.ac.uk/ih
Irish Family History Foundation	www.irishroots.net
Irish Organisation for Geographic information	www.irlogi.ie
Irish Peatland Conservation Council	www.ipcc.ie
Irish Science Centres Association Network	www.iscan.ie
Irish Science Teachers Association	http://indigo.ie/~istasec
Met Eireann	www.met.ie
National Council for Forest Research & Development	www.coford.ie
National Garden Exhibition Centre	www.clubi.ie/calumet
National Information Server	www.heanet.ie
National Trust	www.nationaltrust.org.uk
Native Woodland Trust	www.nativewoodtrust.ie
Natural Resources Institute Tree Register	www.nri.org
Office of Science & Technology	www.dti.gov.uk/ost
Plant Life	www.plantlife.org.uk
Radiological Protection Institute of Ireland	www.rpii.ie
Rainforest Action Network	www.ran.org
Royal Botanic Gardens	www.rbgkew.org.uk
Royal Entomological Society	www.royensoc.demon.co.uk
Royal Geographical Society	www.rgs.org
Royal Society of Chemistry	www.rsc.org
RSPB	www.rspb.org.uk

Society for Experimental Biology	www.demon.co.uk/SEB
Society for Underwater Exploration	www.underwaterdiscovery.org

wildlife & animals

Amateur Entomologists' Society	www.theaes.org
Birdlife International	www.birdlife.net
Birds Ireland	www.birdsireland.com
Birdwatch (South Dublin)	www.birdweb.ie
British Beekeepers Association	www.bbka.org.uk
British Ornithologists' Union	www.bou.org.uk
Cork Bat Group	www.irishanimals.com/wildlife/16.html
Dublin Society for the Prevention of Cruelty to Animals	www.dspca.ie
Irish Marine Institute	www.marine.ie
Irish Seal Society	www.irishsealsanctuary.com
Irish Whale and Dolphin Group	http://iwdg.ucc.ie
Irish Wildbird Conservancy	www.birdwatchireland.ie
Irish Wildlife Trust	www.iwt.ie
Jane Goodall Institute	www.janegoodall.org
Mammal Society	www.abdn.ac.uk/mammal
Mammals Trust UK	www.mammalstrustuk.org
National Bird of Prey Centre	www.appsearch.com/nbpc
Northern Ireland Bat Group	www.batgroup.fsnet.co.uk
Primate Society of Great Britain	www.psgb.org
Royal Society for the Prevention of Cruelty to Animals	www.rspca.org.uk
Royal Society for the Protection of Birds	www.rspb.org.uk
UK Safari	www.uksafari.com
Waterford Wildlife	www.waterfordwildlife.com
Whale Foundation	www.whale-foundation.org
Wild Ireland	www.wildireland.ie
Wildlife News	www.naturalworldtours.co.uk
Wildlife Trusts	www.wildlifetrusts.org
Wildlifeline	www.wildlifeline.org
WWF International	www.panda.org
Zoological Society of London	www.zsl.org

zoos, wildlife parks and aquaria

Belfast Zoo	www.belfastzoo.co.uk
Blackpool Zoo	www.blackpool.gov.uk/zoo
Bristol Zoo	www.bristolzoo.org.uk
Chester Zoo	www.demon.co.uk/chesterzoo
Colchester Zoo	www.colchester-zoo.uk
Dingle OceanWorld	www.dingle-oceanworld.ie
Dublin Zoo	www.dublinzoo.ie
Dudley Zoo	www.dudleyzoo.org.uk
Edinburgh Zoo	www.edinburghzoo.org.uk

Fota Wildlife Park	www.fotawildlife.ie
Galway Atlantaquaria	http://homepage.tinet.ie ~atlantaquaria
Glasgow Zoo	http://glasgowzoo.topcities.com/
Howletts Wild Animal Park	www.howletts.net
Knowsley Safari Park	www.knowsley.com
Lahinch Sea World	www.lahinchseaworld.com
London Zoo	www.londonzoo.co.uk
Longleat Safari Park	www.longleat.co.uk
Marwell	www.marwell.org.uk
Paignton	www.paigntonzoo.demon.co.uk
Paradise Wildlife Park	www.pwpark.com
Sealife	www.sealife.ie
Twycross	www.timellis.demon.co.uk/tza.htm
West Midlands Safari Park	www.wmsp.co.uk
Whipsnade	www.londonzoo.co.uk/whipsnade
Willersmill Wildlife Park	www.sprout.demon.co.uk/Willersmill.html

shopping

antiques & auctions
books
cars
clothes
computer & electrical retailers
cosmetics & perfumes
department stores
flowers
food & supermarkets
furniture & housewares
gifts & stationery
healthcare, beauty & personal hygiene
home entertainment
irish goods
jewellers
magazines & websites
mother & baby
music, games & video
photography
shoes & accessories
shopping centres
specialist
sports & outdoor
tobacco
toys
watches

shopping

antiques & auctions

Ancient Art	www.ancientart.co.uk
Antique Dealers Directory	www.antique-dealers-directory.co.uk
Antique Shopping Mall	www.antiqueshoppingmall.com
Antiques Ireland	www.antiquesireland.com
Christie's	www.christies.com
de Veres Art Auctions	www.deveresart.com
eBid	www.ebid.ie
French Warehouse	www.french-warehouse.com
Irish Antique Dealers Association	www.antique.collectors-on-line.com
Irish Antiques Online Directory	www.irishantiquesonline.com
Irish Collector	www.irishcollector.com
Kennedy Wolfenden & Co	www.antiquesni.co.uk
Military & Historical	www.militaryandhistorical.co.uk
Olympia Fine Art & Antiques Fairs	www.olympia-antiques.co.uk
QXL.com	www.qxl.com
Sarah Rose Antiques	www.srantiques.co.uk
Sothebys	www.sothebys.com
Whyte's	www.whytes.ie

books

Abebooks	www.abebooks.com
Amazon	www.amazon.co.uk
Barnes & Noble	www.barnesandnoble.com
BBC Shop	www.bbcshop.com
Bigsave.com	www.bigsave.com
Blackwell's	www.blackwells.co.uk
Bol	www.bol.com
Book Centre	www.kilkennybookcentre.com
Booknest	www.booknest.ie
Books Ulster	www.booksulster.com
Books Unlimited	www.booksunlimited.ie
Books Upstairs	www.booksirish.com
Bookshop at Queen's	www.queensbookshop.co.uk
BooksIrish.com	http://booksirish.com
Bookworm.ie	www.bookworm.ie
Borders	www.borders.com
Dorling Kindersley	www.dk.com/uk
Eason & Son	www.easons.com
Greene's Bookshop	www.greenesbookshop.com
Hammicks	www.thebookplace.com
Healy Rare Books	www.healyrarebooks.com
Hughes & Hughes	www.hughesbooks.com
Internet Bookshop	www.bookshop.co.uk
Irish Film Centre	www.fii.ie

Kennys Bookshop	www.kennys.ie
Keohanes Bookshops	www.bookshop.ie
Killarney Book Shop	www.killarneybookshop.ie
Kogan Page	www.kogan-page.co.uk
Mercier Press	www.mercier.ie
Modern Languages	www.modlang.ie
Murder Ink	www.eclipse.ie/murderink
National Gallery of Ireland	www.nationalgallery.ie
Penguin	www.penguin.co.uk
Powells	www.powells.com
The Stationery Office	www.thestationeryoffice.com
Veritas	www.veritas.ie
Waterstones	www.waterstones.co.uk
WH Smith	www.whsmith.co.uk

cars

accessories & repairs

Alpine Electronics	www.alpine1.com
Audioseek	www.audioseek.com
Autoglass	www.autoglass.co.uk
Duckworth	www.duckworth.co.uk
Halfords	www.halfords.co.uk
Kenwood	www.kenwoodcorp.com
Kwik-Fit	www.kwik-fit.com
Michelin	www.michelin.com
Motor Sport and Spares	www.motorsportandspares.com
National Tyres	www.national.co.uk
New Reg Personalised Registration Numbers	www.reg.co.uk
Performance Alloys	www.performancealloys.com
Pirelli	www.pirelli.co.uk
Roaduser	www.roaduser.co.uk
Tracker	www.tracker-network.co.uk
Trafficmaster	www.trafficmaster.co.uk
Unipart	www.unipart.co.uk

magazines and websites

Auto Exchange	www.autoexchange.co.uk
Auto Trader	www.autotrader.ie
BBC Top Gear	www.topgear.com
Buy and Sell	www.buyandsell.net
Car	www.carmagazine.co.uk
Car Buyers Guide	www.cbg.ie
Classic Motor	www.classicmotor.co.uk
Irish Classic Car Collection	www.irishclassiccars.com
Society of the Irish Motor Industry	www.simi.ie
WebCar 2000	www.webcar2000.com/countries/ireland

manufacturers

Alfa Romeo	www.alfaromeo.ie

Aston Martin	www.astonmartin.com
Audi Ireland	www.audi.ie
BMW Ireland	www.bmw.ie
Chevrolet	www.chevrolet.com
Chrysler	www.chrysler.co.uk
Citroën	www.citroen.ie
Daewoo	www.daewoo.ie
Delorean	www.delorean.com
Dodge	www.4adodge.com
Ferrari	www.ferrari.com
Fiat	www.fiat.ie
Ford	www.ford.ie
General Motors	www.gm.com
Honda	www.honda.co.uk
Hyundai	www.hyundai-car.co.uk
Isuzu	www.isuzu.com
Jaguar	www.jaguar.com
Jeep	www.jeep.co.uk
Lamborghini	www.lamborghini.com
Land Rover	www.landrover.com
Lexus	www.lexus.ie
Lotus	www.lotuscars.co.uk
Maserati	www.maserati.it/enghome.htm
Mazda	www.mazda.co.uk
Mercedes Benz	www.mercedes-benz.com
Mini	www.mini.co.uk
Mitsubishi	www.mitsubishi-cars.co.uk
Morgan	www.morgan-motor.co.uk
Nissan	www.nissan.ie
Opel	www.opel.ie
Peugeot	www.peugeot.ie
Pontiac	www.pontiac.com
Porsche	www.porsche.com
Renault	www.renault.ie
Rolls Royce	www.rolls-royceandbentley.co.uk
Rover	www.rovercars.com
Saab	www.saab.com
Subaru	www.subaru.co.uk
Suzuki	www.suzuki.co.uk
Toyota	www.toyota.ie
TVR	www.tvr-eng.co.uk
Vauxhall	www.vauxhall.co.uk
Volkswagen	www.volkswagen.ie
Volvo	www.volvo.com

clothes

A Wear	www.a-wear.ie
Adams Childrens Wear	www.adamschildrenswear.com
Armani	www.armaniexchange.com

Avoca Handweavers	www.avoca.ie
Benetton	www.benetton.com
Bigsave.com	www.bigsave.com
Blacktie	www.blacktie.ie
Burtons	www.burtonmenswear.co.uk
Diesel	www.diesel.co.uk
DKNY	www.donnakaran.com
Dorothy Perkins	www.dorothyperkins.co.uk
Etam	www.etam.co.uk
Evans	www.evans.ltd.uk
Freemans	www.freemans.co.uk
French Connection	www.frenchconnection.com
Gap	www.gap.com
H&M Hennes	www.hm.com
High & Mighty	www.highandmighty.co.uk
Hobo	http://hoboclothing.com
Home Shopping Channel	www.shop-tv.co.uk
Jaeger	www.jaeger.co.uk
Jeffrey Rogers	www.jeffrey-rogers.co.uk
Jigsaw	www.jigsaw-online.co.uk
Karen Millen	www.karenmillen.co.uk
Kays	www.kaysnet.com
Kilkenny	www.kilkennygroup.com
La Redoute	www.redoute.co.uk
Levi's	www.eu.levi.com
Louis Copeland	www.louiscopeland.com
Mango	www.mango.es
Marks & Spencer	www.marksandspencer.com
Monsoon	www.monsoon.co.uk
Moschino	www.moschino.it
Moss Bros	www.mossbros.co.uk
Muji	www.muji.co.jp
New Look	www.newlook.co.uk
Next	www.next.co.uk
Oasis	www.oasis-stores.com
Pamela Scott	www.pamelascott.ie
Paul Smith	www.paulsmith.co.uk
Penneys	www.penneys.ie
Pepe Jeans	www.pepejeans.com
Principles	www.principles.co.uk
Red or Dead	www.redordead.co.uk
River Island	www.riverisland.com
Sasha	www.sasha.ie
Thomas Pink	www.thomaspink.co.uk
Tie Rack	www.tie-rack.co.uk
Tommy Hilfiger	www.tommypr.com
Top Man	www.topman.co.uk
Topshop	www.tops.co.uk
Vero Moda	www.veromoda.dk
Victoria's Secret	www.victoriassecret.com

Vila	www.vila.dk
Virgin Clothing	www.virginclothing.co.uk
Wrangler	www.wrangler.com

computer & electrical retailers

Advantage	www.advantage.ie
Apex	www.apex.ie
Apple	www.apple.ie
Avida Online	www.avida.ie
Beyond 2000	www.beyond2000.ie
Bigsave.com	www.bigsave.com
Carphone Warehouse	www.carphonewarehouse.ie
Cellular World	www.cellularworld.ie
Cometstore Ireland	www.cometstore.ie
Compaq	www.compaq.ie
Compustore	www.compustore.ie
Dabs	www.dabs.com
DCBGroup	www.dcbgroup.ie
Dell	www.dell.ie
Direct Memory International	www.dmi.ie
Dixons	www.dixons.co.uk
Duracell	www.duracell.com
Eircell	www.eircell.ie
Electronics Boutique	www.ebstore.com
Ever Ready	www.everready.co.uk
Evesham Micros	www.evesham.com
Game	www.game-retail.co.uk
Gateway	www.gateway2000.ie
Hewlett Packard	www.hp.com
InfoLive	www.techcentral.ie
Jaguar Computers	www.jaguarcompsys.ie
Jungle	www.jungle.com
Laser Computers	www.laser-computers.ie
Learning Store.co.uk	www.LearningStore.co.uk
Lets Talk Phones	www.letstalkphones.ie
Maplin	www.maplin.co.uk
Marx Computers	www.marx-computer.com
Online IT	www.onlineit.com
PC Source	www.pcsource.ie
PC Superstore	www.pcsuperstore.ie
PC World	www.pcworld.co.uk
Peats	www.peats.ie
PFH Computers	www.pfh.ie
Power City	www.powercity.ie
QVCUK.com	www.qvcuk.com
Scan (Mail order)	www.scan.co.uk
Tempo	www.tempo.co.uk
Time	www.timecomputers.com

cosmetics & perfumes

Avon	www.uk.avon.com
Barry M	www.barrym.co.uk
Beauty.com	www.beauty.com
BeneFit	www.benefitcosmetics.com
Bobbi Brown	www.bobbibrowncosmetics.com
Body Shop	www.thebodyshop.co.uk
Boots	www.boots.co.uk
Chanel	www.chanel.com
Clarins	www.clarins-paris.com
Clinique	www.clinique.com
Color Me Beautiful	www.colorme.com
Dior	www.dior.com
Elizabeth Arden	www.elizabetharden.com
Estée Lauder	www.esteelauder.com
Fragrances of Ireland	www.perfume.ie
Givenchy	www.givenchy.com
Goodebodies	www.goodebodies.com
Gucci	www.gucci.com
Hugo Boss	www.hugo.com
Issey Miyake	www.isseymiyake.com
Jean Paul Gaultier	www.jpgaultier.fr
L'Oréal	www.lorealparis.com
Lacoste	www.lacoste.com/index_uk.htm
Lancaster	www.lancaster-beauty.com
Lancôme	www.lancome.com
Lush	www.lush.co.uk
Max Factor	www.maxfactor.com
Miners	www.miners.co.uk
Oil of Olay	www.olay.com
Paco Rabanne	www.pacorabanne.com
QVCUK.com	www.qvcuk.com
Revlon	www.revlon.com
Stila	www.stila.net
Tommy Hilfiger	www.tommypr.com
Urban Decay	www.urbandecay.com
Yves Saint Laurent	www.yslonline.com

department stores

Argos	www.argos.co.uk
Arnotts	www.arnotts.ie
Bhs	www.bhs.co.uk
Bloomingdale's	www.bloomingdales.com
Clerys	www.clerys.ie
Debenhams	www.debenhams.co.uk
Dunnes Stores	www.dunnes.ie
Fortnum & Mason	www.fortnumandmason.co.uk

Harrods	www.harrods.com
Home Shopping Channel	www.shop-tv.co.uk
House of Fraser	www.houseoffraser.co.uk
Index	www.indexshop.com
John Lewis	www.johnlewis.co.uk
Liberty	www.liberty-of-london.com
Macy's	www.macys.com
Marks & Spencer	www.marksandspencer.com
QVCUK.com	www.qvcuk.com
Selfridges	www.selfridges.co.uk
Woolworths	www.woolworths.co.uk

flowers

A1 Rosary Florists	www.irishflorist.com
Blooms and Balloons	www.bloomsandballoons.ie
Blooms Worldwide	www.bloomsworldwide.com
Ferguson Flowers International	www.fergusonflowers.co.uk
Flora	www.flora.ie
Florabunda	www.florabunda.ie
Flowers By Lucy	www.flowersbylucy.ie
Flowers Direct	www.flowersdirect.co.uk
Flowers Ireland	www.flowers.ie
Interflora	www.interflora.co.uk
Justyne Flowers	www.flowers.ie/flowers/dublin
Sheilas Flower Shop	www.sheilas.ie

food & supermarkets

Aldi	www.aldi-stores.co.uk
Centra	www.centra.ie
Co-op	www.co-op.co.uk
Dunnes Stores	www.dunnesstores.com
FoodIreland	www.foodireland.com
Heinz Direct	www.heinz-direct.co.uk
Iceland	www.iceland.co.uk
Mace	www.mace.ie
Marks & Spencer	www.marks-and-spencer.co.uk
Organics Direct	www.organicsdirect.com
Sainsbury's	www.sainsburys.co.uk
Somerfield	www.somerfield.co.uk
Spar	www.spar.co.uk
Spar Ireland	www.spar.ie
Super Valu	www.supervalu.ie
Superquinn	www.superquinn.ie
Tesco	www.tesco.ie

furniture & housewares

Allied Carpets	www.alliedcarpets.com
Amtico	www.amtico.co.uk

Argus Living	www.living.ie
Assetts Furniture	www.assetsfurniture.com
Axminster	www.axminster-carpets.co.uk
Bedsdirect	www.bedsdirect.ie
Belleek Pottery	www.belleek.ie
Bigsave.com	www.bigsave.com
Buy4Now	www.buy4now.ie
Carpetright	www.carpetright.co.uk
Conran Shop	www.conran.co.uk
Courts	www.courts.co.uk
Creative Wood Fittings	www.creativewood.ie
Dulux Paints Ireland	www.dulux.ie
Flanagan's of Buncrana	www.theflanagan.com
Furniture.ie	www.furniture.ie
FurnitureIreland.com	www.furnitureireland.com
Habitat	www.habitat.net
Hickeys	www.celticlinks.com
Ikea	www.ikea.com
Intersaver.co.uk	www.intersaver.co.uk
Irish Linen Company	www.irishlinenco.com
Irish Trading Co.	www.irishtrading.co.uk
Klimmeck Henderson	www.klimmek-henderson.com
Libris	www.libris.ie
Ligne Roset	www.ligne-roset-usa.com
McCarthy ScanHaus Furniture	www.mccarthy-scanhaus.ie
Ovne Antique Stoves	www.ovnestoves.com
Purves & Purves	www.purves.co.uk
Royal Doulton	www.royal-doulton.com
Sleep Council	www.sleepcouncil.org.uk
Slumberland	www.slumberland.co.uk
The Garden Shop	www.thegardenshop.co.uk
The Holding Company	www.theholdingcompany.co.uk
Waterford Crystal	www.waterford-usa.com
Wedgewood	www.wedgewood.co.uk
Wesley Barrell	www.wesley-barrell.co.uk
World of Leather	www.worldofleather.co.uk

gifts & stationery

All Occasions	www.alloccasions.ie
Amazing Days	www.amazingdays.com
Astrix Promotions	www.astrix.ie
BabyBabóg	www.babybabog.com
Dial a Gift	www.dialagift.net
Hallmark Cards	www.hallmark.com
IBGifts	www.ibgifts.com
Lastminute.com	www.lastminute.com
Red Letter Days	www.redletterdays.co.uk
Shop Irish	www.shopirish.com
Slainte Online	www.slainteonline.com
Tierneys Gift Shops	www.tierneysgiftshops.com

Voucher Express	www.voucherexpress.com

healthcare, beauty & personal hygiene

Aquafresh	www.aquafresh.co.uk
BaByliss	www.babyliss.co.uk
Bic	www.bicworld.com
Bodyform	www.bodyform.co.uk
Boots	www.wellbeing.com
Braun	www.braun.com
Cibavision	www.cibavision.co.uk
Colgate	www.colgate.com
Durex	www.durex.com
Eirpharm	www.eirpharm.com
Fiacla	www.fiacla.ie
Gillette	www.gillette.com
L'Oréal	www.loreal.com
Lanes	www.laneshealth.com
Naturalife	www.naturalife.ie
Nature's Way	www.naturesway.ie
Nelsons	www.nelsons.co.uk
Nicorette	www.nicorette.co.uk
Nicotinell	www.nicotinell.co.uk
Nivea	www.nivea.com
Nurofen	www.nurofen.co.uk
Nutkeg	www.thenutkeg.ie
Oral B	www.oralb.com
Pantene	www.pantene.com
Rennie	www.rennie.co.uk
Seavite	www.seavite.ie
Seven Seas	www.seven-seas.ltd.uk
Shophere	www.shophere.ie
Solgar	www.solgar.com
Strepsils	www.strepsils.com
Tampax	www.tampax.com
ThinkNatural	www.thinknatural.com
Tisserand Aromatherapy	www.tisserand.com
Vitabiotics	www.vitabiotics.com
Weleda	www.weleda.co.uk
Wella	www.wella.co.uk
Wilkinson Sword	www.wilkinson-sword.co.uk

home entertainment

Aiwa	www.aiwa.com
Akai	www.akai.com
Alpine	www.alpine-europe.com
Bang & Olufson	www.bang-olufsen.com
Beyond Hi-Fi	www.beyondhifi.com
Hitachi	www.hitachi.com

Home Shopping Channel	www.shop-tv.co.uk
Intersaver.co.uk	www.intersaver.co.uk
JVC	www.jvc-europe.com
Marantz	www.marantz.com
Nakisha	www.nakisahifi.com
Peats	www.peats.ie
Phillips	www.phillips.com
Pioneer	www.pioneer-eur.com
Power City	www.powercity.ie
Richer Sounds	www.richersounds.ie
Sharp	www.sharp.co.uk
Sony	www.sony.com
Technics	www.technics.com

irish goods

Avoca Handweavers	www.avoca.ie
Blarney Woollen Mills	www.blarney.ie
Carraig Donn	www.carraigdonn.com
Carroll's Irish Gifts and Souvenirs	www.carrollsirishgifts.com
Custy's Traditional Music Shop	www.custysmusic.com
Dunn's of Dublin	www.dunns.ie
Gaeltarra Knitwear	www.gaeltarra.ie
House of Ireland	www.houseofireland.com
Irelands Eye Knitwear	www.ieknit.com
Irish Food Store	www.traditionalirishfoods.com
Irish Shopping	www.weshop.ie
Irishop.com	http://irishop.com
Kilkenny	www.kilkennygroup.com

jewellers

A Hartmann & Son Ltd	www.hartmanns.ie
All Claddagh	www.allcladdagh.com
Asprey & Garrard	www.asprey-garrard.com
Cartier	www.cartier.com
Claddagh Jewellers	www.claddaghjewellers.com
Dublin Gold	http://dublingold.com
Ernest Jones	www.ernestjones.co.uk
H Samuel	www.hsamuel.co.uk
Home Shopping Channel	www.shop-tv.co.uk
James O'Connor Jewellers	www.jsocjewellers.ie
Longines	www.longines.com
Martin's Jewellers	www.martinsjewellers.com
McGivneys	www.mcgivneys.com
Montrose Jewellers	www.montrosejewellers.com
QVCUK.com	www.qvcuk.com
Royal Claddagh	www.claddagh.com
Seymour Jewellers	www.seymour.ie
Tiffany	www.tiffany.com
Weir and Sons	www.weirsofireland.com

magazines & websites

Buy and Sell	www.buyandsell.net
Consumer Choice	www.consumerassociation.ie/choice.html
ConsumerLine	www.consumerline.org
European Consumer Centre	www.ecic.ie
Exchange & Mart	www.exchangeandmart.co.uk
Inshop.com	www.inshop.com
Loot	www.loot.com
Office of the Director of Consumer Affairs	www.odca.ie
Shops on the Net	www.sotn.co.uk
Which?	www.which.net

mother & baby

Avent	www.avent.co.uk
Babies 'R' Us	www.babiesrus.co.uk
Babog Knitwear	www.babogknitwear.com
Bébé Confort	www.bebeconfort.com
Blooming Marvellous	www.bloomingmarvellous.co.uk
Britax	www.britax.co.uk
Chicco	www.chiccousa.com
Cosatto	www.cosatto.com
Graco	www.gracobaby.com
Huggies	www.huggies.com
Irish Childbirth Trust (Cuidiú)	www.cuidiu-ict.ie
Johnson's	www.yourbaby.com
Klippan	www.klippan.co.uk
Mamamondo	www.mamamondo.com
Mamas & Papas	www.mamasandpapas.co.uk
Mothercare	www.mothercare.com
National Childbirth Trust	www.nct-online.org
Pampers	www.pampers.com
Real Nappy Association	www.realnappy.com
Tony Kealy's Baby Products	www.tonykealys.com
Urchin	www.urchin.co.uk

music, games & video

Bigsave.com	www.bigsave.com
Blackstar	www.blackstar.co.uk
Britannia Music Club	www.britmusic.co.uk
CD Now	www.cdnow.com
CD Paradise	www.cdparadise.cjb.net
Celtic Note	www.celticnote.ie
Charles Byrne Musick Instrumente	www.charlesbyrne.com
DMGDirect	www.dmgdirect.com
DVDplus	www.dvdplus.co.uk
Electronic Boutique	www.ebstore.com

Game	www.game-retail.co.uk
Gameplay	www.gameplay.com
Gamestop	www.gamestop.com
Golden Discs	www.goldendiscs.ie
HMV	www.hmv.com
Jungle.com	www.jungle.com
Music & Games	www.musicandgames.com
Music City	www.musiccity.ie
Music Ireland	www.musicireland.com
Nice Price	www.niceprice.net
Our Price	www.ourprice.co.uk
Tower Records	www.towerrecords.co.uk
Virgin Megastore	www.virginmega.com
WH Smith	www.whsmithonline.co.uk

photography

Cork Camera Repair Services	http://www.camerarepairs.ie
The Camera Shop	www.thecamerashop.ie/
Dixons	www.dixons.co.uk
Dublin Camera Exchange	http://www.cameraexchange.ie
Fahy Photo	www.fahyfoto.com/
Photographics Repair Services	http://www.prs.ie
Staunton's Camera Centre	http://www.stauntons.ie

shoes & accessories

Birkenstock	www.birkenstock.co.uk
Carl Scarpa	www.carlscarpa.com
Clarks	www.clarks.co.uk
Dolcis	www.dolcis.co.uk
Jones Bootmaker	www.jonesbootmaker.com
Louis Vuitton	www.vuitton.com
Pied a Terre	www.piedaterre.com
Samsonite	www.samsonite.com
Schuh	www.schuh.co.uk
Skechers	www.skechers.com
Timberland	www.timberland.com

shopping centres

Arnotts	www.arnotts.ie
Blanchardstown Shopping Centre	www.blanchardstowncentre.ie
Bluewater	www.bluewater.co.uk
Buttercrane Shopping Centre	www.buttercraneshopping.co.uk
Covent Garden	www.coventgardenmarket.com
Cribbs Causeway	www.cribbs-causeway.co.uk
Eyre Square Shopping Centre	www.eyresquarecentre.com
Forestside	www.forestside.co.uk
Foyleside	www.foyleside.co.uk
Galleria Outlet Centre	www.factory-outlets.co.uk

Golden Island Shopping Centre	www.goldenislandsc.com
Jervis Shopping Centre	www.jervis.ie
Lake Point Retail Park	www.lakepointpark.com
Outlet Centres International	www.outletcentres.com
Shops on the Net	www.sotn.co.uk
St. Stephen's Green Shopping Centre	www.stephensgreen.com

specialist

Ann Summers	www.annsummers.com
Anything Left Handed	www.anythingleft-handed.co.uk
Gadget Shop	www.gadgetshop.com
Green People	www.greenpeople.org
Innovations	www.innovations.co.uk
Left Hand	www.thelefthand.com
Oxfam Ireland	www.oxfamireland.org

sports & outdoor

Allsports	www.allsportsretail.co.uk
Blacks	www.blacks.co.uk
Camping Ireland	campingireland.com
Champion Sports	www.champion.ie
Eirsport	www.eirsport.com
JD Sports	www.jdsports.co.uk
JJB Sports	www.jjb.co.uk
Lifestyle Sports	www.lss21.com
Lowe Alpine	www.thealpineshop.ie
McGuirks Golf	www.mcguirksgolf.com
Millets Online	www.millets.co.uk
Snow & Rock	www.snowandrock.com DOWN
Stauntons & Elverys Sports Store	www.stauntonsintersport.com
Gaelweb	www.gaelweb.com

tobacco

Davidoff	www.davidoff.com
Rizla	www.rizla.co.uk

toys

Action Man	www.actionman.com
Barbie	www.barbie.com
Beanie Babies	www.eurobeanie.co.uk
Bigsave.com	www.bigsave.com
Corgi	www.corgi.co.uk
Crayola	www.crayola.com
E-Toys	www.etoys.co.uk
Early Learning Centre	www.earlylearningcentre.co.uk
Fisher Price	www.fisher-price.com
Furby.com	www.furby.com
Game Store	www.tgs.co.uk
Hamleys	www.hamleys.co.uk
Hasbro	www.hasbro.com
Hobbycraft	www.hobbycraft.co.uk

Hornby	www.hornby.co.uk
Knex	www.knex.co.uk
Lego	www.lego.com
Little Tikes	www.rubbermaid.com/littletikes
Matchbox	www.matchboxtoys.com
Mattel	www.mattel.com
Meccano	www.meccano.co.uk
Playmobil	www.playmobil.com
Pokémon	www.pokemon.com
Scalextric	www.scalextric.co.uk
Smyth's Toys	www.toys.ie
Tiger Toys	www.tigertoys.co.uk
Tomy	www.tomy.co.uk
Toy City	www.toycity.com
Toys 'R' Us	www.toysrus.co.uk
Toys-n-Ireland	www.ireland-now.com/toys
TP Activity Toys	www.tptoys.com

watches

Baume & Mercier	www.baume-et-mercier.com
Breitling	www.breitling.com
Casio	www.casio.co.uk
Citizen	www.citizenwatch.com
G-Shock	www.g-shock.ie
Longines	www.longines.com
Omega	www.omega.ch
Rotary	www.rotarywatches.com
Seiko	www.seiko.co.uk
Sekonda	www.sekonda.com
Swatch	www.swatch.com
Timex	www.timex.com
Tissot	www.bme.es/tissot/ingles

sport

american football
athletics
basketball
boating
bowls
climbing
combat
cricket
cycling
football
gaelic games
golf
gymnastics
hockey
horseracing
ice hockey
inline hockey
inline skating
international games
motor racing
netball
personalities
promotion & education
rugby (irish)
sailing & watersports
showjumping
snooker
sportswear & equipment
squash
sub-aqua
swimming
target sports
tennis
winter sports

sport

american football

National Football League	www.nfl.com
NFL at Sporting News	www.sportingnews.com/nfl
NFL on Fox	www.foxsports.com/nfl
NFL Players	www.nflplayers.com
Super Bowl	www.superbowl.com
The Red Zone	www.theredzone.org

athletics

Athletics Association of Ireland	www.athleticsireland.ie
British Triathlon Association	www.britishtriathlon.co.uk
International Amateur Athletics Federation	www.iaaf.org
International Olympic Committee	www.olympic.org
International Triathlon Union	www.triathlon.org
Irish Runner	www.irishrunner.com
Irish Triathlon Association	www.clubi.ie/triathlon
London Marathon	www.london-marathon.co.uk
Sports News - Athletics	www.athleticsnews.com

basketball

Basketball News	www.basketballnews.com
Basketball Players Association	www.woods.demon.co.uk/BPA
British and Irish Total Basketball	www.britball.com
Global Basketball News	www.eurobasket.com
International Basketball Federation	www.fiba.com
Irish Basketball	www.irishbasketball.com
Irish Basketball Association	www.iba.ie
Irish Schools Basketball Association	www.iol.ie/~isba
National Basketball Association	www.nba.com

boating

Amateur Rowing Association	www.ara-rowing.org
Boat Race	www.boatrace.co.uk
Galway Rowing Club	www.galwayrowingclub.com
Henley Royal Regatta	www.hrr.co.uk
Irish Rowing	www.irishrowing.com
Rowing in Ireland	www.ul.ie/~rowing
Skerries Sea Scouts	www.geocities.com/skerriesseascouts
UCC Rowing Club	www.ucc.ie/ucc/socs/rowing

bowls

Belfast Indoor Bowls Club	www.belfastindoorbowls.com
Bowls Clubs	www.bowlsclubs.co.uk
Lawn Bowls	www.lawnbowls.com
Official Lawn Bowls	www.lawnbowls.co.uk

climbing

Climbing Magazine	www.climbing.com/
Indoor Ireland Climbing Gyms	www.indoorclimbing.com/ireland.html
Irish Climbing online	www.climbing.ie
Mountaineering Council of Ireland	www.mountaineering.ie

combat

boxing

International Boxing Organisation	www.iboboxing.com
Irish Amateur Boxing Association	www.aiba.net
Irish Boxing	www.irish-boxing.com
Irish Boxing News	www.irishboxingnews.com
World Boxing Association	www.wbaonline.com

judo

Irish Judo association	www.irishjudoassociation.ie
World Judo Organisation	www.worldjudo.org

karate

Irish Karate Union	www.nichiai.com/shindokan/irish_karate_union.html
Irish Taekwondo Headquarters	www.ith.koreaone.net
Kenpo Karate Ireland	www.kenpo.ie

kickboxing

Bushido Kick Boxing	www.geocities.com/bushidogendi
World Kickboxing Association	www.worldkickboxing.com

martial arts

Irish Aikido Association	www.geocities.com/HotSprings/6550
Irish Aikido Federation	http://indigo.ie/~aikido

other

Bujinkan	www.bujinkan.ie
Irish Martial Arts Commission	www.martialarts.ie
School of Gom Wong Fu	www.geocities.com/fulungchuan/
Yang's Martial Arts Association	www.chinahand.homestead.com/

wrestling

NCAA Wrestling	www.ncaawrestling.com
WCW Wrestling	www.wcwwrestling.com
World Wrestling Federation	www.wwf.com

cricket

clubs

Derbyshire	www.dccc.org.uk
Durham	www.durham-ccc.org.uk

Essex	www.essexcricket.org.uk
Hampshire	www.hampshire.cricket.org
Kent	www.kentcountycricket.co.uk
Lancashire	www.lccc.co.uk
Larne Cricket Club	www.nireland.com/ larnecricketclub
Leicestershire	www.leicestershireccc.com
Leinster Cricket Club	www.leinstercc.com
Lincolnshire	www.btinternet.com/ ~Lincs.Cricket
Melbourne	www.mcc.org.au
Middlesex	www.middlesexccc.co.uk
Northamptonshire	www.nccc.co.uk
Nottinghamshire	www.trentbridge.co.uk
Portlaoise Cricket Club	http://ireland.iol.ie/ ~pmlewis/cricket/
Sandyford Cricket Club	http://homepage.eircom.net/ ~sandyfordcc/
Somerset	www.somerset.cricket.org
Surrey	www.surreyccc.co.uk
Sussex	www.sccc.demon.co.uk
Warwickshire	www.warwickccc.org.uk
Worcestershire	www.wccc.co.uk
Yorkshire	www.yorkshireccc.org.uk

grounds

Lord's	www.lords.org
Sydney	www.scgt.oz.au

magazines & websites

BBC Cricket	http://news.bbc.co.uk/hi/ english/sport/cricket
CNN Cricket	www.cnnsi.com/cricket
Cric Info	www.cricket.org
Cricket @ sports.com	http://cricket.sports.com
Cricket World	www.cricketworld.com
Cricketer International Magazine	www.cricketer.com
Guardian Sport Unlimited	http://sport.guardian.co.uk/ cricket
Live from Lord's Webcam	http://www-uk2.cricket.org/ link_to_database/ NATIONAL/ENG/
Sky Sports Cricket	www.sky.co.uk/sports/cricket
Total Cricket	www.total-cricket.com
Wisden	www.wisden.com
World of Cricket	www.cricket.com

organisations

Australian Cricket Board	www.acb.com.au
English Cricket Board	www.ecb.co.uk

Federation of International Cricketers	www.ficahof.com
International Cricket Council	www.cricket.org/link_to_database/NATIONAL/ICC
Irish Cricket Union	www.theicu.org
Minor Cricket Counties Association	www.mcca.cricket.org
New Zealand Cricket Board	www.nzcricket.co.nz
Sri Lanka Cricket Board	www.lanka.net/cricket
United Cricket Board of South Africa	www.rsa3.cricket.org
World Blind Cricket Council	www.dialognet.com/score

trophies

World Cup	www.ecb.co.uk/worldcup

cycling

Apollo Cycling Team	www.apolloct.com
Association of Cycle Trades	www.cyclesource.co.uk
BMX	www.ebmx.com
Cyclists' Touring Club	www.ctc.org.uk
Irish Cycle Racing	www.iol.ie/~sshortal
Irish Cycling Federation	www.icf.ie
Irish Cycling Homepage	www.irishcycling.com
Mountain Biking UK	www.bikinguk.net
Prutour	www.prutour.co.uk
Raleigh	www.raleighbikes.com
Road Time Trials Council	www.rttc.org.uk
Tour de France	www.letour.fr
Trail Cyclists Association	www.trailquest.co.uk
Ulster Cycling	www.ulstercycling.com

football

clubs

Aberdeen	www.afc.co.uk
AC Milan	www.acmilan.com
Arsenal	www.arsenal.co.uk
Aston Villa	www.astonvilla-fc.co.uk
Birmingham City	www.bcfc.com
Blackburn Rovers	www.rovers.co.uk
Bohemians FC	www.bohemians.ie
Bradford City	www.bradfordcityfc.co.uk
Bray Wanderers FC	www.braywanderers.ie
Bristol City	www.bcfc.co.uk
Cambridge United	www.cambridgeunited.com
Carlisle United	www.cufconline.org.uk
Celtic	www.celticfc.co.uk
Charlton Athletic	www.charlton-athletic.co.uk
Chelsea	www.chelseafc.co.uk
Cheltenham Town	www.cheltenhamtown.co.uk
Colchester United	www.cufc.co.uk

Cork City FC	www.corkcityfc.com
Coventry City	www.ccfc.co.uk
Crewe Alexandra	www.s-cheshire.ac.uk/cafc
Crystal Palace	www.palace-eagles.com
Derby County	www.dcfc.co.uk
Dunfermline Athletic	www.fife.co.uk/pars
England	www.englandfc.com
Everton	www.evertonfc.com
FAI	www.fai.ie
Fulham	www.fulhamfc.co.uk
Glasgow Rangers	www.rangers.co.uk
Heart of Midlothian	www.heartsfc.co.uk
Huddersfield Town	www.htafc.com
Hull City	www.hullcityonline.com
Ipswich Town	www.itfc.co.uk
Leicester City	www.lcfc.com
Limerick FC	www.limerickfc.com
Lincoln City	www.redimps.com
Linfield FC	www.linfieldfc.org.uk
Liverpool	www.liverpoolfc.org
Longford Town FC	http://homepage.tinet.ie/ ~longfordtown
Macclesfield Town	www.mtfc.co.uk
Manchester City	www.mcfc.co.uk
Manchester United	www.manutd.co.uk
Middlesbrough	www.mfc.co.uk
Millwall	www.millwallonline.co.uk
Motherwell	www.motherwellfc.co.uk
Newcastle United	www.nufc.co.uk
Northampton Town	http://web.ukonline.co.uk/ntfc
Norwich City	www.canaries.co.uk
Nottingham Forest	www.nottinghamforest.co.uk
Notts County	www.nottscounty.net
Plymouth Argyll	www.argyll.org.uk
Queens Park Rangers	www.qpr.co.uk
Rangers	www.rangers.co.uk
Reading	www.readingfc.co.uk
Scunthorpe United	www.scunthorpe-united.co.uk
Shamrock Rovers FC	www.shamrockrovers.ie
Sheffield United	www.sufc.co.uk
Sheffield Wednesday	www.swfc.co.uk
Shelbourne FC	www.shelbournefc.ie
Shrewsbury Town	www.shrewsburytown.co.uk
Sligo Rovers FC	www.sligorovers.com
Southampton	www.saintsfc.co.uk
St. Patricks Athletic FC	www.stpatsfc.com
Sunderland	www.sunderland-afc.com
Tottenham Hotspur	www.spurs.co.uk
Waterford United FC	www.waterford-united.ie
Watford	www.watfordfc.com

West Bromwich Albion	www.wba.co.uk
West Ham United	www.westhamunited.co.uk
Wimbledon	www.wimbledon-fc.co.uk
Wolverhampton Wanderers	www.wolves.co.uk
York City	www.yorkcityfc.co.uk

magazines & websites

Fanzine	www.soccer-fanzine.co.uk
Football 365	www.football365.com
Nationwide League	www.football.nationwide.co.uk
Planet Football	www.planetfootball.com
Roy of the Rovers	www.royoftherovers.com
Soccernet	www.soccernet.com

organisations

FIFA	www.fifa.com
Football Association	www.the-fa.org
Football Supporters' Association	www.fsa.org.uk
Irish Football Message Board	http://transfer.to/IrishFootball
Irish Football Site	www.clubi.ie/fpage
Northern Irish Football Association	www.irishfa.com
Scottish Football Association	www.scottishfa.co.uk
UEFA	www.uefa.com

tournaments

FA Carling Premiership	www.fa-carling.com
UEFA Euro 2000	www.euro2000.org

gaelic games

Armagh GAA Site	www.armagh-gaa.com
Cavan GAA	http://cavan.gaa.ie
Dromina GAA Club	www.dromina.com
Dublin GAA	www.hoganstand.com/dublin
Dublin GAA	www.hill16.ie
GAA with RTE Interactive	www.rte.ie/sport/gaa
GAA World	www.gaa-world.co.uk
Gaelic Athletic Association	www.gaa.ie
Irish Handball	http://homepage.eircom.net/~sligohandball
Kerry GAA	http://kerry.gaa.ie
Ladies Gaelic Football Association (Cumann Peile Gael na MBan)	www.ladiesgaelic.ie
Monaghan GAA	http://monaghan.gaa.ie
Olympic Council of Ireland	www.olympic-council.ie
Setanta sport	www.setanta.com
Tipperary GAA	http://tipperary.gaa.ie
Wexford GAA	www.wxgaa.com

golf

associations

English Golf Union	www.englishgolfunion.org
Golf Foundation of Britain	www.golf-foundation.org
GolfclubIreland	www.golfclubireland.com
Golfing Union of Ireland	www.gui.ie
Ladies' Professional Golf Association	www.lpga.com
Pitch & Putt Union of Ireland	www.iol.ie/ppui
Professional Golf Association of America	www.pga.com
Scottish Golf	www.scottishgolf.com
Scottish Golf Schools	www.golfscotland.co.uk
US Golf Association	www.usga.org

courses

Ballina Golf Club	www.ballinagolfclub.com
Beech Park Golf Club	www.beechpark.ie
Carnoustie Golf Course Hotel & Resort	www.carnoustie-hotel.com
Carton House Golf Club	www.carton.ie
Castle Warden Golf Club	www.castlewardengolfclub.com
Clover Hill Golf Club	www.cloverhillgc.com
Druids Glen	www.druidsglen.ie
Eden Derry Golf Club	www.edenderrygolfclub.com
Gleneagles	www.gleneagles.com
K Club	www.kclub.ie
Malahide Golf Club	www.malahidegolfclub.ie
Mount Juliet	www.mountjuliet.ie
Mount Temple Golf Club	www.emerald-golf.com
Portmarnock	www.portmarnockgolfclub.ie
Royal Birkdale	www.royalbirkdale.com
Royal Dublin Golf Club	www.theroyaldublingolfclub.com/
Royal Troon	www.royaltroon.co.uk
St Andrews	www.standrews.org.uk

gymnastics

British Amateur Gymnastics Association	www.baga.co.uk
Irish Sports Acrobatics Homepage	http://homepage.tinet.ie/~irishacro/
Tydavnet Gym Club	http://homepage.eircom.net/~blillis/

hockey

East Antrim Hockey Club	www.eastantrim.co.uk
Field Hockey	www.fieldhockey.com

Field Hockey Foundation	www.fieldhockeytournament.com
Hockey Net	www.empresa.co.uk/hockeynet
Hockey Player Magazine	www.hockeyplayer.com
Leinster Hockey	www.leinsterhockey.ie
Pembroke Wanderers	www.pembrokewanderers.ie
Planet Field Hockey	www.planetfieldhockey.com

magazines, websites & tv

Fore Magazine	www.scga.org/fore
Golf	www.golfonline.com
Golf Channel	www.thegolfchannel.com
Golf Digest	www.scga.org/fore
Golf in Ireland - Clubs	www.golfeurope.com/clubs/ireland.htm
Golf Journey's in Ireland	www.irishgolf.com
Golf Monthly	www.nexusinternet.co.uk/gm
Golf Plus	www.golfplus.ie
Golf Today	www.golftoday.co.uk
Golf.com	www.golf.com
Irish Golf Tours	www.irishgolftours.com

tournaments

British Open	www.opengolf.com
LPGA Classic	www.lpgaclassic.com
Masters	www.masters.org
Open Championship	www.opengolf.com
PGA European Tour	www.europeantour.com
Times Mees Pierson Corporate Golf Challenge	www.timescorpgolf.com
US Open	www.usopen.org

horseracing

Association of Irish Racecourses	www.air.ie
Equestrian Directory	www.equestriandirectory.com
Equestrian Federation of Ireland	www.horsesport.ie
Horse Ireland	www.horseireland.com
Horse Riding Ireland	www.horseridingireland.net
Irish Bloodstock	www.irishbloodstock.net
Irish Horseracing Authority	www.iha.ie
Irish Horses	www.irish-horses.com
Irish Thoroughbred Marketing	www.itm.ie
Irish Thoroughbred Breeders' Association	www.itba.ie
Turf club	www.turfclub.ie

betting

Barry Dennis	www.barrydennis.co.uk
Bet.ie	www.bet.ie
BetZone - Online Betting	www.betzone.com

Blue Sq	www.bluesq.com
EirBet	www.eirbet.com
IG Index	www.igindex.co.uk
InterBet	www.inter-bet.com
Ladbrokes	www.bet.co.uk
Littlewoods Bet247	www.bet247.co.uk
Online Betting Guide	www.onlinebettingguide.com
Paddy Power	www.paddypower.com
Sean Graham	www.seangraham.com
Sporting Index	www.sportingindex.com
Sportingbet.com	www.sportingbet.com
Sports Online Betting	www.sportsonlinebetting.com
Sunderlands	www.sunderlands.co.uk
Surrey Racing	www.surreyracing.co.uk
Totalbet.com	www.totalbet.com
Victor Chandler	www.victorchandler.com
William Hill	www.williamhill.co.uk

magazines and websites

Channel 4 Racing	www.channel4.com/sport/racing
Irish Racing	www.irish-racing.com
Race Horses.com	www.race-horses.com
Racenews	www.racenews.co.uk
Sporting Life	www.sportinglife.co.uk

organisations

British Betting Office Association	www.bboa.co.uk
British Bloodstock Agency	www.bba.co.uk
British Horseracing Board	www.bhb.co.uk
Football Association of Ireland	www.fai.ie
Horserace Betting Levy Board	www.hblb.org.uk
Irish Horseracing Authority	www.iha.ie
Jockey Club	www.jockeyclub.com
National Trainers Federation	www.martex.co.uk/racehorsetrainers
Racecourse Association	www.comeracing.co.uk
Weatherbys	www.weatherbys-group.com

racecourses (irish)

Ballinrobe Racecourse	www.mayo-ireland.ie/Mayo/Towns/BallinR/Racecourse.htm
Down Royal Racecourse	www.downroyal.com
Fairyhouse Racecourse	http://indigo.ie/~fairyhse
Galway Racecourse	www.iol.ie/galway-races
Leopardstown Racecourse	www.leopardstown.com
Tramore Racecourse	www.tramore-racecourse.com

racecourses (uk)

Aintree	www.aintree.co.uk
Ascot	www.ascot.co.uk

Ayr	www.ayr-racecourse.co.uk
Catterick	www.catterick.com
Cheltenham	www.cheltenham.co.uk
Chepstow	www.chepstow-racecourse.co.uk
Chester	www.chester-races.co.uk
Cork Race Course	www.corkracecourse.ie
Curragh	www.curragh.ie
Epsom	www.epsomderby.co.uk
Goodwood	www.goodwood.co.uk
Haydock Park	www.haydock-park.com
Huntingdon	www.huntingdonracing.co.uk
Kempton Park	www.kempton.co.uk
Market Rasen	www.demon.co.uk/racenews/marketrasen
Musselburgh	www.musselburgh-racecourse.co.uk
Newmarket	www.newmarketracecourses.co.uk
Newton Abbot	www.newton-abbot-races.co.uk
Nottingham	www.nottinghamracecourse.co.uk
Perth	www.perth-races.co.uk
Punchestown	www.punchestown.com
Sandown Park	www.sandown.co.uk
Towcester	www.demon.co.uk/racenews/towcester
Uttoxeter	www.uttoxeterracecourse.co.uk
Warwick	www.warwickracecourse.co.uk
Wetherby	www.wetherby.co.uk
Wincanton	www.wincantonracecourse.co.uk
Windsor	www.windsorracing.co.uk
Wolverhampton	www.parkuk.freeserve.co.uk

ice hockey

leagues & associations

AZ of Ice Hockey	www.azhockey.com
Canadian Hockey	www.canadianhockey.ca
Ice Hockey Superleague	www.iceweb.co.uk
International Ice Hockey Federation	www.iihf.com
National Hockey League (NHL)	www.nhl.com
Scottish Ice Hockey Association	www.siha.net
USA Hockey	www.usahockey.com

teams

Anaheim Mighty Ducks	www.mightyducks.com
Atlanta Thrashers	www.atlantathrashers.com
Ayr Scottish Eagles	www.scottish-eagles.com

Belfast Giants	www.belfastgiants.com
Boston Bruins	www.bostonbruins.com
Bracknell Bees	www.bees.nu
Buffalo Sabres	www.sabres.com
Calgary Flames	www.calgaryflames.com
Cardiff Devils	www.cardiffdevils.co.uk
Carolina Hurricanes	http://carolinahurricanes.com
Chicago Blackhawks	www.chicagoblackhawks.com
Colorado Avalanche	www.coloradoavalanche.com
Columbus Bluejackets	www.columbusbluejackets.com
Dallas Stars	www.dallasstars.com
Detroit Red Wings	www.detroitredwings.com
Edmonton Oilers	www.edmontonoilers.com
Florida Panthers	www.floridapanthers.com
London Knights	www.knightice.co.uk
Los Angeles Kings	www.lakings.com
Manchester Storm	www.manchesterstorm.com
Minnesota Wild	www.wild.com
Montreal Canadiens	www.canadiens.com
Nashville Predators	www.nashvillepredators.com
New Jersey Devils	www.newjerseydevils.com
New York Islanders	www.newyorkislanders.com
New York Rangers	www.newyorkrangers.com
Newcastle Jesters	www.newcastlejesters.com
Nottingham Panthers	www.panthers.co.uk
Ottawa Senators	www.ottawasenators.com
Philadelphia Flyers	www.philadelphiaflyers.com
Phoenix Coyotes	www.phoenixcoyotes.com
Pittsburgh Penguins	www.pittsburghpenguins.com
San Jose Sharks	www.sj-sharks.com
Sheffield Steelers	www.steelers.co.uk
St Louis Blues	www.stlouisblues.com
Tampa Bay Lightning	www.tampabaylightning.com
Toronto Maple Leafs	www.mapleleafs.com
Vancouver Canucks	www.canucks.com
Washington Capitals	www.washingtoncaps.com

websites

A-Z Encyclopaedia of Ice Hockey	www.azhockey.com
Ice Hockey UK	www.icehockeyuk.co.uk

inline hockey

Irish Inline hockey Association	www.clubi.ie/smeaton/hockey.html

inline skating

Inline Skating in Ireland	http://inlineskating.about.com/cs/ireland
Inliners	www.inliners.co.uk

international games

British Olympic Association	www.olympics.org.uk
Commonwealth Games	www.commonwealthgames2002.org.uk
Olympic Games	www.olympics.com

motor racing

circuits

Anglesey	www.anglesey-race-circuit.co.uk
Brands Hatch	www.brands-hatch.co.uk
Castle Combe	www.castlecombecircuit.co.uk
Donington Park	www.donington-park.co.uk
Knockhill	www.knockhill.co.uk
Le Mans	www.24h-le-mans.com
Mallory Park	www.mallorypark.co.uk
Monaco	www.monaco.mc/monaco/gprix
Monza	www.monzanet.it
Nürburgring	www.nuerburgring.de
Oulton Park	www.oultonpark.co.uk
Pembrey	www.barc.net/pembrey.htm
Silverstone	www.silverstone-circuit.co.uk

events

Monaco Grand Prix	www.f1-monaco.com

magazines and websites

F1 Today	www.f1today.com
Irish Motorsport Index	www.irl-motorsportindex.com
Northern Ireland Motorsport	www.nimotorsport.co.uk
Lola Cars International	www.lolacars.com

organisations

Federation Internationale de l'Automobile (FIA)	www.fia.com

teams

Arrows	www.arrows.com
BAR-Honda	www.britishamericanracing.com
Ferrari	www.shell-ferrari.com
Gauloises Prost-Puegeot	www.prostgp.com
Jaguar	www.jaguar-racing.com
Jordan	www.jordangp.com
McLaren	www.mclaren.co.uk
Mild Seven Benetton Playlife	www.benettonf1.com
Minardi	www.minardi.it
Prost	www.prostgp.com
Red-Bull Sauber	www.redbull-sauber.ch
Williams	www.williamsf1.co.uk

netball

International Netball Association	www.netball.org

personalities

Andre Agassi	www.andresite.com
Anna Kournikova (Fan Club)	www.annak.org
Ayrton Senna	www.ayrton-senna.com
Babe Ruth	www.baberuth.com
Chris Bonington	www.bonington.com
Damon Hill	www.damonhill.co.uk
David Leadbetter	www.leadbetter.com
Don Bradman	www.bradman.sa.com.au
Eddie Irvine (Fan Club)	www.exclusively-irvine.com
Evel Knieval	www.evel.com
Gary Player	www.garyplayer.com
Jack Nicklaus	www.nicklaus.com
Jacques Villeneuve	www.jacques.villeneuve.com
Lee Westwood	www.westy.com
Lennox Lewis	www.lennox-lewis.com
Michael Jordan	http://jordan.sportsline.com
Michael Schumacher	www.michael-schumacher.com
Mika Hakkinen	www.hakkinen.com
Nadia Comaneci (Fan Club)	www.nadiacomaneci.com
Pelé	www.pele.net
Pete Sampras	www.sampras.com
Phil Mickelson	www.phil-mickelson.com
Prince Naseem Hamed	www.princenaseem.com
Ralf Schumacher	www.ralf-schumacher.de
Sonia O'Sullivan	soniaosullivan.com
Steffi Graf	www.steffi-graf.com
Steve Waugh	www.stevewaugh.com.au
Tiger Woods	www.tigerwoods.com

promotion & education

Irish Sports Council	www.irishsportscouncil.ie
Sports Council (Northern Ireland)	www.sportni.org

rugby (irish)

Ballymena RFC	www.ballymena.rfc.mcmail.com
Belfast Harlequins	www.belfastharlequins.com
Buccaneers RFC	www.buccaneersrfc.com
Cork Constitution RFC	www.corkcon.ie
Garryowen RFC	www.garryowen-rugby.com
IRFU	www.irfu.ie
Rugby Ulster	www.rugbyUlster.co.uk
Shannon RFC	www.shannonrfc.com
St Mary's RFC	www.stmarysrfc.com
Terenure College RFC	www.terenurecollegerfc.com

Aer Lingus RFC	www.aerlingusrfc.com
Belfast Harlequins	www.belfastharlequins.com
Bucaneers RFC	www.buccaneersrfc.com
CIYMS RFC	www.ciyms.com
Dungannon	www.dungannonrugby.co.uk
Old Wesley RFC	www.oldwesley.ie
Rugby Munster	www.rugbymunster.com
Skerries RFC	www.skerries.com/rfc

clubs (uk)

Avonvale	www.avonvalerfc.co.uk
Bath	www.bathrugby.co.uk
Bedford	www.bedfordrugby.co.uk
Bristol Rugby	www.bristolrugby.co.uk
Cardiff	www.cardiffrfc.com
Coventry	www.coventryrugby.co.uk
Gloucester	www.kingsholm-chronicle.org.uk
Harlequins	www.quins.co.uk
Henley	www.henleyrugbyclub.org.uk
Leeds	www.leedsrugby.co.uk
Leicester	www.tigers.co.uk
Llanelli	www.scarlets.co.uk
London Irish	www.london-irish.com
London Welsh	www.london-welsh.co.uk
Manchester	www.manchester-rugby.co.uk
Neath	www.k-c.co.uk/neathrfc
Newcastle Falcons	www.newcastle-falcons.co.uk
Northampton Saints	www.northamptonsaints.co.uk
Pontypridd	www.pontypriddrfc.co.uk
Richmond	www.rrfc.bc.ca
Sale	www.salerugby.com
Saracens	www.saracens.com
Swansea	www.swansearfc.co.uk
Vulcan	www.vulcanrufc.co.uk
Wakefield	www.rugbysupporters.co.uk
Wasps	www.wasps.co.uk
West Hartlepool	www.west-rugby.org.uk
Worcester	www.wrfc.co.uk

magazines and websites

Rugby World	www.rugbyworld.com
Scrum.com	www.scrum.com

organisations

English Rugby Union	www.rfu.com
International Rugby Board	www.irb.org
Irish Rugby Union	www.irfu.ie
Scottish Rugby Union	www.sru.org.uk
Welsh Rugby Union	www.wru.co.uk

tournaments

Allied Dunbar Premiership	www.rugbyclub.co.uk
Rugby League	www.rleague.com

sailing & watersports

Irish rowing	www.irishrowing.com

boats & equipment

Catamaran.ie	www.catamaran.ie
Corsair Marine	www.corsairuk.com
Garmin	www.garmin.com
International Coatings	www.yachtpaint.com
Irish Boats.net	www.irishboats.net
Laser	www.lasersailing.com
Moody	www.moody.co.uk
Nauquip	www.nauquip.com
Online Marine	www.on-line-marine.com
Raytheon Marine	www.raymarine.com
Sobstad Sailmakers	www.sobstad.co.uk
Suzuki Marine	www.suzukimarine.co.uk
Tenrag	www.tenrag.com
Tri Sailing	www.trisailing.ie
Yacht Finder	www.yachtfinder.ie
Yamaha Motor	www.yamaha-motor.co.uk

clubs & organisations

British Marine Industries Federation	www.marinedata.co.uk/bmif
British Universities Sailing Association	www.busa.co.uk
Clontarf Yacht and Boat Club	www.cybc.itgo.com
Glandore Harbour Yacht Club	www.glandoreyc.com
Howth Yacht Club	www.hyc.ie
Inland Waterways Association of Ireland	www.iwai.ie
International Sailing Federation	www.sailing.org
Irish National Sailing Club	www.inss.ie
Irish Sailing Association	www.sailing.org/isa
Jubilee Sailing Trust	www.jst.org.uk
National Federation of Sea Schools	www.nfss.co.uk
Ocean Youth Club	www.oyc.org.uk
Royal Institute of Navigation	www.rin.org.uk
Royal Irish Yacht Club	www.royalirishyachtclub.ie
Royal St. George Yacht Club	www.rsgyc.ie
Royal Yachting Association	www.rya.org.uk
Team Philips	www.teamphilips.com
Trinity House	www.trinityhouse.co.uk

events, regattas & trophies

America's Cup	www.americascup.org
America's Cup Jubilee	www.amcup2001.org

BT Global Challenge	www.btchallenge.com
Champagne Mumm Admiral's Cup	www.champagne-mumm.com
Cowes Week	www.cowesweek.co.uk
Fastnet Race	www.fastnet.org
Hamble Week	www.hamble-week.org.uk
Millennium Round the World Yacht Race	www.millennium-rtw.co.uk

holidays

Intersail	www.intersail.co.uk
Moorings	www.moorings.co.uk
Nautilus	www.nautilus-yachting.co.uk
Sail for Gold Holidays	www.sailforgold.co.uk

magazines and websites

Classic Boat Magazine	www.classicboat.co.uk
Dinghy Trader	www.dinghytrader.co.uk
Good Old Boat	www.goodoldboat.com
Ireland Afloat	www.afloat.ie
Motor Boat & Yachting	www.ybw.co.uk
Sailing Magazine	www.sailnet.com/sailing
Sailing Today	www.sailingnet.co.uk
SeaHorse	www.seahorse.co.uk
UK Harbours Guide	www.harbours.co.uk
UK Sailing Index	www.uksail.com
Yachting & Boating World	www.ybw.co.uk
Yachting World	www.yachting-world.com

showjumping

Eventing Ireland	www.eventingireland.com
Horse Ireland	www.horseireland.com
Irish Draught Horse Society	www.irishhorseboard.com
Irish Piebald & Skewbald Association	www.castlepook.com/ipsa
Irish Thoroughbed Marketing	www.itm.ie
Irish Thoroughbred breeders' Association	www.itba.ie
Royal Dublin Society	www.rds.ie
Show Jumping Association of Ireland	www.sjai.ie

events

Hickstead	www.hickstead.co.uk
Horse of the Year Show	www.hoys.co.uk
Mid America Showjumping Cup	www.mascup.com

magazines & websites

British Dressage	www.britishdressage.co.uk

organisations

British Horse Society	www.bhs.org.uk
British Horse Trials Association	www.bhta.co.uk
Pony Club	www.pony-club.org.uk

snooker

Billiards Congress of America	www.bca-pool.com
Crucible Theatre	www.shef.ac.uk/city/theatres/crucible
Embassy World Snooker	www.embassysnooker.com
International Billiards & Snooker Federation	www.the-ibsf.org
Irish Snooker	www.irishsnooker.f2s.com
Peradon	www.peradon.co.uk
Pot Black Magazine	www.potblack.co.uk
Snooker Market	www.snookermarket.co.uk
Snooker Net	www.snookernet.com
Snooker Scene	www.rileyleisure.com
World Snooker Association	www.wpbsa.com

sportswear & equipment

Adidas	www.adidas.com
American Golf Discount	www.americangolf.co.uk
Armour	www.armourgolf.com
Belfe	www.belfe.com
Berghaus	www.berghaus.com
Bogner	www.bogner.com
Chase Sport	www.chase-sport.co.uk
Columbia	www.columbia.com
Couloir	www.couloir.com
Crag Hoppers	www.craghoppers.com
Fat Shaft	www.wilsonsports.com/golf
Footjoy	www.footjoy.com
Golf Pride Grips	www.golfpride.com
Gryphon	www.gryphonhockey.com
Head	www.head.com
Helly Hansen	www.hellyhansen.com
Hi-Tec	www.hi-tecsports.com
Hill Billy Powered Golf Trolleys	www.hillbilly.co.uk
JJB Sports	www.jjb.co.uk
Luhta	www.luhta.com
Maxfli	www.maxfli.com
Mitre	www.mitre.com
Mizuno	www.mizunoeurope.com
Monarch	www.monarch-hockey.com
Nevada Bob Golf Superstores	www.nevadabob.co.uk
Nike	www.nike.com
North Face	www.thenorthface.com
O'Neill	www.oneilleurope.com
Oakley	www.oakley.com
Ping	www.pingeurope.com
Pinnacle	www.pinnaclegolf.com
Powakaddy	www.powakaddy.com
Proline	www.proline-sports.co.uk
Puma	www.puma.com

Reebok	www.reebok.com
Riley Leisure	www.rileyleisure.com
Salomon	www.salomonsports.com
Schöffel	www.schoffel.com
Slazenger	www.slazenger.co.uk
Speedo	www.speedo.com
Taylor Made	www.taylormadegolf.com
TearDrop	www.teardropgolf.com
Tenson	www.tenson.com
Titleist	www.titleist.com
Top Flite	www.topflite.com
Umbro	www.umbro.com
Wilson	www.wilsonsports.com
Zevo	www.zevogolf.com

squash

Irish squash	www.ucc.ie/ucc/socs/squash/irish_squash.html
Irish Squash Resources	www.irishsquash.com
Squash Player	www.squashplayer.com
Squash Talk	www.squashtalk.com
World Squash	www.squash.com
World Squash Federation	www.squash.org

sub-aqua

Irish Underwater Council	www.scubaireland.com
National Diving School	www.nds.ie
PADI	www.padi.com
Rodale's Scuba Diving	www.scubadiving.com
UK Diving	www.ukdiving.co.uk

swimming

Federation Internationale de Natation Amateur (FINA)	www.fina.org
Galway Swimming Club	www.galwayswimmingclub.com
Speedo	www.speedo.com
Swim Info	www.swiminfo.com
Swim Ireland	www.swimireland.com
Swim Ulster	www.swim-ulster.com
Web Swim	www.webswim.com

target sports

British Field Sports Society	www.bfss.org
Clay Shooting Magazine	www.clubclayshooting.com
European & Mediterranean Archery Union	www.emau.com
Field Magazine	www.thefield.co.uk
Grand National Archery Society	www.gnas.org
International Archery Federation	www.archery.org

International Practical Shooting Confederation	www.ipsc.org
Irish Amateur Archery Association	http://www.adventuresports.ie/approval-scheme/archery.html
Northern Ireland Archery Society	www.ni-archery.co.uk

tennis

ATP Tour	www.atptour.com
AXA Cup	www.axatenniscup.com
Ballinlough Tennis Club	www.ballinloughltc.com
Champions Tennis	www.championstennis.com
International Tennis Federation	www.itftennis.com
Landsdown Lawn Tennis Club	www.lansdowneltc.com
Lawn Tennis Association	www.lta.org.uk
Real Tennis Association (Irish)	www.real-tennis.com
Tennis for You	www.tennis4you.com
Tennis Ireland	www.tennisireland.ie
Tennis Organisation UK	www.tennis.org.uk
US Open	www.usopen.org
Wimbledon Official Site	www.wimbledon.com
WTA Tour	www.wtatour.com

winter sports

Aviemore & Cairngorms Experience	www.aviemore.co.uk
British Ski & Snowboard Federation	www.complete-skier.com
Cross Country Skier Magazine	www.crosscountryskier.com
Ski Club of Ireland	www.skiclub.ie
Ski Magazine	www.skinet.com/ski
Ski World Cup	www.skiworldcup.org
Skier & Snowboarder Magazine	www.skimag.com

technology

cable providers
internet service providers
magazines and websites
manufacturers & resellers
search engines
telecommunications

technology

cable providers

Cable and Wireless	www.candw.ie
Chorus	www.chorus.ie
NTL\CableLink	www.ntl.ie
Royelectric Cablecom	www.cablecom.ie

internet service providers

AOL	www.aol.co.uk
Blue Chip	www.bchip.com
BT Click	www.btclick.net
BT Highway	www.highway.bt.com
BT Internet	www.btopenworld.com
Buy & Sell.net	www.buyandsell.net
Clara.net	www.clara.net
ClubI	www.clubi.ie
Connect Free	www.connectfree.co.uk
Demon	www.demon.net
Eircom Net	www.eircom.net
Esat Net	www.esatfusion.ie
Fish	www.fish.co.uk
Freeserve	www.freeserve.com
GTS Netcom	www.netcom.net.uk
Indigo	www.indigo.ie
IOL	www.iol.ie
MSN	www.msn.com
OceanFree	www.oceanfree.net
Pipex	www.pipex.net
Rednet	www.red.net
Telewest	www.blueyonder.co.uk
Tiscali	www.tiscali.co.uk
UTV	www.utv.ie/netservices
Virgin Net	www.virgin.net

magazines and websites

.net	www.netmag.co.uk
ClubMac Ireland	www.clubmac.ie
Computer Business Review	www.cbronline.com
Computer Buyer	www.comp-buyer.co.uk
Computer Shopper	www.compshopper.co.uk
ElectricNews.net	www.enn.ie
Infolive	www.infolive.ie
Internet Magazine	www.internet-magazine.com
Irish Computer	www.irishcomputer.com
Irish Linux User's Group	www.linux.ie
MacUser UK	www.macuser.co.uk
Macworld	www.macworld.co.uk
Micro Mart	www.micromart.co.uk
Online.ie	www.online.ie

PC Plus	www.pcplus.co.uk
PCLive	www.pclive.ie
Yahoo UK & Ireland	www.yahoo.ie
ZDNet	www.zdnet.co.uk

manufacturers & resellers

Advantage	www.advantage.ie
Apex	www.apex.ie
Apple	www.apple.ie
Beyond 2000	www.beyond2000.ie
Compaq	www.compaq.ie
Compustore	www.compustore.ie
Dabs	www.dabs.com
DCBGroup	www.dcbgroup.com
Dell	www.dell.ie
Direct Memory International	www.dmi.ie
Gateway	www.gateway2000.ie
Hewlett Packard	www.hp.com
Jaguar Computers	www.jaguarcompsys.ie
Laser Computers	www.laser-computers.ie
Marx Computers	www.marx-computer.com
Packard Bell	www.packardbell.com
PC Source	www.pcsource.ie
PC Superstore	www.pcsuperstore.ie
PC World	www.pcworld.co.uk
Peats	www.peats.ie
PFH Computers	www.pfh.ie
Scan (Mail order)	www.scan.co.uk
Seiko Epson Corporation	www.epson.co.jp/e/index.htm
Sony Computing	www.ita.sel.sony.com
Sun Microsystems	www.sun.com
Toshiba	www.toshiba.co.jp
Unisys	www.unisys.com

search engines

4NI	www.4ni.co.uk
Altavista	www.altavista.com
BritishInformation.com	www.britishinformation.com
Browse Ireland	www.browseireland.com
Curry Guide	www.curryguide.com
CybEire	www.cybeire.com
CyberBritain.com	www.cyberbritain.co.uk
Google	www.google.com
Index Eireann	www.index-eireann.com
IrishSearch	www.irishsearch.net
Lycos	www.lycos.co.uk
NiceOne	www.niceone.com
Northern Ireland Portal	www.niportal.co.uk
NorthernLight	www.northernlight.com
Search Engine	www.searchengine.ie

Searching Ireland	www.searchingireland.com
Shamrock	www.ireland-information.com/engine
Yahoo UK & Ireland	www.yahoo.ie

telecommunications

BT	www.bt.com
Cable & Wireless	www.cw.com
Eircom	www.eircom.ie
Esat	www.esat.ie
NTL	www.ntl.co.uk
Ocean	www.ocean.ie
World Telecom	www.worldtelecom.co.uk

travel

- accommodation
- airlines
- airports
- bed & breakfast
- bus & coach companies
- camping/caravan sites
- car hire
- ferries
- hostels
- hotels
- magazines & websites
- professional bodies and trade associations
- resorts
- trains
- travel agents and tour operators

travel

accommodation

I Click Reservations	www.1clickreservations.net
Active Ireland	www.activeireland.ie
Ireland's Blue Book	www.irelands-blue-book.ie
Irish Accommodations	www.transatlan.com/ireland
Sligo Accommodation	www.sligoaccommodation.com
Travel Directories Ireland	www.dirl.com

airlines

AB Airlines	www.abairlines.com
Aer Arann	www.aerarann.ie
Aer Lingus	www.aerlingus.ie
Aeroflot	www.aeroflot.co.uk
Aerolineas Argentinas	www.aerolineas.com.ar
Air 2000	www.air2000.co.uk
Air Canada	www.aircanada.ca
Air China	www.airchina.com.cn
Air Fiji	www.airfiji.net
Air France	www.airfrance.co.uk
Air India	www.airindia.com
Air Jamaica	www.airjamaica.com
Air Malawi	www.africaonline.co.ke/airmalawi
Air Malta	www.airmalta.com
Air Mauritius	www.airmauritius.com
Air New Zealand	www.airnz.com
Air Portugal	www.tap-airportugal.pt
Air UK	www.airuk.co.uk
Alitalia	www.alitalia.it
All Nippon Airways	www.ana.co.jp/eng
American Airlines	www.americanair.com
Ana Europe	www.ana-europe.com
Ansett	www.ansett.com
Asiana Airlines	www.asiana.co.kr/english
Austrian Airlines	www.aua.com
Avro	www.avro.co.uk
Bahamasair	www.bahamasair.com
BMI British Midland	www.flybmi.com
Britannia	www.britanniaairways.com
British Airways	www.british-airways.com
British European	www.british-european.com
British World Airlines	www.british-world.co.uk
Buzz	www.buzzaway.com
BWIA	www.bwiacaribbean.com
Cathay Pacific	www.cathaypacific.com
Cayman Airways	www.caymanairways.com
China Airlines	www.china-airlines.com
Continental	www.flycontinental.com

Crossair	www.crossair.ch
Cyprus Airways	www.cyprusair.com
Czech Airlines	www.csa.cz/en
Delta	www.delta-air.com
Dragon Air	www.dragonair.com
Eastern Airways	www.easternairways.com
EasyJet	www.easyjet.com
El Al	www.elal.co.il/worldwide/uk
Emirates (UAE)	www.ekgroup.com
EVA Air	www.evaair.com.tw/english
Finnair	www.finnair.co.uk
Garuda Indonesia	www.garudausa.com
Go	www.go-fly.com
Gujarat Airways	www.gujaratairways.com
Gulf Air	www.gulfairco.com
Guyana Airways	www.turq.com/guyana/guyanair.html
Iberia	www.iberia.com
Icelandair	www.icelandair.co.uk
Japan Airlines	www.jal.co.jp
JAS Japan Air System	www.jas.co.jp
Jersey European Airways	www.jea.co.uk
Kenya Airways	www.kenyaairways.co.uk
Kiss Air	www.kissair.com
KLM	www.klm.uk.com
Lauda Air	www.laudaair.com
Loganair	www.loganair.co.uk
LOT Polish Airlines	www.lot.com
Lufthansa	www.lufthansa.co.uk
Malaysia Airlines	www.malaysiaairlines.com.my
Malev	www.malev.hu
Manx Airlines	www.manx-airlines.com
Middle Eastern Airlines	www.mea.com.lb
Monarch	www.monarch-airlines.com
Northwest Airlines	www.nwa.com
Pakistan International	www.piac.com
Pan Am	www.panam.org
Philippine Airlines	www.philippineair.com
Polynesian Airlines	www.polynesianairlines.co.nz
Portugália Airlines	www.pga.pt/uk
Qantas	www.qantas.com.au
Royal Air Maroc	www.royalairmaroc.com/ver_en
Royal Jordanian Airlines	www.rja.com.jo
Ryanair	www.ryanair.com
Sabena	www.sabena.com
SAS Scandanavian Airlines	www.flysas.co.uk
Saudi Arabian Airlines	www.saudiarabian-airlines.com
ScotAirways	www.scotairways.co.uk

Singapore Airlines	www.singaporeair.com
SkyKing Airlines	www.skykingairlines.com
South African Airways	www.saa.co.za
Star Alliance	www.star-alliance.com
Swiftair	www.swiftair.com
Swissair	www.swissair.ch
Thai Airways	www.thaiair.com
Turkish Airlines	www.turkishairlines.com
TWA	www.twa.com
United Airlines	www.ual.com
VARIG Brazil	www.varig.com.br/english
Virgin Airways	www.fly.virgin.com
World Airways	www.worldair.com

airports

Aberdeen Airport	www.baa.co.uk/main/airports/aberdeen/
Aer Rianta	www.aer-rianta.ie
Belfast City Airport	www.belfastcityairport.com
Belfast International	www.bial.co.uk
Birmingham	www.bhx.co.uk
Bristol International Airport	www.bristolairport.co.uk
British Airports Authority	www.baa.co.uk
Cork Airport	www.cork-airport.com
Donegal International Airport	www.donegalairport.ie
Dublin International Airport	www.dublin-airport.com
Galway Airport	www.galway-airport.com
Gatwick	www.gatwickairport.co.uk
Glasgow Prestwick International	www.glasgow.pwk.com
Heathrow	www.heathrow.co.uk
Kerry Airport	www.kerryairport.ie
Knock International Airport	www.knockinternationalairport.ie
Leeds Bradford International Airport	www.lbia.co.uk
Liverpool	www.livairport.com
London City	www.londoncityairport.com
London Luton Airport	www.london-luton.com
Manchester	www.manairport.co.uk
Newcastle International Airport	www.newcastle-airport.co.uk
Shannon Airport	www.shannonairport.com
Sligo Regional Airport	www.sligoairport.com
Southampton Airport	www.baa.co.uk/main/airports/southampton
Stansted	www.baa.co.uk/stansted
Waterford Regional Airport	http://homepage.tinet.ie/~wra/

bed & breakfast

Bed & Breakfast Ireland	www.bedandbreakfastireland.net

bus & coach companies

Aircoach	www.aircoach.ie
Arriva	www.arriva.nl
Bus Eireann	www.buseireann.ie
Chambers Coaches	www.coachireland.com
CIE Tours	www.cietours.ie
Citybus, Belfast	www.translink.co.uk
Cityexpress	www.cityexpress.ie
Citylink	www.citylink.ie
Coachlink	www.coachlink.co.uk
Coras Iompar Eireann	www.cie.ie
Dublin Bus	www.dublinbus.ie
Duelway Coach	www.duelwaycoaches.com
Eirebus	www.iol.ie/~eirbus/index.htm
First Group	www.firstgroup.com
Irish Coaches	www.irishcoaches.ie
National Express	www.nationalexpress.co.uk
Stagecoach	www.stagecoachholdings.com
The City Connector	www.thecityconnector.com
Ulsterbus	www.translink.co.uk

camping/caravan sites

British Holiday & Home Parks Association	www.ukparks.co.uk
Caravan & Camping Ireland	www.camping-ireland.ie

car hire

Abraham Car Rentals	www.howardabraham.co.uk
Argus Car rental	www.argus-rentacar.com
Atlas Car Rentals	www.atlascarhire.com
Autorental	www.autorentals.ie
Avis	www.avis.ie
Budget	www.budgetcarrental.ie
Budget	www.budget-ireland.co.uk
Capital Car Rental	www.capital-car-hire.ie
Dan Dooley Car Hire	www.dan-dooley.ie
Enterprise	www.erac.com
Eurodrive Car Rentals	www.eurodrive.com
Europcar	www.europcar.com
Europcar Ireland	www.europcar.ie
Hamill Rent-A-Car	www.hamills.com
Hertz	www.hertz.co.uk
Holiday Autos	www.holidayautos.com
Limousine Company Ireland	www.limousine.ie
Malone Car Rental	www.malonecarrental.com
McCausland Car Hire	www.mccausland.co.uk

Murrays	www.europcar.ie
National	www.nationalcar-europe.com
Newmarket Motors	www.newmarketmotors.ie
Payless Bunratty Car Rentals	www.iol.ie/paylessbcr
Pierse Motors	www.piersemotors.ie
Windsor Thrifty	www.thrifty.ie

ferries

Brittany	www.brittany-ferries.com
Calmac	www.calmac.co.uk
Channel Hoppers	www.channelhoppers.com
DFDS Seaways	www.dfdsseaways.co.uk
Emeraude Lines	www.emeraudelines.com
Hoverspeed	www.hoverspeed.co.uk
Irish Ferries	www.irishferries.ie
Island Ferries Teo	www.aranislandferries.com
P&O European	www.poef.com
P&O North Sea	www.ponsf.com
P&O Scottish	www.poscottishferries.co.uk
P&O Stena Line	www.posl.com
Scandinavian Seaways	www.scansea.com
Sea France	www.seafrance.co.uk
Seacat	www.steam-packet.com
Seaview	www.seaview.co.uk/ferries
Stena	www.stenaline.co.uk
Swansea Cork	www.commerce.ie/cs/scf

hostels

Celtic Budget Accommodation	www.celtic-accommodation.com
England & Wales	www.yha.org.uk
Hosteling International, Northern Ireland	www.hini.org.uk
Oige	www.irelandyha.org
Scotland	www.syha.org.uk
Youth Hostelling International	www.iyha.org
Youth Hostelling, Ireland	www.irelandha.org

hotels

international hotels & chains

Choice Hotels	www.choicehotels.com
Fitzwilliam Hotels	www.fitzwilliamh.com
Flynn Hotels	http://flynnhotels.com
Four Seasons	www.fourseasons.com
Gleneagles	www.gleneagles.com
Grand Heritage Hotels	www.grandheritage.com
Great Southern Hotels	www.gsh.ie
Hilton	www.hilton.com
Holiday Inn	www.holidayinn-ireland.com

Intercontinental Hotels & Resorts	www.interconti.com
Jury's Hotels	www.jurys.com
Le Meridien	www.lemeridien-hotels.com
Mandarin Oriental	www.mandarin-oriental.com
Marriott Hotels	www.marriott.com
Novotel	www.novotel.com
O'Callaghan Hotels	www.davenporthotel.ie
Oberoi	www.oberoihotels.com
Posthouse Hotels	www.posthouse-hotels.com
Queens Moat Houses	www.queensmoat.com
Radisson	www.radisson.com
Raffles Singapore	www.raffles.com
Red Carnation	www.redcarnationhotels.com
Regal	www.regal-hotels.com
Regency Hotels	www.regencyhotels.com
Ritz	www.theritzhotel.co.uk
Ryan Hotels	www.ryan-hotels.com
Savoy	www.savoy-group.co.uk
Travel Lodge	www.travellodge.co.uk

northern ireland

Beech Hill Country House Hotel, Londonderry	www.beech-hill.com
Benedicts Hotel, Belfast	www.benedictshotel.co.uk
Best Western White Horse Hotel, Londonderry	www.whitehorse-hotel.com
Canal Court Hotel, Newry	www.canalcourthotel.com
Causeway Coast Hotel, Portrush	www.causewaycoast.com
Clandeboye Lodge Hotel, Belfast	www.clandeboyelodge.com
Crawfordsburn Inn, Bangor	www.theoldinn.com
Donard Hotel, Newcastle	www.donardhotel.com
Dukes Hotel, Belfast	www.dukes-hotel-belfast.co.uk
Fitzwilliam International Hotel, Belfast	www.fitzwilliaminternational.com
Galgorm Manor Hotel, Ballymena	www.galgorm.com
Glenavna House Hotel, Newtownabbey	www.glenavna.com
Golf Links Hotel, Portrush	www.kellys-portrush.com
Hastings Hotels	www.hastingshotels.com
Killyhevlin Hotel, Enniskillen	www.killyhevlin.com
La Mon Hotel, Belfast	www.lamon.co.uk
Londonderry Arms Hotel, Carnlough	www.glensofantrim.com
Malone Lodge Hotel	www.malonelodgehotel.com
Manor House Country Hotel, Enniskillen	www.manor-house-hotel.com
Marine Court Hotel, Bangor	www.marinecourthotel.net
McCausland Hotel, Belfast	www.mccauslandhotel.com
Mooney Hotel Group	www.mooneyhotelgroup.com
Park Avenue Hotel, Belfast	www.parkavenuehotel.co.uk

Peninsula Hotel, Portrush	www.peninsulahotel.co.uk
Royal Hotel, Bangor	www.the-royal-hotel.com
Seagoe Hotel, Co. Armagh	www.seagoe.com
Trinity Hotel, Londonderry	www.thetrinityhotel.com
Tullyglass House Hotel, Ballymena	www.tullyglass.com
White Gables, Hillsborough	www.whitegableshotel.co.uk

republic of ireland

Aberdeen Arms Hotel, Co. Clare	www.aberdeenarms.ie
Agaghdoe Heights, Co. Kerry	www.aghadoeheights.com
Ambassador Hotel, Cork	www.ambassadorhotel.ie
Arlington Hotel, Dublin	www.arlington.ie
Ashford Castle, Co. Mayo	www.ashford.ie
Assolas Country House, Co. Cork	www.assolas.com
Ballymaloe House, Co. Cork	www.ballymaloe.ie
Ballynahinch Castle Hostel, Co. Galway	www.commerce.ie/ballynahinch
Belleek Castle, Co. Mayo	www.belleekcastle.com
Brooks Hotel, Dublin	www.brookshotel.org
Cabra Castle, Co. Cavan	www.cabracastle.com
Cashel Palace Hotel, Co. Tipperary	www.cashel-palace.ie
Clarence Hotel, Dublin	www.theclarence.ie
Clontarf Castle Hotel, Dublin	www.clontarfcastle.ie
Conrad International, Dublin	www.conrad-international.ie
Cromleach Lodge Country House, Co. Sligo	www.cromleach.com
Dolmen Hotel, Co. Carlow	www.dolmenhotel.ie
Dromoland Castle, Co. Clare	www.dromoland.ie
Dromquinna Manor Hotel, Co. Kerry	www.dromquinna.com
Dublin Hotels	www.dublinhotels.org
Fitzwilliam Park Hotel, Dublin	www.fitzpark.ie
Galway Bay Hotel, Galway	www.galwaybayhotel.net
Glenlo Abbey, Co. Galway	www.glenlo.com
Grafton Capital Hotel, Dublin	www.graftonplazaie
Gregans Castle Hotel, Co. Clare	www.gregans.ie
Hayfield Manor Hotel, Co. Cork	www.hayfieldmanor.ie
Hibernian Hotel, Dublin	www.slh.com/hibernia
Killeen House, Co. Galway	www.killeenhousegalway.com
Kelly's Hotel, Co. Wexford	www.kellys.ie
Lord Bagenal Inn, Co. Carlow	www.lordbagenal.com
Lutrellstown Castle, Dublin	www.luttrellstown.ie
Merrion Hotel, Dublin	www.merrionhotel.ie
Morrison Hotel, Dublin	www.morrisonhotel.ie
Mount Juliet	www.mountjuliet.ie
Moyglare Manor Hotel, Co. Kildare	www.moyglaremanor.ie
Old Bank House, Co. Cork	http://indigo.ie/~oldbank
Park Hotel	www.parkkenmore.com
Sand House Hotel, Co. Donegal	www.sandhouse-hotel.ie
Sheen Falls, Co. Kerry	www.sheenfallslodge.ie

Shelbourne Hotel, Dublin	www.shelbourne.ie
Temple Country House Health Spa	www.templespa.ie
Park Hotel Kenmare, Co. Kerry	www.parkkenmare.com

magazines & websites

Backpackers Australia	www.backpackers.com.au/bpaus.htm
Bridgestone Guides	www.bridgestoneguides.com
Condé Nast Traveller	www.cntraveller.co.uk
Discover Northern Ireland	www.discovernorthernireland.com
Fodor's Guide	www.fodors.com
Footprint Guides	www.footprintbooks.com
Good Holiday Guide	www.goodholidayguide.com
Good Ski Guide	www.goodskiguide.com
Holiday Ireland	www.nci.ie/holiday
Holiday Which?	www.which.net/holiday
Ireland of the Welcomes	www.irelandofthewelcomes.com
Irish America	www.irishamerica.com
Lonely Planet	www.lonelyplanet.com
National Geographic	www.nationalgeographic.com
Public Transport Information	www.pti.org.uk
Rough Guide	www.roughguides.com
Virgin Net Travel	www.virgin.net/travel

professional bodies and trade associations

ABTA	www.abtanet.com
Association of Independent Tour Operators	www.aito.co.uk
Irish Association of Travel Agents	www.itaa.ie

resorts

Butlins	www.butlins.co.uk
Center Parcs	www.centerparcs.co.uk
Club Mark Warner	www.markwarner.co.uk
Club Med	www.clubmed.com
Disneyland (Paris)	www.disneylandparis.com
Disneyworld (Florida)	www.disney.co.uk/usa-resorts/wdw
Mosney	www.mosney.ie
Share Centre (Northern Ireland)	www.sharevillage.org

trains

Amtrak	www.amtrak.com
Docklands Light Rail	www.dlr.co.uk
Eurostar	www.eurostar.com
Gatwick Express	www.gatwickexpress.co.uk

Heathrow Express	www.heathrowexpress.co.uk
Irish Rail	www.irishrail.ie
London Transport	www.londontransport.co.uk
NI Railways	www.nirailways.co.uk
Railtrack	www.railtrack.co.uk
Scotrail	www.scotrail.co.uk
Virgin Trains	www.virgintrains.co.uk

travel agents and tour operators

Airtours	www.airtours.com
American Holidays	www.american-holidays.com
Atlas Travel Services	www.atlas.ie
Budget Travel	www.budgettravel.com
Budget Travel	www.budgettravel.ie
Carribbean Connection	www.caribbean-connection.com
Club 25	www.club25.ie
Cruise World	www.trtravel.ie/cruise.htm
Cunard	www.cunardline.com
Disney Cruises	www.disney.com/DisneyCruise
E-Bookers	www.ebookers.com
Eclipse	www.eclipsedirect.com
Elegant Resorts International	www.elegantresorts.com
First Choice	www.first-choice.com
Flightline	www.flightline.ie
Golfing in Ireland	www.golfingireland.com
Hostel Ireland	www.hostelireland.com
Internet Travel Services	www.its.net
Irish Travel Agents Association	www.itaa.ie
JWT	www.joewalshtours.ie
Lastminute.com	www.lastminute.com
Orient Express Trains & Cruises	www.orient-expresstrains.com
Royal Carribean Cruise Line	www.royalcaribbean.com
Silversea	www.silversea.com
Simply Travel	www.simply-travel.com
Skidream	www.skidream.com
Sovereign	www.sovereign.com
Sunsail Holidays	www.sunsail.com
Thomas Cook	www.thomascook.com
Thomson Holidays	www.thomson-holidays.com
Toolin Travel	www.toolintravel.ie
Topflight	www.topflight.ie
Trailfinders	www.trailfinders.ie
Travel for the Arts	www.travelforthearts.co.uk
Voyages Jules Verne	www.vjv.co.uk
Windjammer	www.windjammer.com
World Travel Center	www.worldtravel.ie
Dream Travel Africa	www.dreamtravelafrica.co.uk
P&O Stena Line	www.posl.com
Tour America	www.touramerica.ie

A

B

C

D

G

I

J

K

L

M

N

Q

R

S